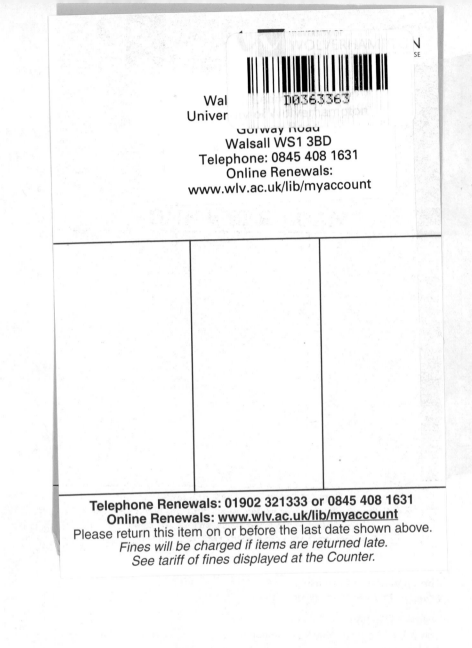

Politics and Culture

A Theory, Culture & Society series

Politics and Culture analyses the complex relationships between civil society, identities and contemporary states. Individual books will draw on the major theoretical paradigms in politics, international relations, history and philosophy within which citizenship, rights and social justice can be understood. The series will focus attention on the implications of globalization, the information revolution and postmodernism for the study of politics and society. It will relate these advanced theoretical issues to conventional approaches to welfare, participation and democracy.

SERIES EDITOR: Bryan S. Turner, *University of Cambridge*

EDITORIAL BOARD

J. M. Barbalet, *Australian National University*
Mike Featherstone, *The Nottingham University*
Stephen Kalberg, *Boston University*
Carole Pateman, *University of California, Los Angeles*

Citizenship and Identity

Engin F. Isin and Patricia K. Wood

SAGE Publications
London • Thousand Oaks • New Delhi

First published 1999

 SAGE Publications Ltd
6 Bonhill Street
London EC2A 4PU

SAGE Publications Inc.
2455 Teller Road
Thousand Oaks, California 91320

SAGE Publications India Pvt Ltd
32, M-Block Market
Greater Kailash – I
New Delhi 110 048

British Library Cataloguing in Publication data

A catalogue record for this book is available from the British Library

ISBN 0 7619 5828 2
ISBN 0 7619 5829 0 (pbk)

Library of Congress catalog card record available

Typeset by Engin F. Isin

CONTENTS

PREFACE

...to see differently, and to *want* to see differently to that degree, is no small discipline and preparation of the intellect for its future 'objectivity'—the latter is understood not as 'contemplation without interest' (which is, as such, a non-concept and absurdity), but as *having in our power* our 'pros' and 'cons': so as to be able to engage and disengage them so that we can use the *difference* in perspectives and affective interpretations for knowledge....There is *only* a perspective seeing, *only* a perspective knowing; the *more* affects we allow to speak about a thing, the *more* eyes, various eyes we are able to speak about the same thing, the more complete will be our 'concept' of the thing, our 'objectivity'.

Nietzsche, *On the Genealogy of Morality*, III, 12

Although this book draws upon theoretical studies on citizenship and identity, it is neither theoretical nor normative, but diagnostic and reflexive. It is diagnostic because we take theoretical and normative attempts to transcend the conflict between citizenship and identity and work out their possibilities and dangers in specific forms of citizenship. What happens when we take the ethos of *pluralization* seriously in specific fields of politics today against a fear of *fragmentation*? What would an ethos of pluralization look like when we examine citizenship from multiple, intersecting and overlapping perspectives? Those who address the issue of group-differentiated or overlapping citizenship make their arguments still from a singular perspective without taking into account plural perspectives and challenges. What happens when we take seriously the ideas of multiple subject-positions and the necessity of developing a multilayered conception? Our response was to delineate further forms of citizenship. In the end, we raise more questions than answers for each form of citizenship and its relationship to others. But this diagnostic approach allows us to accomplish two goals: first, to introduce our readers into debates across disciplines over different forms of citizenship and group-rights; and, second, to confront conceptual difficulties without raising false hopes for a promised land where citizenship and identity are forever reconciled.

We are considering one of the most fundamental and challenging questions: group rights and their just distribution. We might argue that liberal democracy has brought Western nation-states closer to justice than previous polities through its emphasis on equality, its commitment to the participation of the citizen, its appeal to due process and rule of law. But we also believe that these ideals have served as masks to disguise forms of discrimination, oppression and misrecognition based on class, gender, race, ethnicity, age and ability. Unpacking the relationship between citizenship and identity under advanced capitalism challenged us to find an analytical framework. Liberals insist on the supremacy of the individual *à la* Bill of Rights and dismiss the possibility of assigning any legal or political meaning to group rights; communitarians assert the group as the defining centre of identity that all individuals imagine themselves only in relation to the larger 'community' as the basis of a common ground. Meanwhile, 'republican liberals', 'civic republicans' and 'radical democrats' claim to synthesize or transcend the vexing tension between group and individual identities, and between the polity and the person, while still succumbing to binary oppositions. Politics, culture and philosophy get tangled up in our definitions of ourselves and our position in the world in which we live The views created by an either/or construction of identity have clearly become inadequate to reflect upon ourselves and our subject-positions.

Taking the idea of multiple subject-positions seriously pushed us to carry the ethos of pluralization to its limits and thus to expose its promises and dangers. It also demanded a multidisciplinary and interdisciplinary study. The conceptual difficulties of the relationship between citizenship and identity reverberate across different fields such as social and political theory, international relations theory, ecological theory, feminist theory, cultural theory, urban theory and postcolonial theory. For example, the debate over essentialism versus constructivism in cultural studies has affinities with the debate over structure versus agency in social theory, or liberalism versus communitarianism in political theory.

In our negotiation of these concepts and diverse fields, we found ourselves returning to T.H. Marshall, to his *Citizenship and Social Class* (1950), but also to his lesser known works. Marshall's concept of citizenship described its development in terms of hierarchies of power and his framework resonates in our circumstances. But Marshall's work does not go far enough: we want to build on Marshall's analysis, in order to address new political struggles and bring ourselves to the present day. We are encouraged by the fact that feminist theorists have also critically returned to Marshall (Lister, 1997a; Marston, 1990), as have others (Bulmer and Rees, 1996; Manning, 1993).

What does it mean to say that we are building on the work of T.H. Marshall? We are building a deeper conception of citizenship. Marshall delineates the evolution of civil, political and social rights, and illustrates how that evolution was shaped by the development of modern capitalism. We want to go beyond the forms of citizenship he mentions and advocate ethnic, sexual, technological, ecological and cultural forms. At first glance, it may appear that we are merely endorsing the extension of civil, political and social rights to marginalized groups of ethnicity, race and gender. But this is only the first step. We argue that the initial forms of citizenship, due to their connection to capitalism, were articulated in such a way as to oppress and silence such groups that interfered with the relentless pursuit of accumulation. The focus of early citizenship was the specificity of particular rights and freedoms, which were to reside in the individual. The actual practice and process of these rights were only ever conceived in the abstract. Moreover, they were not conceived with any recognition of the relevance of space, that is, the locations from which people exercise their citizenship rights. As advanced liberalism continues its socio-economic reorganization, there is a renewed attempt, often in the language of new technologies, to obliterate (in word, if not in fact) the difference space makes. Our examination of the importance—indeed, the centrality—of space to questions of identity and citizenship is a further way in which we build on, but go far beyond, Marshall.

Our exploration of ethnic, sexual, cultural, cosmopolitan and technological forms of citizenship is underlined by a belief in the necessity of taking group rights seriously. This evolves parallel to the citizenship needs developed by Marshall; that is, new concepts of citizenship are emerging as modern capitalism is transformed in new ways and thereby dislocates us as producers and consumers. But to understand citizenship rights in terms of the right to an identity (i.e., the right to have rights), as opposed (or in addition) to the passive right of status, involves, first, a reconception of the meaning of citizenship, and, second, a reconception of the means of allocating citizenship rights and the polities from which such rights draw legitimacy, from polis to cosmopolis. This is where our emphasis on the process of rights-claims, rather than the rights themselves, becomes crucial. What we hope to achieve here is to emphasize the process of citizenship, in the sense of allocation of rights rather than the actual substance of those rights.

The several forms of rights we examine here are only the beginning of the list. With more skill, time and space, we might also have considered religious citizenship, ability citizenship, children's citizenship, senior citizenship, and so on. Citizenship is a legal status and practice that progressively widens its sphere to include various rights. It is a contested field and democracy ensures that it will remain thus. Again, by focusing on the process, we aim to avoid becoming preoccupied with the specifics of any particular form of cultural politics and to resist the temptation to declare any rights as 'universal' and somehow immune to the contingencies of era and place.

We could not have started the list we have built here without the support of others. We are thankful for our fine research assistant, Charlene Fell, whose services were acquired with the financial assistance of the Faculty of Arts and the Division of Social Science at York University. We are grateful to Robert Rojek at Sage Publications for his encouragement and facilitation of the book every step of the way. We would also like to thank our spouses, Evelyn Ruppert and Steve McKinney, for their respect, recognition and extraordinary support. We dedicate this book to them.

1
REDISTRIBUTION, RECOGNITION, REPRESENTATION

Introduction

Nearly a decade ago, when the Berlin Wall came tumbling down, some thought that history had ended. By their reckoning, the master narratives of the twentieth century—capitalism and socialism—and the bipolar world that they defined gave way to a triumph of democracy and capitalism over socialism as the only credible forms of government and economy. Yet, if the fall of the Berlin Wall marked the end of socialism, it had been retreating in intellectual and practical struggles in the West earlier than that. For at least two decades political struggles in the West had no longer been waged solely in the name of socialism, with redistribution and equality as its twin principles. Instead, a cultural politics emerged where various groups demanded rights ranging from political representation to affirmation of group difference. Just as some may have been celebrating the end of history and the triumph of capitalism and democracy, this cultural politics had begun challenging the fundamental assumptions and principles of both. Various social movements, such as those of women, gays, 'racial' and ethnic 'minorities', have charged that behind the veil of 'universal citizenship' and 'equality before the law' there lay systemic forms of domination and oppression that misrecognized and marginalized them. Similarly, behind the veil of 'progress', 'growth' and 'prosperity', ecological movements have argued that capitalism led to exploitation and domination of nature that threatened the very survival of all species on earth.

Over the course of twenty years, cultural politics built up diverse, fluid, effective and surprising tactics and strategies to seek rights from states and corporations, built ephemeral alliances, and formed effective blocs of resistance to capitalism and challenged liberal democratic institutions that sustained it. (We use the term 'cultural politics' to describe these historically and politically diverse movements primarily because they used culture as their battleground and challenged the prevailing images, conceptions, representations and practices that together made capitalism possible. Cultural politics is a general concept meant to include: (i) earlier movements, often called 'identity politics', which were based upon establishing durable group identities; (ii) movements based upon a 'politics of difference', which sought to claim rights on the basis of group difference; and (iii) recent movements that have sought to transcend the tension between politics of identity and difference.) Venturing beyond the liberal and communitarian views that lament the decline of the public sphere and active citizenship, cultural politics forced a relentless ethos of pluralization of taste, identity, politics and being in the world, and opened up new and vital spaces for politics (C. Connolly, 1993; W.E. Connolly, 1995). Lacking—indeed shunning—a centre or party, the cultural politics of recognition sometimes culminated in progressive politics of inclusion and sometimes in regressive politics of exclusion. But, overall, its diversity, plurality, nomadism and culturalism surprised and confused those both on the left and the right (Foweraker and Landman, 1997).

Many have interpreted this shift to cultural politics as a displacement of class politics (Brooks, 1996) or 'disuniting of the nation' (Schlesinger, 1992). The recent debate between Fraser (1997a, 1997b), Iris Young (1990, 1997), Anne Phillips (1997) and Benhabib (1996) has illustrated that even those with similar political and philosophical dispositions have different interpretations of the meaning of cultural politics, and they disagree as to whether to consider cultural politics based upon struggles over representation as part of a politics of redistribution based on struggles over equality. To put it simply, the political question (or perhaps anxiety) of our times is whether cultural politics can form an effective resistance to injustice, inequality, domination and oppression engendered by advanced capitalism and institutionalized by neoliberalism. (We prefer the term 'advanced capitalism' to postfordism, flexible or reflexive accumulation to signal a broader social, political, economic and cultural change than those terms imply. As well, we intend to connect these transformations in the political economy of capitalism with those transformations in regimes of government defined as 'advanced liberalism'.) To some, cultural politics is too fragmented, incoherent and 'merely cultural'—that is, too far removed from the economic realm—to mount such resistance. They believe the main object of struggle should not be a divisive cultural politics, but the redistribution of economic capital. To others, the fragmentation, incoherence and symbolism of cultural politics are precisely its political strengths. They believe that groups suffer injustices and inequalities on the basis of unequal and unfair distribution not only of economic capital but also of symbolic, social and cultural capital. Perhaps the important point is that the distinction between culture and economy, cultural and social, and, hence, between redistribution and recognition is an analytical distinction that, in their everyday struggles, the new social movements do not make.

It seems the political question of our times is how to reconcile cultural politics *and* redistribution in a theoretically adequate, empirically sound, politically effective and ethically defensible way. We believe that the debate over citizenship and identity that has gained prominence in social and political theory in the last decade offers pathways to address that question (Hall and Du Gay, 1996; Leca, 1992; Rajchman, 1995). This book addresses citizenship and identity as two different windows on the same questions: what conceptual tools are available to define a deep conception of citizenship that can recognize group rights; and what happens when we take group-differentiated or multilayered citizenship seriously under advanced capitalism?

To begin to answer these questions we must first question the desire to eradicate the tension between citizenship and identity as antinomic attachments and loyalties that are incompatible and incommensurable, and are thus irreconcilable. This assumption is quite widely held, although often latent. Discussing 'the clash of identities', for example, James Littleton asserts that 'many people are preoccupied with the attempt to fulfil their political aspirations by placing increasing emphasis on the particular social groups with which they identify.' He adds: 'Instead of regarding themselves as citizens of sovereign nation-states, much less citizens of the world, many people have come to see themselves primarily as members of a racial, ethnic, linguistic, religious or gender group.' Under such circumstances Littleton laments that 'rather than pursuing the common interests of humanity—equality of rights, the satisfaction of material needs, universal respect for the dignity of the individual—their efforts are directed mainly at asserting the rights of their own group' (Littleton, 1996: 1). The belief in the basic conflict between citizenship and identity arises from a specific conception of each: citizenship as universal and identity as particular.

Many others seem to hold the same assumption that group identities such as those based on racial, gender, ethnic and linguistic aspects conflict with citizenship because while citizenship signifies 'universal' attachments, group identities are particularistic. Jonathan Friedman, for example, observes 'the weakening of former national identities and the emergence of new identities, especially the dissolution of a kind of membership known as "citizenship" in the abstract meaning of membership in territorially defined, state-governed society and its replacement by an identity based on "primordial loyalties", ethnicity, "race", local community, language and other culturally concrete forms' (Friedman, 1989: 61–62). Similarly, in their recent work on the new spaces of identity in Europe, with respect to nationalism, David Morley and Kevin Robins also regard identity and citizenship as conflictual attachments. They recognize that the rise of nationalism is a complex and contradictory phenomenon and accept that it can be seen as an expression of the revitalization of civil society, even an assertion of more meaningful collective identities against bureaucratic and technocratic visions of society. Nevertheless, they fear that 'there can also be a dangerously narrow and parochial quality in these attachments. They mobilise warm feelings of mutuality and ideals of community created from within and sustaining familial and kinship relations. The danger in this neo-nationalism is that questions of identity eclipse those of citizenship and democracy' (Morley and Robins, 1995: 186). They clearly consider questions of identity as incompatible with those of citizenship and democracy.

Similarly, Derek Heater has argued that citizenship entails status, loyalty, duties and rights 'not primarily in relation to another human being, but in relation to an abstract concept, the state' (Heater, 1990: 2) and thus derives its power from 'identity and virtue' (182). From this view, citizenship as a form of identity is based on social reciprocity and common interests, which may themselves be based on a sense of tradition, ethnicity or lifestyle, and heightened by systems of beliefs, ceremonies and symbols. Citizenship is one amongst many identities an individual will feel, but is distinguished by its necessity for moral maturity, and by its potential to moderate the divisiveness of other identities—

gender, religion, race, class and nation: 'citizenship helps to tame the divisive passions of other identities' (184).

This book takes a different tack. We approach the relationship between citizenship and identity from a perspective that sees modern citizenship not only as a legal and political membership in a nation-state but also as an articulating principle for the recognition of group rights. We conceive of citizenship broadly—not only as a set of legal obligations and entitlements which individuals possess by virtue of their membership in a state, but also as the practices through which individuals and groups formulate and claim new rights or struggle to expand or maintain existing rights. Rather than regarding citizenship and identity as antinomic principles, we recognize the rise of new identities and claims for group rights as a challenge to the *modern* interpretation of universal citizenship, which is itself a form of group identity. Instead of either eradicating or flattening the tension between citizenship and identity, we aim to make a productive use of it. We seek a new conception of citizenship (and thus the state), with an emphasis on the practice of democracy, that would meet the needs of a diverse citizenry facing the challenges of advanced capitalism.

Citizenship: Status, Rights, Redistribution

Citizenship can be described as *both* a set of practices (cultural, symbolic and economic) and a bundle of rights and duties (civil, political and social) that define an individual's membership in a polity. It is important to recognize both aspects of citizenship—as practice and as status—while also recognizing that without the latter modern individuals cannot hold civil, political and social rights. In the same vein, many rights often first arise as practices and then become embodied in law as status. Citizenship is therefore neither a purely sociological concept nor purely a legal concept but a *relationship* between the two—an important theme to which we shall return later in this book. While, then, citizenship can be defined as a legal and political status, from a sociological point of view it can be defined as competent membership in a polity, thus emphasizing the constitutive aspect of citizenship (Turner, 1994b). But those who do not possess the civil, political and social rights to exercise such citizenship would be denied to become such a competent and full-fledged member of the polity in the first place. Thus, the sociological and politico-legal definitions of citizenship are not mutually exclusive but constitutive (Turner, 1990, 1997).

Since the late eighteenth century, the polity that has 'colonized' everyday life in the world has been the nation-state. Every nation-state in the world today identifies individuals based on set criteria (birth, blood, nationality) and registers them with identity papers such as passports and citizenship certificates. Each nation-state also has elaborate rules and regulations governing naturalization (accepting those who are not born in the state) and the rights of immigrants who are not citizens. Each also has elaborate rules of acceptance to its territory either as visitors, temporary or permanent workers, refugees and 'aliens'. Such issues as how many immigrants to accept, what rights they should possess, under what conditions and criteria they should be granted citizenship, and whether such citizenship should be the same as native born and naturalized citizens are hotly contested (Brubaker, 1992, 1996; Soysal, 1994; Spinner, 1994). Therefore, although it may be considered rather ethnocentric not to make the usual distinction between the 'Western' and 'non-Western' worlds, citizenship has become a widely used institution throughout the world. Regardless of the prevailing form of government and constitution (e.g., democracy, oligarchy, dictatorship), citizenship has been instituted in almost every nation-state around the world. Of course, as many works in the burgeoning field of citizenship studies have shown, the composition of civil, political and social rights and the sphere of its cultural, symbolic and economic practices vary widely from one nation-state to the other (Janoski, 1998). Nevertheless, modern citizenship is no longer an institution unique to the West.

Yet, it is widely believed that citizenship originated in the West. It is impossible today to discuss its various aspects without some reference to its origins and history. Weber (1927) consistently argued that citizenship originated in the West and that the 'oriental' civilizations such as Chinese, Indian and Middle Eastern 'lacked' such a concept. This claim is problematic, if not ethnocentric, because what Weber was searching for in these civilizations was an already worked-out conception of citizenship as a legal status. It can be argued, however, that each of these civilizations had a different conception of political membership and status and, thus, a different conception of citizenship. In other words, Weber made citizenship originate in the West in the sense that he worked out an ideal type and searched for its origins. But this ideal type was of 'Western' civilization or, rather, of those times and spaces of history that have been appropriated as 'Western'. This points towards two problems we wish to avoid when we discuss citizenship: naturalism and historicism. It is very important to recognize that the status and practice of citizenship emerged in specific places in response to specific struggles and conflicts. It is a contested and contingent *field* that allowed for the mediation of conflict, redistribution of wealth and recognition of various individual and group rights throughout history. The fact that it eventually became universal should be interpreted not as 'natural' but rather as contingent and political. Similarly, its widespread use today cannot be taken as a sign of its future durability or stability. Even in recent memory citizenship rights have been suspended or radically altered by groups who have established their hegemony and imposed their view of the world on other groups.

The boundaries of citizenship in the sense of who does and does not have access to its membership and the nature of the rights and obligations associated with that membership have always been contested. Even the Ancients wrestled with such debates: the Greek warriors and peasants fought bloody wars for centuries and there was never a long period where the institution was stable and durable. Similarly, Roman patricians and plebeians fought violent battles to define and redefine citizenship. In the modern era, citizenship involved various group and class conflicts as well. The rise of the welfare state and the securing of social rights for the working class are relatively new that attacks on such social rights by various neoliberal regimes remind us their fragility (Morris, 1994; Roche, 1992). Faulks (1998), for example, convincingly demonstrated how neoliberal regimes in Britain between 1979 and 1997 scaled back not only social rights, as is well known, but even civil and political rights that are thought to be 'sacred' in liberal democracies. Thus, not only is citizenship an unstable concept throughout history, but it has also been a highly contested and constantly changing institution (Mann, 1987; Turner, 1993b).

Another assumption to avoid when discussing citizenship is historicism. Modern Western law constitutes the individual, among other things, as a sovereign subject vested with inalienable rights and freedoms such as speech and the possession of private property. By contrast, in Ancient Greece, the individual's political existence was drawn from political association. For the Greeks, this association preceded the individual, whereas for moderns the individual is believed to exist before the state. To claim that the Western conception of citizenship originated with the Greeks is a 'historicist' claim where a consonance is assumed between 'their' and 'our' conception of citizenship. Claims of affinity between a modern concept and practice of citizenship and those of historical forms should be regarded with scepticism. This is not to say there are no affinities, but rather to emphasize that they are not self-evident (Isin, 1997).

Today, citizenship is widely debated both among scholars and political leaders (Beiner, 1995; Kymlicka and Wayne, 1994; Shafir, 1998; Steenbergen, 1994; Tilly, 1996; Turner, 1993a). The boundaries and the meaning of modern citizenship are currently being challenged. Why has modern citizenship been contested? Our era has been variously described as 'postmodern', 'global' or 'late modern'. Whatever the merits of such definitions and declarations, the fact that they point to transformations in economy, culture and society is important. As Benhabib says, 'our lived time, time as imbued with symbolic meaning, is caught in the throes of forces of which we only have a dim understanding at the present. The many "postisms", like posthumanism, post-structuralism, postmodernism, postfordism, post-Keynesianism, and post-Histoire circulating in our intellectual and cultural lives, are at one level only expressions of a deeply shared sense that certain aspects of our social, symbolic and political universe have been profoundly and most likely irretrievably transformed' (Benhabib, 1992: 1). During such transformation, citizenship defined as both practice and status becomes a field of contest. And, when there is such a contest in the field of political and social power, of course, a similar contest takes place in the field of theory and ideas.

Many now believe that our era is marked by an increasing fragmentation and differentiation of culture, which is a consequence of the multiplication of lifestyles and social differentiation; the use of irony, allegory, pastiche and montage as argumentative styles and as components of rhetoric; the decline of 'grand narratives' of legitimation in politics and society; the celebration of the idea of difference and heterogeneity; the globalization of culture with telecommunications networks; the emphasis on flexibility and reflexivity in lifestyle; a decline in the idea of coherence as a norm of personality; and the decline of 'industrial society' and its replacement by 'postfordism' and 'postindustrialism' (Harvey, 1989; Turner, 1994b).

Each of these interpretations is contested and we shall return to them with certain scepticism throughout the book. The important point here is that a number of specific social, political, cultural and economic transformations have placed citizenship on the political agenda. The nation-state as a sovereign polity is under pressure from both below and above (Sassen, 1996a). Especially among the emerging cosmopolitan classes, globalization is also undermining the personal attachment to membership in the state. In Turner's words: 'The state is caught between these global pressures, which challenge its monopoly over the emotive commitments of its citizens, and local, regional and ethnic challenges to its authority. The question of political sovereignty is of paramount importance for understanding the nature of citizenship and human rights' (Turner, 1994b: 157). Thus, while the various social movements waging struggles of recognition in the past two decades have exposed the limits of modern citizenship, transnational movements ranging from multinational corporations to ecological issues have strained the effective capacity of the nation-state to govern.

To put it simply, three perspectives have emerged in political theory that advance a specific conception of citizenship: liberalism, communitarianism and civic republicanism (Delaney, 1994; Frazer and Lacey, 1993; Mulhall and Swift, 1996; Oldfield, 1990). Although this debate has become familiar to students of politics, it maps out the terrain rather uneasily because many scholars do not exactly fit into these categories. Sandel (1998), for example, who is considered a communitarian, expresses discomfort with such a label. Similarly, Charles Taylor (1989) does not explicitly address the debate. And Kymlicka (1995), who considers himself a liberal, may be considered a radical, given his insistence on group rights. The matter is further confused by American public discourse, where 'liberal' is most often a pejorative term for left-wing politics. It is, therefore, more appropriate to think these perspectives as ideal types rather than water-tight categories to which we can assign scholars. Liberalism denotes those theories that consider the individual as preceding polity and citizenship as specific rights that protect the individual. The bearer of rights is individual and the granter is the nation-state. As Oldfield argues: 'The function of the political realm is to render service to individual interests and purposes, to protect citizens in the exercise of their rights, and to leave them unhindered in the pursuit of whatever individual and collective interests they might have' (Oldfield, 1990: 2). Under liberalism political arrangements are thus seen in utilitarian terms. To participate in the political realm is a right and citizens choose—on the assumption that they have the resources and the opportunity—when and whether to exercise this right. Their status of citizen is not derogated or jeopardized if they choose not to be so active. While citizens are assumed to be skilled in debate and procedure and empowered to express their views on political matters, to propose alternative political or social arrangements, let alone work towards achieving them, is not considered part of citizenship (Gilbert, 1996: 45).

Although many assume that what liberalism purports as a doctrine also happens to be the established legal and political practice in modern democracies in the West, this assumption has been persuasively challenged (Frazer and Lacey, 1993: 41–42; Oldfield, 1990). As we shall see later, there is a cogent literature on governmentality, inspired by Foucault, that interprets liberalism as a practice rather than a philosophy (Barry, Osborne and Rose, 1996; Burchell, Gordon and Miller, 1991). In this view, liberalism emerges as a series of technologies of government that does not quite resemble liberalism as defended or attacked by philosophers. Moreover, scholars such as Kymlicka (1995) argue that modern liberalism has been at best ambiguous about group rights, and its future as a credible philosophy of government will depend on its ability to accommodate such rights. Similarly, the new social movements and resultant cultural politics have severely criticized the liberal conception of citizenship in practice (Jordan, 1994; Kriesi, 1995). They have demonstrated that individual freedom conceived in negative terms (freedom *from*) is not an adequate conception of political life in which many citizens also seek positive liberties (freedom *to*) to alter their conditions of existence as a group, which we shall call later the third form of liberty. As well, the assumption of the individual as the sole bearer of rights is challenged by the formation of effective sub-national groups that seek rights by virtue of membership in these groups. It is, therefore, problematic to claim that liberal philosophy describes the prevailing practices in 'liberal' democracies.

Communitarianism denotes those theories that critique the liberal conception of self-regarding or sovereign individual as debilitating and demeaning for the 'common good'. While communitarianism takes issue with the assumption that the individual exists prior to polity, it does not contest the principle that the individual is the sole bearer of rights. These two political theories are at odds with each other in the sense that the conceptions of the individual they depict and desire are fundamentally different. While liberalism advances a model of the self-regarding individual protecting and advancing his or her interests, communitarianism claims that individuals are situated and embedded and thus not isolated and independent. In other words, communitarianism adheres to a strong view of community, in the sense that 'to say that the members of a society are bound by a sense of community is not simply to say that a great many of them profess communitarian sentiments and pursue communitarian aims, but rather that they conceive their identity—the subject and not just the object of their feelings and aspirations—as defined to some extent by the community of which they are a part' (Sandel, 1998: 150). While a communitarian vision asserts that '[t]he civic virtue distinctive to our time is the capacity to negotiate our way among the sometimes overlapping, sometimes conflicting obligations that claim us, and to live with the tension to which multiple loyalties give rise' (Sandel, 1996: 350), how such loyalties and obligations are formed remains unanswered. In the end, the debate revolves around the extent to which individuals are formed under the influence of community.

Civic republicanism has asserted that there does not need to be a contradiction or conflict between a self-regarding individual and an egalitarian one. For example, Beiner defines citizenship as a problem of 'what draws a body of citizens together into a coherent and stably organized political community, and keeps that allegiance durable' (Beiner, 1995: 1). By appealing to Jürgen Habermas, he identifies a series of political crises such as ethnic conflict, changing sovereignties of states in Europe and elsewhere, dislocating shifts of identity provoked by mass migration and economic integration that raise deep questions about 'what binds citizens together into a shared political community' (3). Beiner criticizes both universalistic claims of liberalism, which argues for the virtues of the individual, and communitarian and postmodern claims of group identity and pluralism (6–8). On the one hand, there are the various kinds of universalism that exalt the inviolable moral worth of individuals above and beyond any collective or civic identity. On the other hand, there are the forces of exclusivity and particularism that celebrate and affirm just those forms of group identity that distinguish individuals from one another. These particularisms, according to Beiner, 'tend to...generate the kind of ethnic and nationalist outbursts whose outcome, as we have seen more and more in the last few years, is the self-dissolution of citizenship' (12). Therefore, 'to recover a coherent idea of citizenship we must go back to older categories of political thought (available from Aristotle, Rousseau, or Hegel, for instance, rather than from Nietzsche or Foucault)' (10). Beiner argues that both approaches undermine citizenship, the former because it conflates ethnic and civic identity, the latter because its 'extreme pluralism' does not leave any room for 'common' identity. Beiner puts forth a third theoretical perspective, which he believes overcomes the flaws of liberalism and communitarianism. His civic republicanism advocates a concept of citizenship that is neither individualist nor collectivist, and makes a clear distinction between civic identity and ethnic identity (14). Beiner thinks that Habermas is moving in this direction with his concept of 'constitutional patriotism'.

Assuming there is a conflict between group identity and citizenship, Beiner also believes there is a 'civic identity' that *all* citizens can share in pursuit of the *common* good while also pursuing their individual ends. The problem with such a view is that it assumes a unitary and singular conception of political community. Many groups that demand rights today are not merely interested in abstract arguments about the common good. They are seeking legitimate recognition and citizenship rights. To claim that we all share a civic identity is inadequate to deal with deeply sustained forms of oppression and discrimination in society. Similarly, Kymlicka's attempt to develop a group-differentiated conception of citizenship is a laudable, if unsuccessful, attempt to respond to this question (Kymlicka, 1995). He argues that liberalism can accommodate group rights as long as we make a clear distinction between self-government rights, polyethnic rights and special representation rights. If a further distinction is made between group rights that pertain to internal sanctions and to external protections, group-differentiated rights are compatible with a liberalism understood as a commitment to the freedom and equality of individual citizens. The details of his argument and the question of whether, once we make these moves, the resultant view can still be called liberalism will be explored in Chapter 3.

While these three perspectives struggle for a new conception of citizenship that resolves the tension between universalism and particularism, there is also an ostensibly radical view of democracy that sees such a tension as constitutive of the democratic process. Among these commentators Mouffe (1993) has been prominent. She argues that a radical democratic conception of citizenship 'can only be adequately formulated within a problematic that conceives of the social agent not as a unitary subject but as the articulation of an ensemble of subject positions, constructed within specific discourses and always precariously and temporarily sutured at the intersection of those subject positions'. She advocates developing a non-essentialist conception of the subject and regarding identity as identification with groups rather than as essential properties of the subject (Mouffe, 1993: 71; 1996). It is clear from her language that although she positions herself within the debate over citizenship and community, her theoretical resources are drawn from postmodern political and cultural theory.

In order to formulate a satisfactory concept of the political community, Mouffe argues, political theory must go beyond liberal individualism to questions of justice, equality and community. Such a concept must be responsive to the new political demands, which social democracy was unable to address and which have contributed to its crisis. It has to meet the challenge of the 'new movements' and acknowledge as legitimate concerns relating to ecology, gay issues, ethnicity and others, as well as the struggles around class, race and gender (Mouffe, 1992b: 4). The emergence of new political subjects, and the creation of new forms of identity and new types of community, has rendered inadequate a conception of justice centred principally on economic inequality. Its failure to address other means of domination makes it inappropriate for capturing the imagination of the new movements (Mouffe, 1992b: 7). Yet, Mouffe warns, while the rediscovery of citizenship is undoubtedly a very positive move, we should be careful that we do not become nostalgic about the Greek polis or any other idealized form of community (Mouffe, 1992b: 5; D.L. Phillips, 1993). According to Mouffe, 'The question at stake is to make our belonging to different communities of values, language, culture and others compatible with our common belonging to a political community whose rules we have to accept' (1995: 34).

Mouffe contends that exclusive concern with individual rights cannot provide guidance for the exercise of those rights. In other words, 'The limitation of democracy to a mere set of neutral procedures, the transformation of citizens into political consumers, and the liberal insistence on a supposed "neutrality" of the state have emptied politics of all its substance. It is reduced to economics and stripped of all its ethical components' (Mouffe, 1996: 22). To recover the political moment in rights, Mouffe argues for an 'antiessentialist theoretical framework according to which the social agent is constituted by an ensemble of "subject positions" that can never be totally fixed in a closed system of differences. It is constructed by a diversity of discourses, among which there is no necessary relation but a constant movement of overdetermination and displacement.' The identity of such a multiple and contradictory subject is therefore 'always contingent and precarious, temporarily fixed at the intersection of those subject positions and dependent on specific forms of identification' (Mouffe, 1995: 33). Mouffe's concept of the individual is neither the self-regarding individual of liberalism nor the constituted individual of communitarianism. Moreover, it does not require the civic republican allegiance to the common good.

Thus, Mouffe rightly does not see group rights in conflict with citizenship. Rather, radical democratic citizens depend on a collective form of identification among the democratic demands found in a variety of movements: women, workers, black, gay and ecological as well as other oppositional movements. Her conception of citizenship aims to construct a 'we', a chain of equivalence among various demands to articulate them through the principle of democratic *equivalence* without eliminating *difference* (Mouffe, 1995: 38). She agrees that the civic republican criticism of the self-regarding individual has been instrumental in demonstrating the serious problems of liberalism. The conception of the citizen who uses her rights to promote her self-interests, for example, leaves no room for a constitutive or intersubjective community, which would constitute the very identity of the individuals. However, the civic republican insistence on the priority of community is also problematic (Mouffe, 1992a: 226). Mouffe argues that one must be wary of this notion of community in civic republicanism in that it does not acknowledge the novelty of modern democracy with its principles of pluralism, individual liberty, the separation of church and state, and the development of civil society. It is very difficult, if desirable, to dream of organizing a community around a single idea of common good (227). She concludes that despite the very useful criticism of liberal and communitarian principles of political agency by the traditions of civic republicanism, the emphasis placed upon liberty and equality by liberalism should not be lost or ignored. A radical conception of citizenship must therefore come to terms with the modern conception of the self-regarding individual while accepting its limits.

For Mouffe the question then becomes how to formulate a conception of citizenship that does not regard political community as incompatible with individual liberty, or, in other words, how to reconcile positive and negative conceptions of liberty (228). She suggests that the distinction made by Michael Oakeshott (1975) between *universitas* and *societas* allows for such a reconciliation. These are two modes of polity, where the former is understood as composed of individuals with a common purpose and the latter of individuals with common interest (232). In Mouffe's words, *societas* 'is a form of association that can be enjoyed among relative strangers belonging to many purposive associations and whose allegiances to specific communities is not seen as conflicting with their membership in the civil association' (232–233). This would not be possible if such an association were conceived as *universitas*, as purposive association, because it would not allow for the existence of other genuine purposive associations.

While Oakeshott constructs a conservative view from this idea and imagines the political association as a conflict-free realm, Mouffe argues that the idea of *societas* can be employed more fruitfully for radical purposes by introducing conflict and antagonism into the conception. In this view, individuals would not be construed as peacefully pursuing their interests, but would be engaging each other over the meaning and definition of their common interests. The object of politics would be the association itself. There will never be a homogeneous unity in such an association since there will always be a need for a constitutive other (235).

What would be the idea of citizenship emerging out of a radical *societas*? Radical democratic citizenship can be a form of identification, not simply a legal status. The citizen is neither, as in liberalism, someone who is a passive bearer of rights nor, as in civic republicanism, someone who accepts submission to the rules prescribed by the political association (235). To put it another way, citizenship is not just one identity among others, as in liberalism, or the dominant identity that overrides all others, as in civic republicanism. Rather, 'it is an articulating principle that affects the different subject positions of the social agent...while allowing for a plurality of specific allegiances and for the respect of individual liberty' (235). The underlying conception of the social agent of this idea of citizenship is 'not a unitary subject but as the articulation of an ensemble of subject positions, constructed within specific discourses and always precariously and temporarily sutured at the intersection of those subject positions' (237). These multiple subject-positions have evolved in the last few years in movements demanding democratic rights, such as black, gay, ecological and other social movements. Radical democratic citizenship does not simply extend the sphere of rights in order to include these groups but allows for the radical mutual restructuring of these identities and the polity (236). Radical democratic citizenship becomes the common political identity of these multiple subject-positions.

The affinities between the multilayered or deep conception of citizenship being developed in this book and the radical democratic citizenship proposed by Mouffe should be apparent. Her emphasis on meeting the challenges of new social movements and identities; her willingness to expand the conception of citizenship; her insistence on non-essential and unstable identities and plurality of subject-positions; her warnings about the common good, unity and nostalgic community, are all welcome attributes.

We part with Mouffe, however, because she ultimately conflates citizenship and identity. While she aims to develop a conception of radical citizenship that is not unitary, she eventually succumbs to a conception where citizenship becomes a master political identity. While Mouffe claims that citizenship as a political identity should be strictly distinguished from ethnic, religious or racial identity, she implies the latter should be subordinate to the former (Mouffe, 1992b: 9). Mouffe believes that, for example, gender should be irrelevant to the practice of citizenship: 'It is true that the modern category of the citizen has been constructed in a way that, under the pretence of universality, postulated a homogeneous public, which relegated all particularity and difference to the private, and that it has contributed to the exclusion of women. But that does not mean that the answer is to introduce women's so-called specific tasks into the very definition of citizenship' (Mouffe, 1992b: 9). But if gender difference becomes irrelevant to citizenship, then what is the point of arguing for a gender-differentiated citizenship? This conflation between citizenship and identity takes Mouffe back to the 'political liberalism' of Rawls (1996), where a sharp distinction is drawn between citizenship as political identity and other identities, attachments and loyalties. Her argument that gender difference should be irrelevant is contradictory to her ostensible aims (Mouffe, 1992b: 9–10). Moreover, her appeal to Berlin's characterization of negative and positive liberties is problematic; if Mouffe had paid attention to Berlin's third concept of liberty, she may have avoided the conflation between citizenship and identity. We shall elaborate on Berlin's third concept of liberty in Chapter 3.

To make gender, ethnicity, 'race', region, language or any other identity irrelevant is problematic. Mouffe ignores the specific history where 'women' have been habituated to be women and 'men' have been habituated to be men. To focus on these differences does not mean we essentialize them; it means we recognize that certain identities are built as durable dispositions via practices which should be used as resources rather than differences to be effaced. It is when Mouffe ignores the relatively durable dispositions of social agents that she conflates citizenship and identity. In the end, Mouffe is unable to come to grips with the question of group rights and still considers the only bearer of rights as the individual. Interestingly, although Kymlicka is considered a liberal, we think his attempt to theorize group rights is more radical than the purported radicalism of Mouffe. We will elaborate on this issue in Chapter 2 when we discuss Iris Young (1990) and Bourdieu (1984, 1986, 1987).

So far this discussion has illustrated that the debates over citizenship inevitably spill into the issues of identity and that also overcoming the tensions between the particular and the universal, and between the specific and the general, is a generative notion in the debate. The tension is between those attempts to establish essential attributes of groups and those who claim that there are no durable group attributes at all, only socially constructed identities. The late modern condition may possibly mean that 'stable' identities are giving way to new and fragmented identities, that the rise of these new identities is part of a wider process of change of which postmodernization and globalization are the twin pillars, and that the self has emerged as a project, giving rise to a new level of reflexivity and a proliferation of lifestyles. To discuss citizenship means to critically explore these claims of a fragmented, decentred subject as well as of shifting group rights and identities without succumbing to either essentialist or constructivist views of identity. It means to examine whether these new identities must be seen to eclipse citizenship as a principle. In other words, without an understanding of sociological issues of belonging, recognition and solidarity we cannot adequately address the political issues of status, rights and equality.

Identity: Belonging, Solidarity, Recognition

As we have seen, while citizenship has been associated with the universal, identity is associated with the particular. Citizenship and identity appear to be incompatible, incommensurable and antinomic concepts. Although there is a tension between the two, their antinomic relationship rests on a problematic conception of identity.

The question of identity is not new. But, as Bauman (1996) argued, the modern question of identity is distinctive. This is not to say that before the late eighteenth century individuals did not have a conception of their selves, but identity as a social *question* emerged out of modernity. It has now gained a new urgency through a significant transformation towards the postmodern condition characterized by at least three intertwined shifts since the 1970s: (i) to a postmodern politics where the struggles over wealth, political status and access that characterized bourgeois and working-class politics throughout the nineteenth century and the first half of the twentieth century were complicated by struggles over race, ethnicity, sexuality and ecology, represented by novel groups rather than traditional parties; (ii) to an increasing aestheticization of everyday life where consumption has become a constitutive aspect of identity formation; and (iii) to a postindustrial economy where production of images, sounds, experiences and knowledge gained primacy over production of material commodities (Featherstone, 1988, 1990, 1993; Giddens, 1990, 1991; Harvey, 1989; Jameson, 1991; Robertson, 1992; Turner, 1994a).

As we mentioned earlier, we describe the politics arising from the new social movements as cultural politics, which began forming new forms of group identities and sought new group rights (Cohen and Arato, 1993; Eder, 1993; Giddens, 1990; Lyman, 1995). In what could be considered the first wave of cultural politics ('identity politics'), groups identified with general characteristics such as race, gender or nationality contended that discriminatory distinctions should not be based on those categories. More recently, several movements rejected this politics of inclusion and began asserting a 'politics of difference' or 'politics of recognition'. The argument was that identity politics obscured cultural and political differences between these groups and 'society'. A proliferation of movements based on identity began proudly to (re)assert, or perhaps reclaim, their identities as difference—as, for example, African-American, Asian-American, Latino or Native American, as female, as gay, or lesbian, as disabled and so forth. Eventually, identity politics called upon hegemonic groups to acknowledge their position in social space as well, so that some began classifying others or themselves as white, male, as straight and so forth.

There is, however, in what might be called a third wave of cultural politics, a growing dissatisfaction with these efforts to accentuate difference and a desire for thinking affirmatively about identity without either *freezing* or *dissolving* difference among groups (Bammer, 1994; Hall and Du Gay, 1996; Rajchman, 1995). In response to the choice between treating identity as a manifestation of essential *differences* or as an effect of social *prejudice* to be transcended, scholars now articulate a set of strategies that acknowledge a simultaneous and ambivalent desire both to *affirm* identities and to *transcend* them (Lister, 1997a: 197; Voet, 1998). This is a very difficult task and it is questionable if it can be resolved theoretically. It is an ongoing struggle for recognition waged by various groups around the world against each other as well as against the hegemonic 'other'. Some of these groups succeed in affirming while transcending identities while others succumb to essentialism and produce various forms of oppression. As well, the literature often neglects to note that identities are not only formed by groups seeking recognition but also by groups that seek domination. As studies on governmentality have shown, forms of classification and representation of various groups as pathological and deviant are powerful instruments of domination that themselves constitute groups (Ericson and Haggerty, 1997; Hacking, 1986).

Theories employed as conceptual tools can take stock of these successes. failures and dangers, and invest them with meanings that can be articulated as claims for rights. This is the reason why we think different claims to identity can be formulated as various forms of citizenship rights (Fraser, 1997a; Honneth, 1996b; C. Taylor, 1994). Or, as Lister put it, citizenship can be reconstructed along pluralist rather than dualist lines (1997a: 197). The discussion in the above section illustrates that to do that we have to develop a robust conception of identity. The literature on identity is vast. What we propose to do here is to draw upon key contributors and highlight the elements of a vigorous conception of identity. It becomes quickly obvious that the central problem that beset the literature is how to transcend essentialist *and* constructivist views of identity, leading some to believe that it may be theoretically impossible to achieve such a feat and some others to propose to drop the concept of altogether.

Although Stuart Hall agrees that the concept is rife with theoretical difficulties, he provides two convincing arguments for its continued use. First, he suggests that a critique should not simply aim to displace a concept which it critiques. 'Unlike those forms of critique which aim to supplant inadequate concepts with "truer" ones, or which aspire to the production of positive knowledge, the deconstructive approach puts key concepts "under erasure". This indicates that they are no longer serviceable—"good to think with"—in their originary and unreconstructed form. But since they have not been superseded dialectically, and there are no other, entirely different concepts with which to replace them, there is nothing to do but to continue to think with them' (S. Hall, 1996: 1). Hall refers to this as 'thinking at the limit or as thinking in the interval'. Identity is such a concept, operating under critical but stable conditions, in the interval between reversal and emergence, 'which cannot be thought in the old way, but without which certain key questions cannot be thought at all' (2). Thus, we would continue to use the concept although in a reflexive and critical fashion, more attuned to open up possibilities with it, rather than ascribing certainties to it.

Hall's second response highlights the fact that identity is a political concept, and, although the term is not new, at present it responds to the historical problem of agency in social theory and the need to reconceptualize it (2). Like Mouffe,

Hall thinks that the concept of identification is perhaps more appropriate. It refers to a process of articulation, a suturing, an over-determination not a subsumption (3). The identification process, Hall argues, continues throughout the life of the individual and is never stable, fixed or unified. Especially in late modern times, 'identities are fragmented and fractured, never singular but multiply constructed across different, often intersecting and antagonistic, discourses, practices, and positions' (4). Individual and group 'identities are about questions of using the resources of history, language and culture in the process of becoming rather than being: not "who we are" or "where we came from", so much as what we might become, how we have been represented and how that bears on how we might represent ourselves' (4). This is neither an active nor a passive conception of identity. To Hall, '[i]dentities are ... points of temporary attachment to the subject positions which discursive practices construct for us' (5–6). Individuals are neither passive recipients hailed into specific roles nor free subjects who constitute themselves without constraint. 'The notion that an effective suturing of the subject to a subject-position requires, not only that the subject is "hailed", but that the subject invests in the position, means that suturing has to be thought of as an *articulation*, rather than a one-sided process, and that in turn places *identification*, if not identities, firmly on the theoretical agenda' (6).

The importance of this point is the recognition that the individual cannot be conceived as either an author of her destiny (subjectivism) or a bearer of subject-positions (objectivism). (Hall argues that Foucault eventually moved from his earlier studies where the subject or agency was simply an effect of power or discourse to a position where subjectivities were actively produced.) Hall warns against two forms of struggle over representation and identity. The first assumes that there is some intrinsic and essential content to any identity which is defined by either a common origin or a common structure of experience or both. Struggling against existing constructions of a particular identity takes the form of contesting negative images with positive ones, and of trying to discover the 'authentic' and 'original' content of the identity. Basically, representations of identity here take the form of displacing one essential identity with another. The second struggle, while emphasizing the impossibility of such distinct identities, denies the existence of authentic identities based in a shared experience. Identities are always in some way relational and incomplete, in the process of being formed. Any identity depends upon its difference from, its negation of, some other term, even as the identity of the latter term depends upon its difference from, its negation of, the former. Identity is thus formed not against difference but in relation to difference. Identity is always a temporary and unstable effect of relations which define identities by marking differences. Thus the emphasis here is on the multiplicity of identities and differences rather than on a singular identity and on the connections or articulations between the fragments or differences. The fact of multiple identities has given rise to the recognition of race, class, ethnicity and gender as constitutive of the subject.

While Hall has been crucial in developing non-essentialist views of identity, his view of multiple subjects and the construction of identity leave open the gap in understanding why groups feel so strongly about their identities and invoke essentialist notions in their struggles for recognition. As Calhoun (1994a: 14–16) argued, such social constructivism can become exclusionary when every effort of group identification is criticized for essentialism. This becomes clear in Bhabha's criticism of Charles Taylor's celebrated essay which identifies the politics of recognition with the essentialist conceptions of identity and argues against the possibility of authentic identities (C. Taylor, 1994). Bhabha argues that Taylor's definition of culture as an expression of large numbers over a long period of time is arbitrary and states that, 'obviously, the dismissal of partial cultures, the emphasis on large numbers and long periods, is out of time with the modes of recognition of minority or marginalized cultures' (Bhabha, 1996: 57). Bhabha also criticizes him for his use of Bakhtin's dialogical reasoning, whereby Taylor 'deprives the "dialogic" of its hybridizing potential. The most telling symptom of this is that despite his "presumption of equality" Taylor always presents the multicultural or minority position as an imposition coming from the "outside" and making its demands from there' (Bhabha, 1996: 57). In other words, Taylor himself holds an authentic view of identity while arguing against it; to him authentic community is defined by its durability, but he fails to acknowledge the technologies of power that produce such durability.

Clearly, the concept of identity is troublesome. To address some of its conceptual difficulties and to address inadequacies of essentialism and constructivism, a number of concepts have been proposed, the most important of which include difference, fragmentation, hybridity and diaspora. The concept of difference, for example, describes a particular constitutive relation of negativity in which the subordinate group (the marginalized other or subaltern) is a necessary and internal force of destabilization existing within the identity of the dominant group. The instability of any dominant identity—since it must always and already incorporate its negation—is the result of the very nature of language and signification.

The concept of fragmentation emphasizes the multiplicity of identities and of position within any apparent identity. It thus sees a particular concrete or lived identity as a kind of disassembled and reassembled unity (Haraway, 1991: 174). Identities are thus always contradictory, made up out of partial fragments. Theories of fragmentation can focus on the fragmentation either of individual identities or of the social categories (of difference) within which individuals are placed, or some combination of the two. Further, such fragmentations can be seen as either historical or constitutive, which gives rise to the notion of syncretism (Gilroy, 1993).

The concept of hybridity is more difficult to characterize for it is often used synonymously with other concepts. Nevertheless, it describes three different images of border existences, or subaltern identities, as existing between two competing identities. The first two images are third space and liminality (Bhabha, 1996; Soja, 1996). In both these conceptions, the subaltern is defined by its location in a unique spatial condition which constitutes it as different from either alternative. Neither colonizer nor precolonial subject, the postcolonial subject exists as a unique hybrid which may, by definition, constitute the other two as well (García Canclini, 1995). A third conception of hybridity is that of the 'border-crossing', marking an image of between-ness.

The concept of diaspora is closely related to that of border-crossing, but it is often given a more diachronic inflection. This concept has become increasingly visible through Clifford, Gilroy and Lavie. As Clifford describes it: 'the term "diaspora" is a signifier not simply of transnationality and movement, but of political struggles to define the local—I would prefer to call it place—as a distinctive community, in historical contexts of displacement' (Clifford, 1994: 308). Diaspora links identity to identifications with alternative histories and cosmopolitanisms as networks, and questions the assumption of a necessary or even essential relation between group identity and territory (Massey, 1994).

In this discussion of hybridity and diaspora, we should mention, as well, the rise of the expression 'borderlands'. This term emerged to describe the physical space of areas along political, usually national, borders that have seen a large degree of economic, social and cultural exchange (Applebaum, 1994). In recent studies, it has also come to describe a mental or psychological space. Beginning with a focus on the mentality of those who live in such areas, the literature now extends to encompass those with such a sensibility, regardless of their actual proximity to an official border. It also emphasizes the existence of other borders in society.

The language of 'borderlands' is most popular in the literature on the Mexican–American border and the Latino/Chicano identity in the United States (Gutiérrez-Jones, 1995; Heyck, 1994; Martínez, 1996). 'Borderlands' has also witnessed significant usage in the works on Canadian–American relations. It is most common now in studies on the areas surrounding the 49th parallel, where the Canadian–American border is literally invisible, the 'borderlands' concept has also found a comfortable home in the history of New England and the Maritime provinces (Lecker, 1991; New, 1998). It is also becoming slightly more prominent in current geopolitical discussions of ethnic identity in Europe (Applebaum, 1994).

The idea of borderlands is an attempt to wrestle with identities that do not fit neatly into master discourses of ethnicity, race and nation, particularly in the wake of immigration (Anzaldúa, 1987). The concept is an attempt to address the tensions that arise from the imposition of the legal and political 'big picture' onto a lived, everyday experience of culture that crosses, avoids and even defies those borders. It is important to acknowledge the way social, economic and cultural ties can develop across a border, despite that border (Malcomson, 1994). But ultimately the discussion of a border suggests the constant presence of a divide, or identities that are either/or, always with the possibility of conflict. This may at times be the reality, but it privileges the external perspective, as usual, and reinforces the 'normal' categories. 'Borderlands' does not challenge the existence of the borders nearly as much as it re-entrenches them. It describes the marginalized experience always as irregular, unusual and deviant even as it tries to assert its importance.

While these concepts are themselves worthy of contemplation, as Çağlar (1997) argued, they also raise further questions about the formation of group identities. Although many argue that with postmodernization, the identity of an individual can no longer be assumed to be a unified and unifying construct, many also admit that such identities are formed under constraining conditions. While many argue that an individual is always in the process of being formed and one's identity is an ensemble of values, communities and groups to which one belongs, many others also argue that such a statement ignores the relatively durable and permanent dispositions of individuals. While it is important to recognize that identification is not a simple process, it is also important that 'identity formation' through which individuals incorporate certain characteristics and values is a process involving relatively durable attachments, obligations and promises. Thus, it is inadequate to focus on one aspect (fluidity and multiplicity) of identity at the expense of the other (solidity and relative permanence).

Citizenship and Identity

There are differences and affinities between concepts of citizenship and identity that generate significant problems in addressing both. In terms of differences, citizenship is more of a concept of status than identity (Preuß, 1995). It is expressed in juridical and legal norms that define the rights of the members of a polity. Many scholars argue for a concept of citizenship broader than a juridical and legal status but these arguments do not change the basic fact that ultimately citizenship allows or disallows civil, political and social rights and obligations in a polity. Such arguments for active citizenship or deep citizenship are concerned with deepening the scope of citizenship but they nevertheless presuppose that the status of citizenship already exists.

While identity does not need to have a legal and juridical basis, it may become the subject of legal dispute and struggle. Although identity formation is a process that begins outside the purview of legal rules and regulations, it is often quickly drawn into the legal field. This is also its strength. 'Identity' is a concept that presupposes a dialogical recognition of the other; it is a relational concept. But it is also a concept that presupposes identification in the sense that individuals recognize attributes or properties in each other that are construed as identical or at least similar. These properties, then, are used as an index of individual position and disposition. Identity is therefore a concept not so much of uniqueness or distinction as of resemblance and repetition (Jenkins, 1996). By contrast, an individual is a distinct assemblage of identities. Thus, individuality should be kept distinct from identity. When we use the concept identity we inevitably invoke a classification that places and positions an individual within a social space by virtue of his or her various identities.

Thus, the formation of group identity is a process whereby individuals recognize in each other certain attributes that establish resemblance and affinity. This becomes the basis of identification whereby individuals actively produce and reproduce equivalent dispositions. The dialogical process of recognition is an ongoing negotiation of habituating, inculcating, defining, redefining and reproducing these dispositions. Identity allows for the effective formation of groups which sometimes but not necessarily may lead to claim for legal entitlements. Although identity too can become a status concept, especially a social status, it should rather be thought as the basis of recognition demanded by groups excluded from the scope of citizenship. In other words, groups do not form out of individual properties and attributes that pre-exist groups. On the contrary, individual attributes of identity are formed via the group. But, at the same time, individual attributes can only form under material constraints. There are limits to both essentialist and constructivist views of identity in that they conflate individual and group identity. The affinity between citizenship and identity is that they are both group markers. Citizenship marks out the members of a polity from another as well as members of a polity from non-members. Identity marks out groups from each other as well as allowing for the constitution of groups as targets of assistance, hatred, animosity, sympathy or allegiance. As group markers the difference between citizenship and identity is that, while the former carries legal weight, the latter carries social and cultural weight.

A way to transcend the essentialist and constructivist conceptions of identity in modern political and social theory is to develop a sound conception of 'group'. As Iris Young (1990) has observed, our conceptions of social group are remarkably underdeveloped. In other words, the fixed and stable boundaries of identity have become contested by new identities and their fluidity (but also their new rigidity) and raised questions about the nature of social groups. Some have argued that the politics of identity has fragmented the political strength of groups based upon class. In this view, for the purpose of accentuating differences, identity politics weakened the 'common bond' among various oppressed and subordinated groups. Moreover, identity politics may have served to mask class conflicts underlying major struggles. The proponents of identity politics, however, charge that finding common ground under 'master identities' such as 'class' or 'nation' often ends up being a strategy of oppression and levelling of differences. How could a conception of politics recognize and respect group difference but allow for building alliances and blocs to struggle for rights?

This is where the affinities between citizenship and identity become politically and socially significant. Citizenship, despite modern, universalist rhetoric, has always been a group concept—but *it has never been expanded to all members of any polity*. Still today, in modern democratic states there are many members who are denied the legal status of citizenship on the basis of their place of birth. Moreover, many members of polities are excluded from the scope of citizenship even if they are legally entitled to its benefits.

While it is therefore a mistake to conflate citizenship and identity, it is also a mistake to see them as antinomic. There is certainly a tension between the universal aspirations of citizenship and particularistic claims of identity. Nevertheless, since citizenship has never been universal, it is more appropriate to interpret different formation of group identities as claims for recognition of citizenship rights. Many theorists have embraced postmodernism not as a threat but as a potential questioning of modern social and political theory. Those studies (W.E. Connolly, 1988, 1991; Hatab, 1995; Mouffe, 1992c, 1993; Trend,

1996) which have attempted to develop a concept of postmodern or radical democracy, without the essentialist assumptions of modern social and political theory, open more promising avenues than those commentators who are caught in a reactionary or nostalgic mode (Callinicos, 1989; Jameson, 1991). By exploring concepts such as conflict, struggle or agon and arguing that they do not need to be inconsistent with democracy and citizenship, by abandoning the unitary concept of individual and self, by abandoning the possibility of stable cultural identities, by refusing an ethic of ultimate ends, and by avoiding grand narratives and universal assumptions, teleological and evolutionist schemes, these studies begin to form an alternative to liberal democratic, socialist and communitarian conceptions of citizenship, democracy and politics. They also suggest an alternative to immature versions of postmodernism where the death of certainties is celebrated without an ethic of responsibility (O'Neill, 1995). Nevertheless, these theories also run the risk of falling into a constructivist trap where identities appear as an outcome of free or unmediated choice and in which every individual has the same capacity, skill and resources to form identities as any other.

As we have seen, while liberal and communitarian views establish an irresolvable antinomy between citizenship and identity, civic republican views conflate them. While radical democratic views seem to articulate sound principles with which to construct an alternative, multilayered or differentiated conception of citizenship, they are also troubled by theoretical and political problems, especially with respect to group rights. This book does not pretend to solve these problems. *Citizenship and Identity* has two aims. First, it provides a conceptual framework with which to navigate complex and variegated problems of citizenship from the perspective of cultural politics in the late twentieth century. Second, by moving from theoretical and normative views of citizenship to politics and practices of different types of citizenship and identifying problems, dangers and possibilities in each, it attempts to clear a path for further work. While exploring the possibility of a richer and multilayered conception of citizenship understood as an ensemble of different forms of belonging rather than a universal or unitary conception, it addresses the question of what happens to citizenship when we acknowledge the challenge of identity/difference politics. What happens to different types of citizenship when we attempt to accommodate group difference and articulate a broader principle at the same time? What problems may we encounter, for example, when we accept the possibility of ecological citizenship and technological citizenship simultaneously?

This book builds on the radical critiques of liberalism, communitarianism and civic republicanism, but by attempting to make its claim operational, it hopefully also provides some correctives to these critiques. It critically appropriates the debates over postmodern or radical democracy and its conception of citizenship. While drawing upon European, American, Canadian and Australian literatures, the concluding chapter explores the potential and danger of postmodern citizenship with examples, primarily but not exclusively, drawn from the debates over sexual, technological, ecological, ethnic and consumer rights.

Citizenship and Identity proceeds with two principles. First, it acknowledges that postmodernization and globalization force us to abandon the unitary, homogeneous concept of citizenship in favour of a multidimensional and plural concept of citizenship. Improving upon a typology developed by Turner (1990), it develops a typology of forms of radical democratic citizenship, which include the political, civil, social, economic, diasporic, cultural, sexual and ecological. It critically examines the claim that these forms are not mutually exclusive but overlapping and intersecting dimensions of a radical democratic citizen. Being a radical citizen cannot be *merely* associated with being a member of the nation-state and nationality as master identity. Rather, the *identity* of a postmodern citizen is an ensemble of these different forms of citizenship understood as competent membership in various value-spheres or fields such as the sexual or ecological. Second, it accepts that postmodernization and globalization also compel us to move beyond the essentialist and constructivist assumptions of identity. While being a citizen cannot be conceived as a fixed right and privilege but is an ongoing negotiation of identity and difference, the resources available to enter such negotiations are not equally distributed. The constitutive element of being a citizen may well be the restoration of agon in political life, but inequalities in redistribution of resources as well as in recognition of differences force us to reassert citizenship as an institution for reducing and eliminating such inequalities.

By formalizing the tension between citizenship and identity and by expanding the scope of citizenship via recognizing several group rights and identities, would we be running a danger of essentializing identities? When we defend the possibilities of diasporic citizenship, sexual citizenship or cultural citizenship are we opening up a way to freeze and essentialize these categories? These are certainly serious dangers. We address each in related chapters. We think that dangers of not confronting the modern idea and practice of citizenship outweigh the difficulties resulting from the confrontation.

In Chapter 2, we examine the relationship between citizenship and identity in the context of T.H. Marshall's seminal work on class and citizenship. We discuss his basic framework of citizenship, critical views of his model, and the potential responses contained in his later work. While we find his framework useful, especially his focus on class, we also stress the need to go beyond his work by including different forms of citizenship, which he perhaps could not have considered. To do that we first examine a neglected nineteenth-century jurist, Otto Gierke, and his work on the history of group rights. We argue that the followers of Gierke such as Durkheim and Tönnies misappropriated his work and shifted the discussion of group rights into, as Derek Phillips (1993) recognized, a problematic debate over the meaning of community. But his work can be reappropriated to argue that group rights constitute the riddle of modernity, which has been exposed by the new social movements of cultural politics. While Gierke is useful in providing a historical perspective on group rights, his position on the real existence of groups is weighed down with essentialist tendencies. Bourdieu, however, made the most sustained attempt to go beyond the objectivist and subjectivist accounts of groups, and we turn to his work, especially the key concepts of *habitus*, *capital* and *field*, to rework Gierke. This allows us re-evaluate the important work of Iris Young and her attempt to rework the concept of social group. The result is not, we are afraid, a resolution of the tension between community and the individual, the universal and the particular, or even between citizenship and identity. But we hope it is a conceptual outlook that grounds an ethos of pluralization, makes possible a radically plural rather than dual way of thinking about citizenship and identity. and allows us to negotiate a subtle and dangerous but promising line of thought that avoids essentialism, constructivism, universalism and particularism simultaneously.

Chapter 3 explores the possibility of diasporic citizenship. Although this form of citizenship has been called 'multicultural citizenship', we have concerns with not only the implications of the term in contemporary politics but also the theoretical tradition that uses it as a synonym for a thinly veiled politics of 'accommodation'. We argue that diasporic citizenship is not about accommodation of 'minorities' within liberal democracies but about radical, mutual transformation of politics that effectively breaks down barriers and discrimination based upon ethnic, racial, national and Aboriginal identities, while reconstructing citizenship along plural lines. Chapter 4 continues this reconstructing for sexual identities with a keen eye on various subtle but significant differentiations and identities based upon sexual choices, orientations and realities. The argument in both chapters is that while diasporic and sexual identities pose severe challenges to the nation-state and its homogeneous imaginary, they also begin to allow us to imagine a postnational state where citizens negotiate their differences along various allegiances and identities without an appeal to shared values or even a common good or tradition.

If the postcolonial and sexual identities begin to afford the possibility of imagining a postnational state, globalization begins to allow us to imagine a cosmopolitan form of citizenship where groups purposefully negotiate their differences not only within nation-states but also across them as transnational movements and flows. Since this is a vast subject and spans various scholarly terrains, including international theory, in Chapter 5 we take three forms of cosmopolitan citizenship and explore their possibilities. Technological citizenship is one which raises the spectre of not only access to communications technology but also the use of identification technologies. Ecological citizenship raises concerns about the constitution of nature as an object of care. Urban citizenship highlights issues surrounding the increased differentiation and articulation of particular spaces around the globe, forming special type of networks or wired zones.

If globalization is contesting the sovereignty of the nation-state and making its boundaries permeable, giving rise to various forms of cosmopolitan citizenship, postmodernization is creating new forms of social differentiation, establishing new relationships between class and citizenship. Chapter 6 negotiates a position that can be described as a postmarxist political economy, laying out the new relations of social class under advanced capitalism, and setting out a new relationship between citizenship and class. By so doing it draws upon three distinct, but in our view interrelated, literatures on cultural capital, governmentality and consumption studies. The result is a conception of consumer citizenship which neither accepts the consumer citizen as the passive automaton of traditional critical theory, following the rules set out by mass media and advertising, nor constitutes the consumer citizen as the free subject, making unmediated and unconstrained choices.

Throughout this book, space—understood not as metaphor to stand for openings, but as real, material spaces and the struggles to produce, regulate and modulate them—is quite central to our arguments. Whether we are discussing gay rights and how they claim spaces for group expression or discussing the possibilities of cosmopolitan democracy and how geopolitics engender various identities, we consider not only space as a backdrop against which, and perhaps within which, events take place, but how relations of power constitute spaces which produce and reproduce possibilities and dangers for certain individuals and their capacities to claim rights and form themselves as groups (Keith and Pile, 1993).

In Chapter 7, we take stock of the variegated terrain we have navigated over these pages and consider where all this might lead. If all we have done is open new paths of investigation and, thus, resituate the debate, we will have made a useful contribution.

2
MODERN CITIZENSHIP: CIVIL, POLITICAL AND SOCIAL

Introduction

This chapter develops a conceptual outlook necessary to address group-differentiated citizenship. It discusses the limits of modern conceptions of citizenship in the context of T.H. Marshall and his critics and under the twin pressures of postmodernization (fragmentation and pluralization) and globalization (interconnectedness and flows). It focuses on group rights as the 'riddle of modernity'. It sets out the claim that citizenship, far from a universal concept, embodies the multifarious and complex character of the political subject. After critically reviewing the work of Marshall, the chapter proceeds with a discussion of group rights as the riddle of modernity via a focus on the work of the nineteenth-century German jurist Otto Gierke. It then develops a set of conceptual tools via Pierre Bourdieu to link up with Iris Young, whose work constitutes one of the most cogent attempts to rethink social groups and group-differentiated citizenship. The chapter ends by drawing together the themes of Chapters 1 and 2.

Constituting Modern Citizenship

Widely regarded as an important contributor to citizenship studies, T.H. Marshall has nevertheless been criticized for his evolutionary scheme and for his exclusive focus on citizenship as rights. He has also been criticized for his lack of emphasis on the social struggles that surrounded the development of citizenship (Mann, 1987; Turner, 1986, 1990). However, Marshall's *Citizenship and Social Class* (1950) remains what Michel Foucault (1998b) might call the founding document of modern citizenship studies. Thus, Marshall's brief, succinct and powerful analysis is the place where we begin our discussion.

Marshall's own starting point was a lecture delivered by Alfred Marshall in 1873 on the *Future of the Working Classes*. T.H. Marshall believed that this lecture, although delivered by an economist, contained an implicit sociological hypothesis about the relationship between the equality of citizenship and the inequality of class:

> It postulates that there is a kind of basic human equality associated with the concept of full membership of a community—or, as I should say, of citizenship—which is not inconsistent with the inequalities which distinguish the various economic levels in the society. In other words, the inequality of the

social class system may be acceptable provided the equality of citizenship is recognised. (Marshall, 1992: 6)

According to T.H. Marshall, Alfred Marshall wondered to what extent class mobility was a reality, and where the ceiling of such mobility might hang. He concluded that class inequality would never be eliminated, but that all men could nevertheless become gentlemen (4–5). By this he meant that although their heavy physical labour prevented the working classes from developing habits and mentalities that would enable them to share in the social and cultural heritage of the nation, throughout their acceptance of 'the private and public duties of a citizen' they realized 'the truth that they are men, and not producing machines' (5). Citizenship, according to Alfred Marshall, was a status expressing a capacity or competence to be a member of society. Equality of citizenship did not mean equality of class. On the contrary, citizenship could and did maintain class inequality.

Instead of considering citizenship and class as opposing principles, Marshall raised the question of whether modern citizenship had become a condition of class inequality. 'Is it still true', he asked, 'that basic equality, when enriched in substance and embodied in the formal rights of citizenship, is consistent with the inequalities of social class?' (7). This question still haunts us: is citizenship an institution that masks various forms of inequality such as based on gender, race and ethnicity? To answer this question, Marshall articulated a historical typology of citizenship, mapping out its development alongside that of class.

This typology was composed of the civil, the political and the social. Civil citizenship included individual freedoms of speech, thought and faith and rights to property, contract and justice. Political citizenship included the right to participate in public decisions and vote. Social citizenship consisted of the right to security and welfare and to share in the 'social heritage and to live the life of a civilized being according to the standards prevailing in the society' (8). Marshall emphasized that the history of citizenship he is tracing is national rather than local as in medieval cities. In the medieval period, these three types of citizenship were fused together and inseparable, and only existed in cities where it meant the right to the city and its institutions. Outside cities, however, the mark and measure of inequality was status and there was no uniform collection of rights and duties with which all persons were endowed. The specific rights and duties of an individual were drawn from the specific location (whether town or countryside) and situation (noble, common, clergy). Under such conditions, civil, political and social rights were all fused and inseparable. Presumably beginning with the fifteenth century (but Marshall does not say), the three parted ways developing in a rough historical sequence: civil rights in the eighteenth century, political in the nineteenth and social in the twentieth. Marshall cautions that this periodization should be treated with elasticity and given allowance for overlap.

Marshall traces the evolution of civil rights through a series of legislation passed between 1688 and 1832 concerning the freedom of the individual (10). Factory and Poor Laws provided the individual with the ability to participate in the development of the industrial capitalist model. While political rights existed in the eighteenth century, they were far from universal. The nineteenth century saw a greater extension of the franchise in particular, although substantial gains eluded the vast majority until the twentieth century. The franchise remained a group monopoly. Political rights were extended to those who, using their civil rights, had made economic gains and purchased property (13).

Throughout both centuries, social rights were separated from citizenship. The Poor Laws and Factory Acts demonstrated that one could rely on the state's protection only when one abandoned one's civil and political rights. Women and the poor gained protection from the more desperate aspects of modern capitalism only on the assumption that they were unable to be full citizens, with the strength to manage for themselves (14–15). Needing such protection, they were then denied many civil, political and social rights. It was only in the twentieth century, with the rise of trade unionism and the right to bargain collectively, that social rights emerged with respect to the workplace that did not preclude citizenship, what Marshall terms 'industrial citizenship' (26).

The development of state-supported elementary education in the nineteenth century was 'the first decisive step on the road to reestablishment of social rights in the twentieth', yet it, too, emanated from the mutual exclusion of social rights and citizenship. In an unusual departure from free-market capitalism, public schooling became compulsory on the grounds that children, who were not yet citizens, were nonetheless 'citizens in the making'. Previously established civil and political rights, which were supporting modern capitalism, required an educated populace and workforce (16–17).

Marshall does not adequately address the circumstances that brought about the changes in rights and citizenship. The important context he fails to provide is the way in which capitalism was linked to the pursuit of empire. War played a stronger and earlier role than he appreciates (25). The needs brought about by such pursuits, particularly military, played a significant role in the creation of a national imaginary. As the demand for staffing the army and navy increased, British statesmen sought ways by which to encourage the loyal service of the masses. By selling the people a mostly rhetorical share in the nation, state authorities were rewarded with societal support and men in uniform (Colley, 1992). In many cases, we are presented with a dominant group extending certain rights and privileges in exchange for services (military, industrial, etc.) which in turn entrenched the power and prosperity of the dominant group.

After this turn through British labour and social history, Marshall returns directly to his question of the relationship between citizenship and class: 'Citizenship', he asserts, 'is status bestowed on those who are full members of a community. All who possess the status are equal with respect to the rights and duties with which the status endowed' (Marshall, 1992: 18). Class, on the other hand, is a system of inequality. It is reasonable to expect that the impact of citizenship on social class should take the form of a conflict between opposing principles. If modern citizenship has been developing since the seventeenth century, it has been concomitant with the rise of capitalism, which is a system of inequality. How did these seemingly two opposing principles of citizenship and class evolve together? What made it possible for them to be reconciled with one another and to become, for a time at least, allies instead of antagonists? To Marshall these questions were vitally important to residents of the twentieth century, for he believed that citizenship and class were at war again.

Marshall makes a distinction between two types of class. First, he discusses class as order: patricians, plebeians, serfs, slaves and so forth. This type of class dominated early modern societies. The equality implicit in the concept of citizenship would have a profound and disturbing effect on class as order or rank (18–19). Or, as he articulates succinctly: 'No subtle argument is needed to show that citizenship is incompatible with medieval feudalism.' Societal laws and customs do not construct the second type of class Marshall identifies. Rather than an independent institution itself, it is the result of relationships between other institutions. As Marshall sees it, the differences among groups defined by this form of class 'emerge from the interplay of a variety of factors related to institutions of property and education and the structure of the national economy' (19).

In contrast to the first type (class as social order or status), Marshall argued that citizenship did not conflict with a second type of class, which we might call 'modern class'. On the contrary, as we have discussed briefly above, civil and political rights were in fact necessary to the development of capitalism and its class system by giving each adult male the right to engage as an independent agent in economic struggle. Civil citizenship made class differentiation less vulnerable to attack by alleviating its less defensible consequences (20–21). Citizenship 'raised the floor-level in the basement of social edifice, and perhaps made it rather more hygienic than it was before' (20). In short, civil rights did not conflict with the inequalities of capitalist society but were necessary to the maintenance of that particular form of inequality.

According to Marshall, citizenship requires a different bond than kinship; it is a direct sense of polity based on loyalty to a civilization, which is a common possession. It is the loyalty of free men endowed with rights and protected by a common law. The growth of citizenship is stimulated both by the struggle to exercise those rights and by their enjoyment when won (25). It is significant that the core of citizenship at this stage was composed of civil rights. Differential status associated with orders, rank and family was not eliminated in society; rather, such status was replaced by the institution of citizenship. This provided the foundation of status equality—equality of opportunity—on which the structure of class inequality could be built (21). Modern citizenship conferred the legal capacity to strive for the things one would like to possess but did not guarantee the possession of any of them: 'A property right is not a right to possess property, but a right to acquire it, if you can, and to protect it, if you can get it' (21).

The end of the nineteenth century brought the incorporation of social rights into the status of citizenship, for which Marshall singles out three reasons. First, he argues, was the rise of egalitarian principles, which were expressed in the expansion of social citizenship. He identifies a growing interest in equality as a principle of social justice and an appreciation of the fact that the formal recognition of an equal capacity for rights was insufficient (24). Second was the rise of real incomes, which closed the gap between classes. Third was the development of mass production and the widespread incorporation of the working class in mass consumption, which we shall later elaborate as Fordism in Chapter 6. The expansion of social citizenship created a universal right to real income which is not proportionate to the market value of the claimant (28). Marshall argues that the incorporation of social rights had a profound effect on class inequality. The reduction of class conflict was still the aim of social rights, but it had acquired a new meaning: 'It is no longer merely an attempt to abate the obvious nuisance of destitution in the lowest ranks of society. It has assumed the guise of action modifying the whole pattern of social inequality' (28). Moreover, '[t]he political rights of citizenship, unlike the civil rights, were full of potential danger to the capitalist system, although those who were cautiously extending them down the social scale probably did not realise quite how great the danger was' (25).

Marshall argues that the rise of social rights in the twentieth century, however, has made citizenship the architect of a new class inequality. He illustrates this with a review of social services with particular emphasis on housing and education. In planning housing projects with the idea of balanced community, planners created new classification schemes, which become embedded in individuals (35–36). Similarly, education became tied to occupation: 'Great and increasing respect is paid to certificates, matriculation, degrees and diplomas as qualifications for employment, and their freshness does not fade with the passage of the years' (38). Marshall admits that '[t]his development is partly the result of the systematisation of techniques in more and more professional, semi-professional and skilled occupations ...' (38). But it is also fostered by the refinement of the selective process within the educational system itself. Individuals are classified into certain groups of aptitude or profession by an essentially arbitrary system which becomes a system of class differentiation. The repeated classification into groups, followed by assimilation within each group and differentiation between groups, results in the entrenchment of these differences as class differences. To Marshall this is 'precisely the way in which social classes in a fluid society have always taken shape' (39).

The important conclusion to his argument is that 'through education in its relations with occupational structure, citizenship operates as an instrument of social stratification' (39). 'The claims of status are to a hierarchical wage structure, each level of which represents a social right and not merely a market value' (42). Thus, Marshall concludes that 'the preservation of economic inequalities has been made more difficult by the enrichment of the status of citizenship. There is less room for them, and there is more and more likelihood of their being challenged' (45).

Marshall criticizes those who think of the conflict between citizenship and class as merely the result of muddled thinking of legislators and governors. He argues that 'the conflict of principles springs from the very roots of our social order in the present phase of the development of democratic citizenship. Apparent inconsistencies are in fact a source of stability, achieved through compromise which is not dictated by logic' (49). And he adds, 'this phase will not continue indefinitely' (49).

The criticisms of Marshall can be classified into four groups (Birnbaum, 1997; Rees, 1996). First, some thought that Marshall emphasized only how citizenship ameliorated class conflicts but not how citizenship rights were earned as a result of class struggles. Giddens criticizes Marshall for not emphasizing the struggle aspect of the rise of citizenship rights. 'The extension of citizenship rights, in Britain as in other societies, was in substantial degree the result of the efforts of the underprivileged to improve their lot' (Giddens, 1982: 171). Some extended this criticism by arguing that Marshall focused on how citizenship restructures class rather than or perhaps as well as exploring how class conditioned citizenship. Bottomore, for example, argued that 'Marshall recognised that an element of conflict existed, but he expressed it as a clash between opposing principles rather than between classes, and his discussion of class was primarily concerned, as he said, with the impact of citizenship on social class, not with the ways in which the historical development of classes had itself generated new conceptions of citizenship and movements to expand the rights of citizens. But the impact of class on citizenship is unmistakable' (1992: 73). Second, some criticized Marshall for his sequence of rights, arguing that historically citizenship emerged in a circuitous way rather than in a linear fashion as he suggested (Birnbaum, 1997). Third, there are also those who argued that Marshall assumed that class was the only pattern of inequality and did not examine other forms of inequality such as gender and ethnicity (Turner, 1986). Although important, class nevertheless was only one of the inequalities that divided early twentieth-century society. Gender, race and ethnic inequalities were also significant. Marshall had nothing to say about these. As well, since Marshall delivered his influential lecture, new identities have been formed that demand incorporation in an enriched form of citizenship.

To conclude, the sociological question as to whether there is an inherent conflict between citizenship and class formulated by Marshall now needs to be expanded. The sociological question postmodern societies face today is whether there is a conflict between citizenship and different forms of identity. How does citizenship contribute to or ameliorate sexual, gender, national, ethnic and regional identities? As we have seen in Chapter 1, this question goes right to the core question of modernity and group rights.

To an extent, Marshall has responded to some of this criticism. Twenty years after his seminal lecture, for example, he returned to his sociological question in another lecture (Marshall, 1981). His main concern this time was power and rights. In the context of considering which type of rights would prove most effective in averting the threat of the rise of authoritarianism, he elaborated on the differences between these rights (Marshall, 1981: 140). He argued that political rights do not hold the promise of averting such a threat because they are exercised through a centralized body politic and as such easy to undermine. Similarly, social rights are not designed for the exercise of power at all. They reflect the strong individualist element in mass society, but only as individuals are consumers, not actors. We would take issue with this definition of social rights in that they can be construed as precondition of the exercise of political rights by endowing individuals with the capacity to exercise political judgement. Nevertheless, Marshall thought that the character of civil rights was very different. They refer to the individual as actor, rather than as consumer. Civil rights express principles which are internalized in the early stages of socialization. He said, 'They thus become part of the individual's personality, a pervasive element in his daily life, an intrinsic component of his culture, the foundation of his capacity to act socially and the creator of the environmental conditions which make social action possible in a democratic civilisation' (141). Civil rights also permeate the social body, making it very difficult to attack them. Civil rights also, though vested in individuals, are used to create groups, associations, corporations and movements of every kind. They are the basis of political and social pluralism (142).

These reflections indicate that Marshall thought of citizenship as constitutive of subjectivities rather than a passive status (cf. Turner, 1994b: 159). Similarly, his remark on the capacity of civil rights to create groups and movements illustrates that he also regarded citizenship as practice. Civil rights therefore are deeply involved with power. Marshall went on to make a distinction among three forms of power: (i) power over or the power to give orders which will generally be obeyed, (ii) power derived from possession of resources; and (iii) following Weber, power as a potential rather than a quantity. 'The distinction is important because a potential for power may exist without being exercised' (Marshall, 1981: 144). Marshall suggested that the first two are not essential characteristics of power. The third form of power is the use made of the capacity for successful action, where 'capacity' refers both to faculties and to facilities— in fact to their union, for action in a situation in which action of this kind has a chance of success (145). This kind of power 'denotes the sort of action that is possible for citizens whose modes of thought and behaviour, whose assessment of the desirable and the possible, have been fashioned with the help of a well-established system of civil rights and their absorption into their social personality' (145).

Marshall elaborated on this concept of civil rights and power by briefly discussing the civil rights movement in America, which is illuminating. He discussed the thoughts of black leaders such as Malcolm X and concluded that the powerlessness of blacks was due not simply to lack of rights, but to much deeper causes. He argued that it was the way in which the blacks possessed power that made them powerless. He claimed that the leaders were well aware of this and were asking not for power over or redistribution but rather an effective share in the total power of society, which we might now call the politics of recognition. 'The concept of power which runs through the writings of these people and of those who have sought to understand them is one where "power" is the antithesis of frustration—frustration of self and of the group of which one is a member' (150). It is the power to escape anomie, disrespect and alienation to achieve legitimate goals by the use of legitimate means. This was not a demand for civil rights, for the Black movement did not seek admission into American society as it is. Rather, 'The goal is a new kind of society, truly multiracial or, should that prove impossible, then, some would say, composed of independent and equal racial communities' (150). Marshall seemed to anticipate the debate over multiculturalism with an outlook that is much more progressive than those who treat these claims as 'rights for minorities'. We hope to have illustrated that too much focus on a singular text by Marshall led towards a neglect of his larger body of work that not only elaborated upon his earlier work on citizenship but also broadened his conception.

This emphasis on recognition and distribution, self-esteem and domination, as we shall later in this chapter, themes that have been taken up fruitfully by Iris Young (1990), Honneth (1996b) and Fraser (1997a). Nevertheless, group rights and the idea of groups remain undertheorized in political and social theory.

Group Rights: A Third Form of Liberty?

A scholar who explicitly emphasized group rights and who is much less known for this emphasis is Isaiah Berlin (1969). His characterization of liberty in its 'negative' and 'positive' forms is well known. Although it was considered by many to be a vague distinction, Berlin argued that the freedom to individual self-determination was as prominent an aspect of liberty as the freedom from constraints, which is the more common understanding of liberty. What is much less known and discussed about his famous essay 'Two Concepts of Liberty' is that Berlin also raised the possibility of a third form of liberty. Berlin named this as desire of recognition displayed by social groups. 'The lack of freedom about which men or groups complain amounts, as often as not, to the lack of proper recognition' (Berlin, 1969: 155). This view clearly resonates with that of late Marshall on the civil rights movement. While Berlin cautioned against regarding social groups as being literally persons, he asked 'would it be natural or desirable to call the demand for recognition and status a demand for liberty in some third sense?' (155).

Berlin argued that the desire for recognition was different from both forms of liberty and it should be considered as a third form because it was about the assertion of self and agency. Moreover,

> what is true of the individual is true of groups, social, political, economic, religious, that is, men conscious of needs and purposes which they have as members of such groups. What oppressed classes or nationalities, as a rule, demand is neither simply unhampered liberty of action for their members, nor, above everything, equality of social and economic opportunity, still less assignment of a place in a frictionless, organic state devised by the national lawgiver. What they want, as often as not, is simply recognition (of their class or nation, or colour or race) as an independent source of human activity, as an entity with a will of its own, intending to act in accordance with it (whether it is good or legitimate, or not), and not to be ruled, educated, guided, with however light a hand, as being not quite fully human, and therefore not quite fully free. (156–157)

Therefore, this third form of liberty, 'although it entails negative freedom for the entire group, is more closely related to solidarity, fraternity, mutual understanding, [and] need for association on equal terms' (158). Berlin criticized the liberal tradition, especially Mill, for not understanding the desire for group recognition. Berlin was convinced that unless this form of liberty is recognized it would be impossible to understand why individuals belonging to certain groups accept the curtailment of their individual liberties but still feel enjoyment of group liberty (158–159).

We argue that Berlin highlighted a major flaw in liberalism and was trenchant in his assessment of liberalism: '[i]t is the non-recognition of this psychological and political fact (which lurks behind the apparent ambiguity of the term "liberty") that has, perhaps, blinded some contemporary liberals to the world in which they live' (162). Yet, subsequent liberals mostly ignore this deep challenge raised by Berlin. As we shall see in Chapter 3, Will Kymlicka's problem, for example, of how to impose liberal principles on 'illiberal' groups becomes redundant if one recognizes, as Berlin did, the legitimacy of group rights. Ultimately, Berlin thought that '[t]he wish to assert the "personality" of my class, or group or nation, is connected both with the answer to the question "What is to be the area of authority?" (for the group must not be interfered with by outside masters), and, even more closely, with the answer to the question "Who is to govern us?"—govern well or badly, liberally or oppressively—but above all "who?"' (160). Although, as far as we know, Berlin did not further elaborate the problem of group rights he raised, his discussion remains an essential starting point for the recognition of group rights. But to move beyond Berlin we need to develop a history of group rights and a sociology of groups. We will briefly focus on Otto Gierke for the former and on Pierre Bourdieu for the latter.

While many commentators remark that cultural or social identity is a modern problem, the deep historical source of this problematization is rarely discussed. It is often emphasized that the sovereign individual is a modern construct and 'its' identity has been constructed by the state. As we have seen, it has now been recognized that group rights must be seriously considered in an age of postmodernization and globalization (Shapiro and Kymlicka, 1997). Nevertheless, the intriguing history through which the state–individual dichotomy appeared is not examined. It is also often assumed that such a dichotomy is coterminous with the rise of modern capitalism. It can be argued, however, not only that this dichotomy goes further back in history than modern capitalism but that it was also crucial for its emergence. Otto Gierke is the most outstanding contributor to the history of group rights. His main argument is that modernity is built upon the obliteration of the idea of group rights, which was the hallmark of the medieval configuration of power between the eleventh and fifteenth centuries in Europe.

Gierke regarded the modern idea of political association, recognizing only the sovereign individual and sovereign state, as a flawed conception of political life (1900, 1934, 1939, 1977, 1990). He argued that the modern idea of unity was a mythical entity and that political life embodied an irreducible multiplicity, which was expressed through group identity and membership. Writing in the late nineteenth century, he argued that the future of democracy was suspect unless public law recognized group rights mediating between the state and the individual.

Gierke developed his view of group rights on the basis of historical research that took him to ancient, medieval and early modern associations of all sorts, including warrior bands, guilds, cities, leagues and communes. He concluded that throughout history group rights played a significant role in formation of individual identities and that the latter would have been inconceivable without the former. In other words, Gierke refuted the idea that the individual existed before or independent of the group to which he or she belonged. Instead, he argued that group identities were as real as individual identities and they were socially and morally constructed through the intersubjective process of mutual recognition. He insisted that the way people are connected makes a difference to the kind of persons they are as well as to the kind of group to which they belong (Gierke, 1990: xv).

Gierke also demonstrated that until modernity, group rights were significant aspects of social and political life. Drawing upon five stages of European history from the ninth century to the nineteenth, he examined the rise of groups such as guilds and cities. Gierke argued that group rights always battled against unifying and centralizing political forces. He set up several opposing principles as ideal types between fellowship and lordship, and between corporation and institution. Fellowship and corporation expressed principles of group rights as an embodiment of free wills of individuals forming collective identities. The distinguishing characteristic of fellowship and corporation was that they owed their existence neither to an essential, natural origin nor to an external unity imposed by a sovereign. Rather, individuals constructed these identities. He contrasted these with lordship and institution, which expressed the will of sovereigns who imposed particular identities on groups. In the latter case the freedoms and rights of groups were transformed into duties and obligations of its members to a sovereign.

Gierke argued that especially between the twelfth and the fifteenth centuries, Europe was marked by a smorgasbord of guilds, craft guilds, confederacies, associations, chapters, cities, leagues, federations, and numerous multiple and overlapping identities. Since no single sovereign was able to impose a unity, politics was a battle of an 'inexhaustible combination' of identities. Even the so-called 'medieval city' was not so much a unity as a multiplicity of guilds, associations and communities that formed an unstable and constantly changing confederation of such associations. Unlike the contemporary communitarian and civic republican philosophers, Gierke emphasized instability and conflict rather than unity and harmony in medieval cities (Gierke, 1990: 42). Also unlike Marshall, Gierke found civil, political and social rights clearly developed in medieval cities, including both the rights of the city and the rights of citizens (Gierke, 1990: 35).

For Gierke the real historical question was the transformation of Europe from an inexhaustible combination of identities exercising group rights to modernity, where only two sovereignties were recognized: the state and the individual. The details of his explanation, which focused on the adoption of Roman law, need not concern us here (Gierke, 1900, 1934; Maitland, 1898; Ullmann, 1968). Nonetheless, Gierke highlighted the transition from the principle of group rights to the principle of sovereignty, where the absolute state was at the same time a supervisory state. He argued that while the medieval concept of citizen embodied political rights and duties, active and passive participation, and lordship and obedience, the early modern subject was a subject only in the sphere of private law; in public law the subject was merely the object of power (Gierke, 1990: 110). Gierke argued that although the rise of modern civil and political citizenship in the nineteenth century provided for the rights to free association, these rights never recognized group rights. The laws governing the formation of groups and association remained very restrictive and based upon the institution principle rather than the fellowship principle (Gierke, 1990: 168–183).

The significant point that emerges from Gierke's work is that modernity never solved the riddle of group rights and identity. The modern state was able to impose a unity that lasted for a long time and was able to suppress multiplicities with a master national identity. In other words, the modern state exercised hegemony over these multiplicities. Balibar (1995) calls hegemonic those institutions that are capable of imposing a single superior identity on all the individuals who recognize themselves as members of different groups and thereby conferring a universal ethic on the multiplicity of practices. He argues that modern history presents us with two great competing models of a hegemonic institution: the religious and the national. Each is authentically hegemonic because, although it does not suppress the multiplicity of belongings as a totalitarian institution would, it succeeds for a longer or shorter time to impose certain limits to pacify these multiplicities (Balibar, 1995: 180). Similarly, Laclau argues that there is no such thing as universal identity. There are different groups, which struggle with each other for representational hegemony to establish their particularisms as universal (Laclau, 1995). There are obvious echoes of Gierke's discussion of group rights in these arguments.

Gierke's work found earlier echoes in Marx, Durkheim, Weber, Tönnies and many scholars who focused on the struggles for group rights. As Black (1984) has argued, the similarities between Marx and Gierke with their emphasis on solidarity and fellowship are due to the shared sources they drew upon rather than an awareness of each other. The same cannot be claimed for Durkheim, Weber or Tönnies since each acknowledged their debt to Gierke. The well-known distinction, for example, made by Durkheim between mechanical solidarity and organic solidarity is based upon Gierke. Durkheim also appropriated Gierke and argued for the importance of associations and group solidarities between the state and the individual. He argued that political and social problems were directly related to the lack of intermediate associations between the individual and the state (Durkheim, 1992: 96). 'But what are the groups which are to free the state from the individual? Those able to fulfil this are of two kinds. First, the regional groups. We could imagine, in fact, that the representatives of the *commune*s of one and the same *arrondissement*, perhaps even of one and the same *département*, might constitute the electoral body having the duty of electing the members of the political assemblies. Or professional groups, once set up, might be of use for this task' (Durkheim, 1992: 96). Durkheim argues, however, that regional groups no longer have the importance they once had because people are now so mobile and lack loyalties to place. The ties which unite the members of regional groups such as cities, regions, villages, are fairly external and not permanent. There is something artificial about such groups. 'The permanent groups, those to which the individual devotes his whole life, those for which he has the strongest attachment, are the professional groups. It therefore seems indeed that it is they which may be called upon to become the basis of our political representation as well as of our social structure in the future' (Durkheim, 1992: 96–97).

Unlike Gierke, therefore, Durkheim believed that urban communities could not fulfil this function because of the dramatically altered state of interconnections among individuals in modern society. Instead, he argued that occupational and professional groups could fulfil such a role. Similarly, Tönnies' well-known distinction between community and association was based on Gierke (Tönnies, 1963). But it can be argued that by shifting the discussion from group rights to community, Durkheim and Tönnies actually misappropriated Gierke, for whom the issue was which entity was a legitimate bearer of rights. By contrast, Weber's significant chapter on the city as a political association in his *Economy and Society* illustrates that Weber, who was a student of Gierke in Berlin (S.P. Turner and Factor, 1994), read Gierke very closely and responded to his arguments and interpretations.

Although Gierke's conclusions and his recommendations for early twentieth-century Germany have been criticized, his work is full of historical insights for thinking about group rights. Unfortunately, scholars such as Anne Phillips (1993), Iris Young (1989, 1990), Honneth (1996a, 1996b), Fraser (1997a), Charles Taylor (1994) and Kymlicka (1995) do not consider his work. Nevertheless, Gierke can be critically appropriated by suggesting that the boundaries and the existence of groups are always social struggles of recognition and rights. In modernity, since public law does not recognize group rights, these struggles take the form of battles over the existence and identity of such groups. Whereas Gierke and Berlin have raised the issue of group rights in modernity, Bourdieu has developed conceptual tools with which to reflect on such groups.

Classification Struggles and Group Rights

In a wide-ranging empirical work comparable to Marx or Weber, Pierre Bourdieu has developed an impressive vocabulary, an innovative methodology and a philosophy of social research. We shall argue that despite certain empirical and theoretical criticisms of his work, an interpretive analytics of groups is present in his work that is much more advanced than that of Marx or Weber or Foucault.

Bourdieu argues that the most difficult theoretical problem with the existence of a group is that it is itself an instrument of struggle. This is a crucial insight and highlights many conceptual problems that persist in literature on the existence of groups. In a playful move Bourdieu calls the attempts to represent groups symbolically as 'classification struggles' (Bourdieu, 1984, 1987: 3). For Bourdieu classification struggles (in which different groups argue for and against the existence of certain groups in society) and class struggles (in which individuals and groups struggle for their material and ideal interests) reinforce and condition each other. Failing to recognize this aspect of group or class results in either objectivism (assuming that classification of individuals by using such criteria as occupation, employment, income, education or ownership of the means of production can correspond to classes as they exist in reality) or subjectivism (assuming that individuals adequately classify themselves according to their consciousness of the social world). Objectivism treats individuals as things that can be classified while subjectivism denies real existence of class positions unless individuals have consciousness of such positions.

According to Bourdieu, those who assert the 'real' existence of groups take an objectivist stand and assume that groups as described by scholars exist in reality. The difficulty with objectivism, as many scholars have shown, is that the variety of individuals in the real world becomes impossible to classify discretely. This difficulty then makes it possible for others to argue that there are no real social differences among individuals. Bourdieu argues that those who assert that groups exist in reality and those who argue that groups are nothing other than analytical constructs actually subscribe to the same notion of reality as directly available to the intuition of everyday experience. Bourdieu argues that 'it is possible to deny the existence of classes as homogeneous sets of economically and socially differentiated individuals objectively constituted into groups, and to assert at the same time the existence of a space of differences based on a principle of economic and social differentiation' (Bourdieu, 1987: 3). In order to do so, Bourdieu makes a distinction between theoretical groups (or classes) and practical groups (or classes): the former is the work of symbolic or classification struggles while the latter is the result of the practical and political work of organizing and mobilizing. Any homology between theoretical and practical groups is a result of both intellectual and political work. The theoretical classes can be characterized as a group of individuals who, by virtue of the fact that they occupy similar positions in social space, are subject to similar conditions of existence and are endowed with similar dispositions. Intellectual work classifies these individuals, who, being subject to similar conditions, tend to resemble one another and are inclined to assemble practically, to come together as a practical group, and thus to reinforce their points of resemblance. But such assembly is the result of organizing and mobilizing. Just because one can empirically classify individuals does not mean that these individuals will act as a group or class struggling for their material and ideal interests. Marx assumed the practical existence of theoretical classes, while such classes must be seen as only probable classes whose constituent individuals are likely to be brought together and mobilized on the basis of their similar dispositions (Bourdieu, 1987: 6–7). All this labour of group- or class-making involves a recognition that class struggle as such does not exist, that classes can ascend to definite form only as a result of specific practical work, and that such political work is likely to succeed when it is supported with an empirically constructed theoretical groups or classes—all very significant points for understanding groups and group differentiation.

The representation of classes therefore is one of the major stakes in any political struggle. The classification and class struggles are intermingled. It is through the endless work of representation that individuals impose their vision of the world (or the vision of their own position in that world) to define their group identity or membership in a group or class. In the reality of the social world, in the everyday experiences of individuals, there are no straightforward class boundaries. The institutionalization of a permanent organization capable of representing different groups tends to create more durable, recognizable and visible group boundaries. The individual struggles of everyday life become political struggles through a presentation of self in imposing a particular representation through permanent organizations. The ultimate aim of such struggles in modernity has been to control the state institutions.

Symbolic power has been crucial in these struggles. Symbolic power is the power to make groups and to consecrate or institute them in particular through various rites. It is the power to make something exist in the objectified, public or formal state that previously existed only in an implicit state; this happens only when the group is labelled, designated or selected as such. The power of naming or labelling usually comes with the power of representing since the group must now be represented with its organizations, leaders and spokespersons.

So, a group or class exists 'when there are agents capable of imposing themselves, as authorized to speak and to act officially in its place and in its name, upon those who, by recognizing themselves in these plenipotentiaries, by recognizing them as endowed with full power to speak and act in their name, recognize themselves as members of the class, and in doing so, confer upon it the only form of existence a group can posses (Bourdieu, 1987: 15). This involves a paradox. While an individual who identifies with such a group is empowered and recognized, at the same time, one, by virtue of the delegation that representation entails, becomes dispossessed in the sense that one relegates his or her individual powers to others to represent them. This raises a particular problem in our era when 'the symbolic struggles between individuals is for the most part carried out through the mediation of professionals of representation who, acting as spokespersons for the groups at whose service they place their specific competence, confront each other within a closed, relatively autonomous field, namely, the field of politics' (Bourdieu, 1987: 14). The formation of groups is, therefore, always fraught with the danger that, instead of advancing the legitimate claims of its members, it may turn an oppressive power on them. In other words, when groups begin to represent themselves as real as opposed to constructed via social struggles, they tend to essentialize properties of individuals that make up such groups by appealing to nature, God or science.

Bourdieu develops these insights into an interpretive analytics of groups with three interrelated concepts: *habitus*, *field* and *capital*. Bourdieu defines habitus as a 'system of structured, structuring dispositions, which is constituted in practice and is always oriented towards practical functions' (Bourdieu, 1990: 52). The affinity between habitus and identity as concepts to address the social agent are remarkable. Both refute the subjectivist and objectivist notions of the subject. Bourdieu says that to overcome and transcend the false antinomy between objectivism and subjectivism, 'one has to situate oneself *within* "real activity as such", that is, in the practical relation to the world through which the world imposes its presence, with its urgencies, its things to be done and said, things made to be said, which directly govern words and deeds without ever unfolding as a spectacle' (52).

The formation of a group involves the inculcation in individuals of specific ways of being in the world and making sense of that world. 'The conditioning associated with a particular class of conditions of existence produce *habitus*, systems of durable, transposable dispositions, structured structures predisposed to function as structuring structures, that is, as principles which generate and organize practices and representations that can be objectively adapted to their outcomes without presupposing a conscious aiming at ends or an express mastery of the operations necessary in order to attain them' (53). Since habitus is a system of durable dispositions it can be seen as a presence of the past that tends to perpetuate itself with continuity and regularity. It is this regularity that objectivism records without being able to account for it (54). It is also this regularity that leads advocates of groups to essentialize and naturalize habitus. The fact that habitus is a capacity for generating thoughts, perceptions, expressions and actions whose limits are set by the historically and socially situated conditions of its production would require historicizing and contextualizing rather than essentializing it (55). While the habitus excludes and regulates incompatible behaviour with its objective conditions, it is also an embodied history, internalized as a second nature, an active presence of the past of which it is the product (56). This is what the subjectivist approaches such as constructivism miss: while habitus is socially produced, its outcome is embodied in gestures, bodily movements, ways of thinking, manners and a series of very real effects. That is why the formation of group or class habitus results from similarities in the conditions of existence of various individuals without any calculation or conscious reference to a norm and intersubjectively adjusted in the absence of any direct interaction or explicit coordination (58). The practices of the members of a group or class are always better harmonized than the agents know or wish (59).

Nevertheless, Bourdieu argues that it is a mistake to regard all individuals as identical if they happen to display the same habitus. It is unlikely that two or more members of the same group or class habitus would have exactly the same experiences; it is just that each member of a group or class is more likely than any other member of another group or class to have been confronted with the situations familiar to members of the group or class (59–60). While there is a relationship between group habitus and individual habitus, they are not identical but homologous. 'The singular *habitus* of members of the same class are united in a relationship of homology, that is, of diversity within homogeneity reflecting the diversity within homogeneity characteristics of their social conditions of production. Each individual system of dispositions is a structural variant of others, expressing the singularity of its position within the class and its trajectory' (60). 'The principle of the differences between individual *habitus* lies in the singularity of their social trajectories, to which there correspond series of chronologically ordered determinations that are mutually irreducible to one another' (60).

Bourdieu argues that the main purpose of the concept of habitus is to break away from the myth of the rational agent. Instead, he argues, his theory of practice construes practice as a product of practical sense, of a socially constituted sense of the game. (Bourdieu and Wacquant, 1992: 120–121). He suggests that the concept is also designed against objectivism, in the sense that it posits that objects of knowledge are constructed and not passively recorded, and against subjectivism, in that it reminds us that the principle of this construction is found in the socially constituted system of structured and structuring dispositions acquired in practice and constantly aimed at practical functions (121). The habitus aims to escape from the philosophy of the subject without doing away with the agent (121). 'To speak of habitus is to assert that the individual, and even the personal, the subjective, is social, collective. Habitus is a socialized subjectivity' (126). The proper object of social science is neither the individual nor groups as concrete sets of individuals sharing a similar location in social space, but the relation of mutual conditioning between group and individual habitus (126–127). The cases of discrepancy between habitus and field, in which conduct remains unintelligible unless analysis brings habitus and its specific inertia, its hysteresis, into the picture, are what makes the analysis of habitus important (130). This mutual conditioning or intersubjectivity takes place in a field, which is a meaningful world, a world endowed with sense and value, in which it is worth investing one's capital (127).

Bourdieu always insists that it is important not to associate capital only with its economic form (Bourdieu, 1986: 242). For a long time an economistic view of capital persisted in which the only form of capital recognized was economic capital, oriented towards the maximization of profit. Other forms of capital and exchange have been defined as non-economic. But there are principles of conversion of different types of capital to each other. Although Bourdieu speaks about other forms of capital such as symbolic, he primarily makes reference to three forms. Economic capital is immediately and directly convertible into money and may be institutionalized in the form of property rights. Cultural capital can be converted into economic capital under certain conditions and may be institutionalized in the form of educational qualifications. Social capital, made up of social obligations, is convertible under certain conditions into economic capital and may be institutionalized in the form of status symbols. Bourdieu argues that the formation of groups is about appropriation of different forms of capital as resources (Bourdieu, 1986: 244). The value of a form of capital hinges on the existence of a field in which this competency can be employed. A form of capital is what is efficacious in a given field, both as a weapon and as a stake of struggle, that which allows its possessors to wield power, influence, and thus to exist, in the field under consideration (Bourdieu and Wacquant, 1992: 98). The question of the limits of the field is a difficult one because these limits are always at stake in the field itself. There is a production of difference, which is in no way the product of a search for difference (Bourdieu and Wacquant, 1992: 100).

Capital is embodied power and it does not exist except in relation to a field (Bourdieu and Wacquant, 1992: 101). Bourdieu insists that social agents are not passive recipients that are mechanically pushed and pulled about by external forces. They are active users of different forms of capital and, depending on their trajectory and on the position they occupy in the field by virtue of their endowment (volume and structure) in capital, they have a propensity to orient themselves actively either towards the preservation of the distribution of capital or towards the subversion of its distribution (Bourdieu and Wacquant, 1992: 109). The importance of this point for the debates over struggles for redistribution and recognition cannot be underestimated. As we shall see shortly, scholars such as Iris Young (1990, 1997), Fraser (1997b) and Anne Phillips (1997) agree on the need to overcome this dichotomy. We think Bourdieu's reconstruction of group identity and his emphasis on different forms of capital and their interconvertibility effectively breaks down the necessity to make an analytical difference between cultural and economic struggles or between struggles for redistribution and recognition.

Iris Young (1990, 1997) has shown the importance of rethinking group rights. Young argues that at the centre of modern thought about inequality lies the concept of distributive justice. This concept regards inequality in terms of different quantities of wealth, status and power held by different groups and construes these differentials as unjust. According to this 'distributive paradigm', achieving social justice means redistributing these quantities to equalize. Young argues that it is a mistake to reduce social justice to distribution (1990: 15). First, the focus on benefits and jobs tends to ignore the social and institutional relations that determine patterns of inequality. Second, even when the focus shifts to non-material social goods such as education or health, the concept of redistribution represents them as though they were static objects as opposed to social relations.

Young suggests that we shift our focus to oppression and domination in terms of social justice. She defines oppression as the institutional constraint of self-development and domination as the constraint on self-determination (37). Young argues that although these two concepts overlap, it is useful to distinguish them. With its focus on oppression and domination a concept of justice refers not only to distribution but also to the institutional conditions necessary for the development and exercise of individual capacities and group rights (39). She argues that what made this conceptual shift in defining social justice is not a theoretical innovation but the political work of social movements in the last twenty years. Although oppression was traditionally understood as the exercise of tyranny by a ruling group, the social movements of the 1960s and 1970s shifted its meaning to the disadvantage and injustice some people suffer not because a tyrannical power coerces them, but because of the everyday practices of a well-intentioned liberal society (40–41). 'Oppression in this sense is structural, rather than the result of a few people's choices or policies. Its causes are embedded in unquestioned norms, habits, and symbols, in the assumption underlying institutional rules and collective consequences of following those rules' (41).

Young argues that to understand the concept of oppression requires a robust conception of social group, something which neither political nor social theory has developed. Statistical classifications that aggregate individuals into groups based on specific attributes do not necessarily constitute a social group. Regarding individuals within associations as social groups is not adequate either because such a conception presupposes that the individual pre-exists the social group. To arrive at an adequate conception of social group we must contrast it with aggregates and associations (43).

Young argues that a social group is defined not primarily by a set of shared attributes but by a sense of identity. A social group partially constitutes individual identities in terms of cultural forms, social situation and history that group members know as theirs, because these meanings have been either forced upon them or forged by them or both (44). Social groups constitute individuals. An individual's particular sense of history, affinity and separateness, even the individual's mode of reasoning, evaluating and expressing feeling, are constituted partly by his or her group affinities. By contrast, the social ontology underlying many contemporary theories of justice is methodologically individualist or atomist. It presumes that the individual is ontologically prior to the social. This individualist social ontology usually goes together with a normative conception of the self as independent, autonomous, unified, free and self-made, standing apart from history and affiliation choosing its life plan entirely for itself (45).

Young admits that some people consider social groups to be invidious fictions, essentializing arbitrary attributes. The individualist conception of self and its relation to the other tends to identify oppression with group identification. Oppression, in this view, is something that happens to people when they are classified in groups. Rather, people should be treated as individuals, not as members of groups. Resonating with Berlin's third form of liberty, Young takes issue with that position. Despite the modern myth of a decline of parochial attachments and ascribed identities, in modern society group identity remains endemic. 'As both markets and social administration increase the web of social interdependency on a world scale, and as more people encounter one another as strangers in cities and states', she writes, 'people retain and renew ethnic, locale, age, sex, and occupational group identifications, and form new ones in the process of encounter' (47). She argues that social justice requires not the melting away of differences, but institutions that promote reproduction of and respect for group differences without oppression.

Young argues that '[t]his view of group differentiation as multiple, cross-cutting, fluid and shifting implies another critique of the model of autonomous, unified self. In complex, highly differentiated societies like our own, all persons have multiple group identifications. The culture, perspective, and relations of privilege and oppression of these various groups, moreover, may not cohere. Thus individual persons, as constituted partly by their group affinities and relations, cannot be unified, themselves are heterogeneous and not necessarily coherent' (48). In a previous work, Young (1989) has argued that the ideal of universal citizenship stands in contrast to universality as generality and universality as equal treatment. As long as differences exist within a society with certain privileged groups, adherence to the principle of equal treatment tends to perpetuate oppression. The inclusion of everyone requires special rights attending to group differences to undermine oppression. The ideal of a general will excludes. Democracy requires genuine public discussion which requires enabling policies for groups to be heard. This suppression of the 'other' has been supported by the traditional association with the public as general and the private as particular.

A group-differentiated citizenship and heterogeneous public recognizes differences and acknowledges them as irreducible. A social group is defined by a shared sense of identity, understood by relational differentiations. Young understands oppression as including one or more of the following: exploitation; marginalization; powerlessness; cultural imperialism; and the experience of group hatred. Group representation implies institutional mechanisms and public resources to support: (i) self-organization to gain a sense of collective empowerment and experience; (ii) voicing group analysis of how policies affect them, putting forth their own proposals in arenas where these must be taken seriously; (iii) veto power regarding policies that affect them directly.

Such group representation exposes the false claims to universality of the views of the privileged. Based on Habermas' model of communicative ethics the only legitimate decisions are those arrived at by the public in the context of free expression of all points of view. This differs from group rights by insisting that only the oppressed deserve special group representation. These groups are defined by their way of life and not some particular political interest or goal; interest groups are not obliged to consider other interests, while to be compatible with social justice, group representation is. Universality of law and policies equally supports oppression in a group-differentiated society, hence special rights are required. Honneth provided the basis for Young's idea of group-differentiated rights. Honneth argues that the possibility for sensing, interpreting and realizing individual needs and desires as a fully autonomous person—in short, the very possibility of identity formation—depends crucially on the development of self-confidence, self-respect and self-esteem. These three modes of relating practically to oneself can only be acquired and maintained intersubjectively, through being granted recognition by others whom one also recognizes. In this view, recognition is worthless if it does not come from someone whom one views as deserving recognition. As a result, the conditions for self-realization turn out to be dependent on the establishment of relationships of mutual recognition. These relationships go beyond close relationships of love and friendship to include legally recognized rights and networks of solidarity.

These relationships are not historically given but must be established and expanded through social struggles, which cannot be understood exclusively as conflicts over interests. Honneth has argued that 'social-structural upheavals in developed societies have so greatly expanded the possibilities for self-realization that the experience of individual or collective difference has become the impetus for a whole series of political movements. In the long run, their demands can only be satisfied once culture has been transformed so as to radically expand relations of solidarity' (Honneth, 1996b: 179).

While sympathetic to Young and the various forms of oppression that she identifies, Fraser is nevertheless critical of Young's overemphasis of recognition over redistribution. She argues that 'to be a radical democrat today is to appreciate—and to seek to eliminate—two different kinds of impediments to democratic participation. One such impediment is social inequality; the other is the misrecognition of difference. ... Radical democrats will never succeed in untying the Gordian knots of identity and difference until we leave the terrain of identity politics. This means resituating cultural politics in relation to social politics and linking demands for recognition with demands for redistribution' (Fraser, 1997a: 173–174). She further contends that '[w]e are currently spinning our wheels arguing over identity politics, having succumbed to two unfortunate temptations. One is the tendency to adopt an undiscriminating form of antiessentialism, which treats all identities and differences as repressive fictions. The other is the mirror-opposite tendency to adopt an undiscriminating version of multiculturalism, which celebrates all identities and differences as worthy of recognition. In fact, both of these tendencies share a common root: they fail to connect the cultural politics of identity and difference to the social politics of justice and equality' (Fraser, 1997a: 175).

While anti-essentialism is sceptical about all difference and identities because all these are constructed, there is no essential foundation upon which such differences and identities can be defended. Multiculturalism, at least the version Fraser calls pluralist, is premised on a one-sided understanding of difference: difference is viewed as intrinsically positive and inherently cultural. This perspective accordingly celebrates difference uncritically while failing to interrogate its relation to inequality (Fraser, 1997a: 185). 'We must find a way to combine the struggle for an antiessentialist multiculturalism with the struggle for social equality' (Fraser, 1997a: 187).

We have seen that the interpretive analytics of groups developed by Bourdieu provides a way that Fraser is seeking. Nonetheless, Bourdieu is vulnerable to criticisms and corrections. First, Bourdieu seems to assume that individuals have a unitary habitus. As discussed in Chapter 1, critical theories on identity stress the importance of pluralization and fragmentation. Often individuals do not belong to only one group and in their life trajectories they experience a variety of social conditions that may not be compatible. Immigrants, for example, often experience displacement and dislocation in their habitus that result in hybrid identities. In other words, an individual can have different sets of dispositions that become enacted in different social and political conditions. Second, Bourdieu places too much emphasis on the durability of habitus whereas the theories of identity now question such durability and place emphasis on the instability of identity. Finally, as other commentators have pointed out, Bourdieu has been particularly concerned with class habitus while neglecting other forms of habitus such as gender, race, ethnicity and age. As Swartz (1997: 154–156) argues, although Bourdieu attempts to take into account other stratifying factors, his formulations are less than satisfying. Nevertheless, Bourdieu provides an innovative interpretive analytics of group rights in the late twentieth century. Gierke is important in understanding the riddle of modernity and group rights historically, but he is not sufficiently aware of potential dangers of essentialism or naturalism in imputing rights to groups. While Gierke reminds us of the historical, political and constitutional difficulties of group rights, Bourdieu reminds us of sociological challenges.

If critically appropriating Gierke and Bourdieu in addressing group-differentiated citizenship is one aspect of developing a critical responsiveness to the late modern condition, what exactly would group rights mean? What kinds of rights-claims can be advanced by groups? It is important to make here a distinction between rights granted to individuals on the basis of their membership in a group and rights that are granted to groups themselves. While the former has been practised in modern public law, mostly it is the latter that is at issue when we discuss citizenship and identity. Most of the rights-claims classified by Levy (1997), for example, fall in the former category. He identifies eight clusters of rights-claims that have similar normativity and application. These are: (i) exemptions from an ostensibly neutral law which unfairly burdens a cultural group (e.g., Sikhs wearing turbans in police duty); (ii) assistance to overcome unfair disadvantages of burdens when engaging in the same activities as the dominant group (e.g., affirmative action and special funding); (iii) self-government, whether through secession or autonomy within a larger state; (iv) external rules limiting the freedom of non-members in order to protect an endangered culture or cultural practice (e.g., restrictions on the English language in Quebec); (v) internal rules which limit the freedom of members, and which must be obeyed for continued recognition as a member of the group (e.g., disowning children who marry outside the group); (vi) recognition and enforcement of customary legal practices by the dominant legal system (e.g., Aboriginal land rights); (vii) guaranteed representation for group members within government bodies (e.g., Maori voting roll for Parliament); and (viii) symbolic claims about the nature of the polity and the representation of its constituent groups. While this classification is very useful in understanding the variety of rights-claims, it assumes the sole grantor of these rights is the nation-state. What happens when groups also make claims for rights that are across borders? What happens when neither the source of normativity nor the domain of applicability is the nation-state? What happens when one cluster of rights conflict with another? As we shall see in many of the legal and normative debates over rights, the source and domain of law is assumed to be the nation-state while currently many rights-claims also cross borders and identities.

3
DIASPORIC AND ABORIGINAL CITIZENSHIP: POSTCOLONIAL IDENTITIES

Introduction

This chapter considers the impact of global migration on the 'West', the history of exclusionary legislation based on ethnic and racial groupings, and the consequences of subsequent political battles for the citizenship rights of ethnic and racial identities. Noting the increased use of a more global language of 'human rights', the chapter proceeds to discuss the decentring of the nation-state as a homogeneous and homogenizing 'master identity'. The rise of multiculturalism and Aboriginal struggles for land and sovereignty are presented as examples of upward pressures on the modern nation-state and the subsequent challenges for an emerging postnational state. This chapter also seeks to come to terms with the perhaps contradictory fact that even as many minority groups identified themselves in terms of racial and ethnic difference, and challenged discrimination, their language argued for the irrelevance of such difference and for the right to participate. The consequences of a simultaneous emphasis on the irrelevance and importance of difference have complicated cultural politics in a way that many scholars have not been able to come to terms with.

This chapter also begins to expose the limits of liberalism as a regime of government. In our critique of liberalism's attempt to address prejudice, discrimination and injustice in society, we emphasize instead its complicity in the production of inequality along racial and ethnic lines. Many liberals acknowledge this and attempt to revise liberalism. Unfortunately, liberalism is as much practical as philosophical. An examination of the history of liberalism as a regime of government rather than a political philosophy, its development into political practice in the nation-state, and the subsequent treatment of minorities reveals its limits. We conclude that liberal theory cannot address the tensions of diversity without confronting liberal practice.

But, first, a few comments on the vocabulary of this chapter. There are a few terms we struggled with for this particular segment. The first and most central was 'multicultural'. There are several reasons for this. Most difficult is the fact that it has taken on so many meanings in the various contexts, positive and negative, in which authors have placed it (Joppke, 1998). In some instances, particularly with reference to education, 'multiculturalism' has been used to describe not just the presence of many ethnic and/or racial cultures, but also the inclusion of the presence or study of women and feminism (Glazer, 1997). While some groups may celebrate this term, right-wing movements concerned with national unity employ it in a tactical fashion, to attack and belittle it. Leftists, too, have been accused of hiding a 'hypocritical and repressive ideology' behind the term (Hodges, 1998). Will Kymlicka's recent *Multicultural Citizenship* (Kymlicka, 1995) also uses the term in a problematic way. We are convinced that many have come to use this term almost indiscriminately, perhaps to a point where it is no longer clear what the meaning or even the connotation of its use might be (Matustik, 1998). Moreover, 'multiculturalism' seemed incapable of encapsulating all we wanted to put into it. We would like this term to reflect diversity not only within a nation, but within individual citizens as well. We have in mind a usage that depicts the state of diversity but also reflects the social struggle of minorities such diversity has historically produced. In addition, 'multiculturalism', particularly as policy, should have something to say about citizenship, and, thus, we need the word to be open to such a connection. In short, we want it to be descriptive and proscriptive, clear yet flexible. At times, we have wondered whether all this was too much to expect, and whether there was another term more appropriate to our wants and needs.

This is why we prefer diasporic citizenship (Laguerre, 1997). In this chapter we examine how it moves from merely a description of the presence of many cultures to a process whereby those cultures practice citizenship in a radical sense, a sense that goes beyond 'accommodation' and mere 'belonging'. Nor does this meaning conflict incoherently with other uses of the term to the extent where we would feel discouraged. Instead, we optimistically seek to apply the term academically to politics, but to be less political about our application. This usage should not be as caught up in the positive/negative connotative dilemma as 'multicultural' is, but should serve to acknowledge that the West is the terminus of many international migrations. In other words, our use of the concept of diaspora is not intended to add to the debate as to whether the diversity produced by migration is a good or bad thing, but to assert that migration is a political and social reality all citizens of Western states must address.

It is worth clarifying, as well, the use of the terms 'race' and 'ethnicity'. These categorizations, while similar, are distinct from one another. As discussed in Chapter 1, it is a complicated task to determine whether such categories are invented or 'real'. In the end, we argue, they are both. Biologists now inform us that the categorization of race is genetically meaningless, that there are many more scientifically significant ways of grouping human beings. The metamorphosis of the word, from a basis in religion to an emphasis on a random matrix of physical attributes, clearly illustrates that its generation is social rather than scientific. Nevertheless, its social meanings, in flux as they are, have symbolic and material realities that, in turn, have political consequences.

On the surface, ethnicity is more grounded than race. Ethnic identity or identities are understood to be inherited, and in this way immutable. Parental ancestry determines ethnicity and in this way it is often explained in terms of 'blood' or being in the blood. Even when it is truly believed that there is no biological basis for ethnic origin (although genetic characteristics have developed due to limited gene pools), contemporary discourses commonly attribute everything from holiday practices to personality characteristics to ethnicity, and sufficiently blur tradition with genetics to use such categories with little hesitation.

Yet ethnic categories are just as invented as their racial parallels. Certainly any group that has historically shared norms and customs, lived, celebrated and died together, has a set of practices of sociological significance that merit recognition under the term 'ethnicity' (Jenkins, 1997). But the employment of the idea is more often political than analytical. Most ethnic categories today are derived from nation-state of origin, with little regard for or knowledge of actual history and culture (A.D. Smith, 1986; Wood, 1995). In North America at least, ethnic origin is defined as whatever country was the residence of one's ancestors prior to arrival in the northern, industrialized New World. 'Mexican' qualifies as a category; 'Canadian' and 'American' do not. The current collection of categories reflects a desire to target rather than describe. In the best of circumstances, it is of limited use, for example, to describe someone as 'ethnically Chinese', given the variety of language and culture not only in but outside China. Many, if not most, ethnic categories bury differences at least as much as they delineate them. The emerging 'Caribbean' category, which crosses lines of race, language, religion and other cultural postices, and merges groups with divergent histories, particularly in terms of their experience of colonization, illustrates this difficulty. Emigrants from the Caribbean, like many other migrant groups, have found that their experiences of their new home produce sufficient cultural dislocation as to lead them to unite with those they are categorized with by others ignorant of the specifics of their history and culture.

Thus, like race, ethnicity is a contested term. Recognizing that groups use this category, often fundamentally organizing and understanding themselves along such lines, we employ the term here in a manner that reflects our knowledge of the process and use of ethnic categories, but does not take such categories to be essential, immutable or natural. Nor does it mean that they are whimsical, frivolous or immaterial. We need to maintain an active appreciation of the history and process of social movements that can acknowledge their importance and seriousness without leading to essentialist or constructivist conclusions. Similarly, we should keep in mind the perspective of those who have been placed in positions of minority or even victim, without reducing their perspective and self-understanding to that of the victimized minority. Only with such an approach can we hope to make sense of the complexity of diversity. The history of minority groups—their formation and their understanding of themselves—is integral to the development of their identity, from within and without. We start from a position of recognition of a multiplicity of perspectives and move through an acknowledgement of the weight of history towards a process that incorporates both into the practice of citizenship and democracy.

There is also the argument that race and ethnicity became more 'naturalized' explanations for the apparently unnatural phenomenon of class. This appears to have been more prevalent in North America where the democratic language of politics seemed to fly in the face of class inequality: capitalism needed labour, but it needed to justify the divergence between who owned the factory and who went to work on the factory floor. However, nineteenth-century discourses do not support a simplistic argument that reduces race and ethnicity to masks for class. For example, the religious basis of many ideologies of race and ethnicity suggests class is only part of the explanation. The scientific assistance lent to such ideologies complicates the picture even further. Although race and ethnicity have at times been employed as explanatory devices for the unequal distribution of capital, it is dangerous and reductive to conflate the categories. There are important connections and intersections between race, ethnicity and class; in practice these identities inform and shape each other in an often inextricable matrix that may blur their borders. We also acknowledge that distinct social and political movements have been framed in terms of race and ethnicity; to suggest these were only a façade for class is to devalue these movements in terms of their meaning to their participants and society in general. In whatever way we come to understand race and ethnicity, we must respect the reality of the experience of these identities for many people, particularly in terms of discrimination. The social movements that were the results of resistance to such discrimination are undeniably 'real' and political; denying the 'reality' of race or ethnicity does nothing to alter that fact. Such resistance to discrimination over a long period of time establishes its own symbols, narratives and icons and creates relatively durable dispositions in its members. As we discussed in Chapter 2, the formation of groups goes beyond such narratives to produce a habitus that is all too real. As well, before some of these racial and ethnic groups identified themselves, practices of oppression had already marked them out with categories of representation. The principle and practices of group formation are therefore very complex and defy ways of thinking framed by essentialism and constructivism.

Global Diasporas: Geographies of Postcolonialism

Modern citizenship originates with territory, with birth and/or residence in a particular nation-state. Before modern nation-states, citizens were members of a multiplicity of intersecting and overlapping polities ranging from guilds to leagues. There was no such idea as today's United Nations Charter assertion that 'everyone has the right to a nationality'. In modernity, everyone must belong to a state, with all the positive and negative connotations such a condition implies. The origins of the nation-state were necessarily accompanied by 'founding fathers', who identified the political membership and determined the first terms of citizenship. However, the same processes of imperialism and mercantile capitalism that established the nation-state in the first place set into motion another phenomenon that would challenge such foundations. Historic levels of immigration, particularly from non-Western to Western countries, introduced difference into the tidy homogeneous identities that underwrote early modern citizenship.

Modern capitalism and the creation of the nation-state displaced millions of people, temporarily or permanently, from their homelands when their farms were turned into factories or they themselves sought better remuneration in industrial labour. In the cities, they encountered the rise of a bourgeoisie that was turning its economic capital into social, cultural and political capital (Harvey, 1985). While some members of the latter class pursued fortune and adventure in the New World, it was the masses of peasants and workers who comprised the vast majority of those who crowded themselves onto disease-ridden ships of uncertain safety. There were those who left relatively voluntarily, with family contacts waiting for them, others who sold themselves into indentured labour, some who were deported convicts, and at least six million who were kidnapped and sold into slavery. The violence of the migration experience should not overshadow the fact that many immigrants of the eighteenth and nineteenth centuries were forced to flee by the military battles that created modern nation-states. For example, Italy's upheavals sent millions of migrants to the farthest reaches of the New World; even the United States' revolution produced the refugees (the Loyalists) that became the bulk of Canada's English-speaking settlement of the time.

Similarly, emerging industrializing nations today are producing stateless or near-stateless persons as they 'reform' agricultural lands in favour of economic capital interested in large-scale production and/or bringing the rural population to the cities to join an industrial labour force. Postcolonial struggles that have turned violent have created millions of migrants. Immigration, legal and illegal, is now arriving most commonly from Southern and South-East Asia, Africa, and the former Eastern Bloc countries in the wake of the break-up of the Soviet Union.

An even more disruptive and problematic demographic shift is the rapid escalation of refugees in the last two decades. According to the United Nations, the number of refugees in the world in 1978 was about 3 million. By the early 1980s, that number had multiplied more than three times. When the figure peaked in 1993, it had reached 18.2 million persons. These figures did not and do not include the large numbers—currently estimated at between 25 and 30 million people—displaced within their own countries by civil war, famine, environmental disasters or government policies. After migrating, many of these people remain in a precarious state, whereby the place to which they have escaped is no more secure than that which they have left. Even in a more peaceful haven, their legal status and that of any family left behind may remain unresolved for years. The birth of children often goes unregistered, creating enormous obstacles to their achievement of even basic citizenship rights. The situation is rendered more complicated by the fact that the majority of refugees are women, whose relatively weak political and social position compounds their difficulties (Yuval-Davis, 1997: 109).

It is interesting that Western European nations invoke the name of refugees in their discussion of immigration politics and have used such language to increase their restrictions on granting asylum. The refugee 'problem' is still one that is mostly confined to the Third World. As the figures above indicate, the largest numbers of those forcibly displaced move within their home country. The next largest groups of refugees move to neighbouring countries. In 1996, the twelve largest refugee movements documented by the United Nations were all between developing nations; by far the largest single relocation, more than 150,000 refugees, was of those from Burundi who fled to Tanzania, which also received refugees from Zaïre and Rwanda.

The number of legal immigrants is smaller than at other periods in history, but the number of illegal immigrants and refugees is probably at record heights. However, the source of the new diversity in industrialized nations is overwhelmingly legal immigrants, not refugees (Brubaker, 1992; Soysal, 1994). Nevertheless, far-right political organizations frequently raise the spectre of the refugee, otherwise 'unqualified' and thus unacceptable, entering Western nations by virtue of exceptional circumstances, as the threat to the native population. Blurring the distinctions between legal immigrants and refugees, these voices suggest immigration is dangerously unchecked and out of control. This tactic creates difficulties for all foreigners and native-born minorities. We focus here on immigrants arriving through approved channels, who, for all their legality, remain marginalized and vulnerable to political, social and economic discrimination (Modood and Werbner, 1997).

While Canada and the United States are receiving a considerable portion of these migrants, Western Europe is also receiving a share of this transnational movement. Whereas in earlier waves of migration, Western Europe had been the source of migrants, it is now confronted with the reality of racial, ethnic, religious and linguistic diversity within its borders on a scale it had not previously experienced (Castles and Miller, 1993). Britain was probably the first in Western Europe to experience the recent ethnic and racial diversification with the migration of Indian and Pakistani people in the 1960s and 1970s. More recently, British immigration policy was scrutinized for possible racism with its treatment of Hong Kong residents before the return of the colony to China.

Illegal immigrants have been less of a problem for Britain, due to its island geography and strict passport checks and levying of fines at airports and ports. The Eurostar train that runs through the 'Chunnel' has recently created another entry for illegal immigrants as it does not require a passport check before boarding. The summer of 1997 saw more than 1,000 Africans (principally Somalis), Asians, Turks and Eastern Europeans without passports or visas arrive in London's Waterloo station. But these are insignificant numbers relative to legal immigration and the current population of Britain.

France has been facing its own 'crisis of integration' with a significant number of Algerians and other Islamic Africans arriving in the early 1980s to join a small but diverse community already established (Diop, 1997; Nair, 1996). Both legal and illegal immigrants have been subjected to racism. The intolerance has been encouraged by at least one political party, the National Front, whose platform explicitly asserts a racist understanding of French citizenship. The party's municipal and regional electoral success through coalition has brought its anti-immigrant stance into mainstream politics and put some of its policies into practice. Mayors affiliated with the party have already begun purging local libraries of 'leftist' and 'international' books. President Jacques Chirac's regime, however, presents far from an open door: in 1997, the National Assembly passed a law tightening already tough 1993 legislation regarding illegal immigration, enabling authorities 'to fingerprint non-European residence seekers, confiscate passports of suspected illegals, search vehicles and workplaces, and expedite the expulsion process' (Sancton, 1997).

Germany has been wrestling with the issue of integrating the 'other' on several fronts. Following reunification, East and West have had to negotiate the German identity as a people with a common political future. Eastern Europeans from former Soviet bloc states like Poland and break-away republics such as Kazakshtan who consider themselves ethnically German are also returning to the fold, and are awarded citizenship under the terms of a 1913 law that privileges ancestry. However, Germany's *Gastarbeiter* programme, which has supplied the nation with a cheap labour force, has also presented a social and political problem. The population now includes a large component of Turks, who have taken advantage of the opportunity to work in Germany. Their inclination to settle and raise their German-born children in Germany has been met with political and social resistance. Even those born in the country must be naturalized and some Turkish communities have been subject to extreme violence by 'native' Germans. All of these newcomers have raised the question of who is German and who is a foreigner (Faist, 1994; Yalçin-Heckman, 1997). Language, race, history, politics and regionalism have all been raised. And it is not simply a matter of a social or cultural identity. As Barbieri (1998) illustrates these immigrants present legal, political and ethical questions of citizenship.

Italy finds itself confronted with similar problems. From 'too many' African street vendors on the tourist-clogged streets of Florence to the recent selection of a black Miss Italy, the non-white presence in Italy is increasingly visible, and, for some, problematic. In addition to some anti-African immigrant sentiments towards those who settle in Italy, some members of Italian society also raise the concern of becoming a 'gateway to Europe' for these people. There is a reluctance to admit non-white immigrants, but also a worry about Italy's reputation within the European Union. Italy's recent ascent from 'sick man to rich man of Europe' (King, 1992) has gone a long way to maintain the nation's economic credibility within the Union. The issue of non-white immigrants, illegal aliens in particular, is now a political minefield in all the nations of Western Europe. The Italian government does not want Italy to be seen as a 'hole in the fence', a situation that might question its loyalty to the European Union and, perhaps equally importantly, the modern European identity.

In all of these countries, the question of citizenship and, more generally, belonging has not remained an abstract, academic debate. Racial and ethnic minorities have been the targets of nativist discrimination and violence. Anti-immigrant political parties have gained strength not only in France, but also in Austria, Italy and Belgium. In 1996 Germany officially recorded more than 2,500 hate crimes. In the Czech Republic, gypsies have been brutalized by skinheads. Europe's perceived homogeneity has been exposed as fraudulent, and 'foreigners' are taking the blame for social and economic ills (Castles and Miller, 1993).

Although the settler societies of Australia, the United States and Canada have had more time to 'adjust' to immigration and diversity, multiculturalism remains a hotly debated topic and has fuelled the fire of nativism (Stasiulis and Yuval-Davis, 1995). Canada has adjusted its policies to attract 'better qualified' immigrants and has placed stricter limits on family reunification. The state of California has withdrawn all public services, including public schooling, from illegal immigrants and has moved towards similar measures for even legal immigrants. The political career of Pauline Hanson, the leader and founder of Australia's One Nation party, was launched from the encouraging response to a letter to the editor she wrote protesting the overprivileging of Aboriginals. Hanson also proposes a ban on Asian immigration. In June 1998, in its electoral debut, the One Nation party took 23 per cent of the vote in Queensland's state elections.

The issue of diversity is about more than immigration policies, however. When the social and political achievements by African-Americans of the 1960s civil rights movement and others were followed up by curriculum changes in education at all levels, scholars and politicians began speaking out on the issue of national culture. History and literature were particularly sore spots: some were dismayed by the writing and teaching of history that was shameful rather than heroic; others were outraged that the pillars of the Western literary canon might be joined (or even replaced) by texts authored by women, African-American and other marginalized voices. After many of the more petty political spats quieted, another scholar waded into the discussion with his best-selling *The Disuniting of America* (Schlesinger, 1992). Arthur Schlesinger, a respected historian generally considered to be a voice of moderation, took a position with the neoliberals. He warned of the consequences for a nation whose citizens focused on their divergent pasts, instead of on their common present and purpose. Many academics and politicians have held up Schlesinger (often overstating his argument) as proof that diversity is tearing apart the nation. Nathan Glazer, who is somewhat sympathetic to their concerns, suggests such accusations have become overblown in the political arena: 'National disunity is a reasonable fear but perhaps an exaggerated one' (Glazer, 1997: 45).

Why have racial and ethnic tensions been central to many political debates in all these countries? Why does the issue of 'accommodating' all these 'others' still remain unresolved in these settler societies, where the diversity of immigration has been the reality since the explorers found themselves face to face with Aboriginals? And we should not overestimate the homogeneity of Europe before the Second World War; internal migration was the norm for hundreds of years, mixing peoples of varying nationalities, cultures and religions (Hoerder and Moch, 1996; Hoerder, Rössler and Blank, 1994). Indeed, a state of multiculturalism to some degree has been the norm, not the exception, in the Western world for a long time (A.D. Smith, 1986). Most important is that this diversity precedes the modern era. Those who argue that the claims for rights by various groups are disuniting the nation-state overlook a richness of historical experience. The homogeneity some remember was a unity the dominant classes attempted to imagine and impose; it should not be mistaken for the experience of minorities and, as we shall see in Chapter 4, women (see B. Anderson, 1991; Bissoondath, 1994; Gilroy, 1991, 1993; Said, 1993; Takaki, 1993; Wald, 1995; Wood, 1995; R. Wright, 1992).

The history behind cultural politics and our seeming inability to resolve the conflicts they present is entangled with and shadowed by that of other groups and their rights struggles. To return to Marshall here, we should begin with an idea of citizenship as an exclusionary practice. The first principle of exclusion was class: franchise and citizenship were extended to only those with property. The second principle of exclusion was gender: women were denied the franchise. The third principle was ethnic and religious. In England, Canada and the United States, the earliest exclusion was of Catholics and, more quietly, Jews. Slavery within the British Empire (and others) and the post-Revolution United States clearly established a racial hierarchy of citizenship, where race began to evolve from a religious ideology to a purely 'biological' one. Thus, Asian immigrants to North America, too, were similarly excluded from citizenship. In the United States, they were ineligible by virtue of their colour, and remained ineligible even after 1890, when African-Americans gained the right to citizenship. In both Canada and the US, they were banned from voting and owning property, and subjected to discrimination, rioting and other violence. Even the most rudimentary review of the 'justice' experienced by any of these groups demonstrates that none received equal treatment before the law. Certainly there is an argument that many do not receive such treatment today. As argued in Chapter 1, modern citizenship has always been allocated only to select groups, despite its universal language.

What was the purpose of such exclusionary legislation? We would argue that it is a reflection of an imperialist practice that found its strongest expression in citizenship to mark out the Other. Such a practice includes the categorization of land as 'territory' and people as 'races'. Both presuppose ownership and control. At the core of this practice is an invented hierarchy of peoples and nations that attempts to justify the claiming of land and the subjugation of peoples previously foreign to the conqueror. It was from and within imperialism that nations were born, not only as a means to overthrow oppressive empires (Said, 1993). Nations were established and governed by similar groups and classes that had launched empires. As power moved increasingly from monarchies to corporations, the nation-state became the most efficient means by which to solidify and from which to defend modern capitalism. Thus, the trinity of nationalism, capitalism and imperialism was eventuated with the state. Again, we return to the idea of nations as owned and defined by the few and that these few established for themselves a clear idea of who met the standard and who did not. This history, although well documented and known to most historians and other scholars, is frequently implicitly silenced by the manner in which new social movements today are discussed. Cultural politics, in particular, is described as something new and unique to the late twentieth century. Typically, David Morley and Kevin Robins (1995) suggest that the current identity crisis is a product of postmodern globalization, rather than a problem deeply rooted in modernity and merely exposed under the postmodern condition.

Politics of Resistance and Inclusion: Reinventing National Identity

Just as modern nations were founded by and for certain social classes, so too have they been established by and for certain 'races' and ethnic groups (K. Anderson, 1991; Wood, 1999). In the words of the British politician Enoch Powell, as recently as 1995, 'Racism is the basis of nationality.' Aboriginals and immigration—forced and voluntary—have challenged those exclusionary definitions of nations. Initially through legal battles revolving around issues such as property rights and suffrage civil rights, marginalized groups have sought to be included within the definition of their new nation, to see themselves reflected in and defended by its symbols and institutions. From these relatively narrowly defined political and civil legal battles, these groups have moved towards more substantial issues of social justice. In the process, many are attempting to employ an international, perhaps universal—rather than national—rhetoric of rights. In other words, they are trying to articulate a cosmopolitan citizenship that they patently do not have (in the eyes of the 'new class', who patently *do* have it—see Chapter 5).

There have been several theoretical responses to the issues of identity, multiculturalism and citizenship. Many have struggled with the concept of multiculturalism and the issues of identity politics; few have taken on the legal and political specifics of its relevance to citizenship. In Chapter 1, we briefly discussed Charles Taylor and his well-known argument on the politics of recognition. Taylor fails to appreciate the material reality of the history detailed above and, thus, he characterizes the struggles for group rights as merely recognition. While Taylor is correct to assert that '[t]he projection of an inferior or demeaning image on another can actually distort and oppress, to the extent that the image is internalized', he reduces the impact of his discussion of oppression when he completes his thoughts with only the following: 'Not only contemporary feminism but also race relations and discussions of multiculturalism are undergirded by the premise that the withholding of recognition can be a form of oppression' (C. Taylor, 1994: 36). It is true that the social movements speak out against the ways in which they feel their presence has been rendered invisible or their voice silenced. They resent the frustration of their attempts to get their issues onto public political agendas. They appreciate the significance and power of language and representation to their struggle and to their self-identification. All of these largely representational battles do constitute forms of oppression (I. Young, 1990), but they are only part of the discrimination groups have faced. However, nowhere does Taylor acknowledge the material reality of oppression, much less the violence with which that oppression has sometimes been achieved.

Taylor also provides no space for 'hybrids', and more generally, the complexities of these identities. Not everyone fits neatly into categories imposed by others. People with 'mixed parentage' are as old as colonialism, and their communities have stood as a challenge to homogenizing eugenic projects of imperialism, just as they do today (Root, 1996; R. Young, 1995). It has been argued that hybridity was seen as both a necessary part of and an aberration of the colonial project. It has also been suggested that hybridity, particularly with reference to sexual relationships, was a desired part of the colonial project, one that erotically animated imperialism in a fashion similar to images of swashbuckling adventurers. As Robert Young puts it, 'Theories of race were also covert theories of desire' (R. Young, 1995; Said, 1978, 1993).

Taylor's rigidity leaves his discussion insufficient to deal with the political and social aspects of hybridity (not just the sexual ones). For such scholars, there is always the presumption of contradictions among varying identities, instead of an acknowledgement of the flexibility individuals give their identities. We would argue that such contradictions are imposed from without; this is important, but so, too, is the way in which individuals are able to resist such social definitions and resolve apparent contradictions for themselves. On this matter, we prefer to endorse the approach of scholars such as Paul Gilroy, whose *The Black Atlantic* explicitly searches for and attempts to appreciate rather than categorize the dual and multiple identities individuals have historically held (Gilroy, 1993). Gilroy draws on the work of W.E.B. Du Bois for the idea of 'double consciousness' to address what he calls the 'intercultural positionality' of those whose claim 'identities [which] appear to be mutually exclusive' and are compelled to '[occupy] the space between them or [try] to demonstrate their continuity' (Gilroy, 1993: 1, 6). While Gilroy does not explicitly discuss the work of Bourdieu, his emphasis on actual exchanges rooted in place accords with the latter's emphasis on durable dispositions.

Hybridity is key to discussions of identity not only because it complicates and even prevents neat categorization of people, but also because it reasserts the fluidity and contingency of identity. Identities are the products of specific chains of historical events and ideas. An understanding of the history of a given group must enter into the just consideration of its citizenship rights. As we shall see in greater detail below, groups exist in hierarchies of political, cultural, social and economic power. Through an appreciation of the historical process of those power relationships, the blind equalization and sanctification of all identities will be avoided, and the pursuit of justice for marginalized groups will be facilitated.

On the many aspects of identity, multiculturalism and citizenship, Will Kymlicka's *Multicultural Citizenship* (1995) is the most thorough treatment. While overall we have several points of contention with Kymlicka, he does recognize many important things with which we would agree. First, Kymlicka reminds us that despite the idealized images Western political theorists might hold, '[m]ost organized political communities throughout recorded history have been multiethnic', a point many scholars often overlook. As we are trying to illustrate throughout this book, these issues of identity politics have emerged most vividly in the twentieth century as a product of the collapse of modern master narratives rather than any novelty of diversity in our age. Cultural politics is the issue it is today because of its intersection with changing economic and political conditions. Kymlicka also takes a step forward from Taylor in openly acknowledging the often extreme discrimination and prejudice minorities have faced when a dominant group attempts to create the homogeneity it feels will produce the ideal society. On these grounds, Kymlicka believes that liberal theory of social justice must take into account group rights.

Nonetheless, the framing of multicultural citizenship as minority rights, and Kymlicka's understanding of minority primarily derived from the example of the French in Canada quite seriously hampers his focus on group rights. It is telling that Kymlicka introduces his study with a reference to his home base, the University of Ottawa: 'As a bilingual university with a mandate to serve both the anglophone and francophone communities in Canada, it is ideally suited for research on minority rights' (Kymlicka, 1995: v). Despite the conflicts between the English- and French-speaking groups in Canada that have blossomed into a constitutional odyssey, one might also argue that these two groups are each dominant in their own way and circumstances. In the eyes of newer immigrants to Canada, such as Southern European, Asian or African immigrants, the French are not a minority. French language and culture are explicitly protected in the Canadian Constitution; English and French are both official national languages; and the 'Quebec question' has dominated Canadian politics almost constantly for at least the past three decades. As far as issues of citizenship rights and identity are concerned, French Canadians are in a more privileged position than other non-British groups in Canada.

Much of Kymlicka's (and Taylor's) rationale appears to derive from an attempt to address the Quebec question, between two very large groups that, while not equal in power, are nevertheless in positions of economic, social, cultural and political power at the national level. Such a situation cannot hope to compare to the multiplicity of ethnic and racial groups that populate Canada and by now, as sketched above, all Western nations. The diversity of language, religion, dress, social practice and skin colour, combined with the politics of legal and illegal immigration and refugees, presents a much more complicated picture than Kymlicka would perhaps like to recognize. His reduction of the negotiation of multicultural citizenship to two dominant groups also assists him in avoiding what is a necessary acknowledgement of multiple hierarchies of power (B. Walker, 1997). His considerations of multiculturalism, both as a social phenomenon and as a policy, reveal the flaws in his logic, some of which are perhaps rooted in his initial positioning between the English and French.

Kymlicka divides 'multiculturalism' into two categories, making a distinction between the 'multinational', countries that were created, forcefully or otherwise, from previously existing nations, and the 'polyethnic', countries whose population diversified ethnically through voluntary, individual or family immigration. He of course allows that countries like Canada and the United States are both multinational and polyethnic (Kymlicka, 1995: 17). His grounds for this distinction are that the term 'multicultural' 'can be ambiguous, precisely because it is ambiguous between multinational and polyethnic'. He cites examples of what he considers misunderstandings of the term and, specifically, of the Canadian policy of Multiculturalism. These misunderstandings, however, are more accurately described as differing opinions regarding the consequences of the policy. More weakly, Kymlicka cites a 1975 reference to sum up the aims of the 1971 policy, whereas the policy has since been revised by legislation more than once and has been subjected to a greater degree of public scrutiny. It is a policy subject to widely diverging interpretations, yes, but the varying perspectives are legitimate in their own contexts (Bissoondath, 1994).

More confusing is what meaning Kymlicka ascribes to this distinction. It is very close to an us (the established)/them (the newcomers) dichotomy that does not produce the tolerance Kymlicka repeatedly endorses. For him, it appears, the nation-state is not a collective process. As he puts it, 'national membership should be open in principle to anyone, regardless of race or colour, who is willing to learn the language and history of the society and participate in its social and political institutions' (Kymlicka, 1995: 23). This argument raises several questions and implicitly condones an assimilation paradigm. What is hidden in the phrase 'in principle'? Why the emphasis on the theoretical, the abstract and an absence of discussion of 'in practice'? More importantly, who defines these 'social and political institutions' and measures legitimate participation? Who writes the history? Kymlicka is talking about the 'integration' of immigrants into an apparently homogeneous polity; he overlooks the native-born activists and revolutionaries. Furthermore, his idea of integration of newcomers into established institutions is clearly not retroactive. The first immigrants (the colonizers) did not assimilate into Aboriginal culture, but later immigrants should assimilate into that of the colonizers. It is the quintessential logic of maintaining the status quo. Ultimately, then, this is *unequal citizenship*, whereby one's cultural rights are determined by length of residence and access to power, not by legal citizenship. (This is perfectly in line with liberalism; indeed, it points to a central tenet of liberalism as practical inequality.)

As Kymlicka imagines the nation, it is clear that a first come, first served approach is somewhere at work. While he decries the treatment that Aboriginals endured at the hands of colonists, nowhere does he openly acknowledge and condemn the imperialism or imperialist attitudes that led to such treatment. Why? Because ultimately liberalism is in its own way a form of imperialism. This should not surprise anyone; the height of imperialism was accommodated, even enabled—but not challenged—by liberalism. Implicit in imperialism is the notion of hierarchy of people, inherently present in cultural characteristics. These characteristics have ranged from religious to racial to economic (Gogwilt, 1995; Said, 1993); they have been 'legitimated' by the science of geographers, biologists and political scientists. Some sense of superiority was always necessary to justify the claiming of territory and the control of commerce. Liberalism's basic acceptance of the idea of natural hierarchy prevents it from ever providing effective tolerance, equality and justice. We think that Kymlicka, by pushing liberalism to its limits, vividly illustrates the difficulties of transcending those limits due to the philosophy's ahistorical premises. Individual rights were one of imperialism's many tools precisely because *they were never universal*. As we have argued earlier, they were a privilege granted to a select group. To truly move beyond imperialist attitudes, it is necessary to think more radically, more democratically and more collectively.

Kymlicka does attempt to incorporate group rights into liberalism. Rather than a full-scale endorsement of the sovereignty of the individual, he begins his discussion with the assertion that individual rights are essential 'for protecting group difference. These rights enable individuals to form and maintain the various groups and associations which constitute civil society ...' (Kymlicka. 1995: 26). He remains committed to the idea that '[a] liberal democracy's most basic commitment is to the freedom and equality of its individual citizens' (34). And he believes that '[t]he protection afforded by these common rights of citizenship is sufficient for many of the legitimate forms of diversity in society' (26). We would draw attention to his use of 'sufficient' and 'legitimate'. He does allow, however, for 'special legal or constitutional measures, above and beyond the common rights of citizenship' (26). While others may argue that any idea of group rights is diametrically opposed to liberal philosophy, Kymlicka contends that 'many forms of group-differentiated citizenship are consistent with liberal principles of freedom and equality' (34). Thus, the practice of liberal democracy, according to Kymlicka, is not entirely incompatible with 'group-differentiated rights', a term he prefers to 'collective rights'. The reasons for his preference are revealing in themselves: it avoids the inclusion of 'the rights of trade unions and corporations; the right to bring class-action suits; the right of all citizens to clean air, etc.' (34–35).

For the most part, his discussion of group rights indicates that he is thinking of Quebec again. He identifies three forms of group-specific rights: self-government, polyethnic and special representation (27). His discussion of federalism then revolves around whether it can accommodate group rights. He acknowledges the geographic aspect of such disputes of self-determination and takes it beyond the issue of land title. Kymlicka argues that '[w]here national minorities are regionally concentrated, the boundaries of federal subunits can be drawn so that the national minority forms a majority in one of the subunits' (27–28). He uses this suggestion, and his illustrative example of the Canadian province of Quebec, to demonstrate how federalism's multiple tiers can successfully accommodate racial and ethnic diversity within a state. He is, of course, forced to acknowledge that federalism has not served African-Americans nor the Native populations of North America particularly well. He notes that it was a 'deliberate decision' in the United States not to accommodate minorities with self-government rights (24–25, 28–29).

In Kymlicka's final category of 'special representation rights', he addresses a central component of rights literature: the composition of legislative bodies in terms of gender, ethnicity, race, ability and so on. This issue, which overlaps with discussions of affirmative action, is distinct from the others he discusses in its temporary nature. The larger goal, of course, is that 'society should seek to remove the oppression and disadvantage, thereby eliminating the need for these rights' (32). Kymlicka admits that this is idealistic and not a sufficient answer, that there is a need to be much more pragmatic. The liberal demand for a 'just society' means including all those 'others'. When all privileges of power and governing were reserved for the white men, the absence of democratic practice was much less troubling (to those men). Thus, their protesting against affirmative action policies and insistence on a just society *now* is somewhat disingenuous. Moreover, his category disintegrates, as Kymlicka acknowledges, when we realize that 'special representation is sometimes defended, not on the grounds of oppression, but as a corollary of self-government' (32).

A recent experiment with such rights, and the subsequent public and legal response, reveals how the individualized, equality language of liberalism prevents special representation rights from being enacted, particularly when attached to territory. In the 1980s, the lines of congressional districts were redrawn in North Carolina with the express intent of creating two voting territories in which African-Americans would be in the majority. Its designers hoped the new 1st and 12th districts would send black representatives to Congress (for the first time in almost a hundred years) and thus meet two goals: (i) to visually and actively represent the black population (in 1990, 22 per cent of the state); and (ii) to increase the tiny number of visible minorities in Congress. The plan was successful, but the new 12th district did not last. The lines of the district, a 160-mile stretch barely half a mile wide in places, were successfully challenged in the Supreme Court in 1993 as being racially motivated and thus, discriminatory. The district has been redrawn twice since; only 34 per cent of registered voters in the current district are African-American. The Supreme Court will hear North Carolina's appeal of the latest changes in 1999. Several other states have designed similar districts to benefit their black and Hispanic communities; these are equally vulnerable to legal challenge.

Kymlicka's proactive federalism ultimately avoids the problem rather than resolves it. Any territory delineated for the purposes of creating a racial or ethnic majority necessarily creates minority groups who will argue in turn for their right to territory (B. Walker, 1997). His own example of Quebec illustrates the difficulties quite tellingly. Separatists attempt to represent the province as a homogeneous French-Canadian territory, glossing over the English residents, the francophone Haitians, other immigrant groups (many of whom are trilingual) and the Native population. The central problem is that the decision-making process of determining a 'national minority' is implicitly arbitrary. Which minorities should benefit from such self-government through territorial adjustments? Kymlicka makes no suggestions or provisions as to the process of determining size, concentration, historical claim or territory. Nor did the US Supreme Court have any such guidelines and so could find no way to justify the redrawing of districts, much less defend group rights.

These problems are compounded by the separation of 'self-government' rights from polyethnic rights. This separation is not original; liberals, particularly in Canada, often separate the issues of self-government for 'older', more established minorities such as Aboriginals or French Canadians, and those of newer immigrants, whereas a more significant difference is found between Aboriginals and non-Aboriginals, particularly as it concerns the issue of *land*. In his discussion of polyethnic rights, Kymlicka speaks almost exclusively of immigrant groups and their demands 'freely to express their particularity without fear of prejudice...' (30). He describes these issues in a less analytical manner: rather than approach the history of the ethnic and racial aspects of the founding of modern nations, he instead is content to mention what the demands of immigrant groups have been (support for their cultural activities and exemption from certain laws, often on religious grounds). His conclusion reveals part of his motivation for the categories: he argues that 'unlike self-government rights, polyethnic rights are usually intended to promote integration into the larger society.' This is not always the case, as many of his own examples amply show. Pacifist, anti-modern groups such as the Hutterites clearly do not want to integrate. Jews protest the closing of stores on Sundays not to fit in, but to organize their weekly schedule around the maintenance of their Sabbath, without any disadvantage for doing so. In these cases, and many others, it might be more fruitful to merge these two categories.

According to Kymlicka, '[w]e need to distinguish two kinds of claims that an ethnic or national group might make. The first involves the claim of a group against its own members; the second involves the claim of a group against the larger society' (35). Only the latter is acceptable to Kymlicka. He proscribes that 'liberals can and should endorse certain external protections, where they promote fairness between groups, but should reject internal restrictions which limit the right of group members to question and revise traditional authorities and practices' (37). He also sees representation rights as a means to prevent minorities from being ignored or disadvantaged by the majority (or make an occurrence of this less likely) (37). Similarly, 'self-government rights devolve powers to smaller political units so that a national minority cannot be outvoted or outbid by the majority on decisions that are of particular importance to their culture, such as issues of education, immigration, resource development, language and family law' (37–38). Here again, he clearly has Quebec in mind, and is interested in devolving such decision-making powers to a provincial level only. We doubt he would support the devolution of these powers to the municipal level, even though this would logically follow from his argument. 'Each of these three forms of group-differentiated rights helps reduce the vulnerability of minority groups to the economic pressures and political decisions of the larger society' (38). Admittedly, he acknowledges the source of the problems with and threats to diversity: economy and politics, not individualized prejudice. It is important to bear this in mind and not allow liberal and neoliberal regimes to turn the debate to individualized character traits as the cause for the presence or absence of success.

Kymlicka nevertheless deserves credit for this attempt to integrate liberalism with group rights. There is a small but significant group of scholars that points to the existence and, especially, 'encouragement' of diversity as an explicit threat to the nation-state. As much as globalization appears to challenge the nation-state from above, tribalism challenges it from below and threatens to splinter its political unity (Barber, 1995; Bissoondath, 1994; Schlesinger, 1992). These scholars range fairly widely in their politics and their ultimate conclusions. Not all of them fear difference, nor do they harbour prejudicial fears about specific groups. In the case of Schlesinger, it is partly his recognition of the history of racial and ethnic oppression in America that leads him to worry at the consequences of too much contemplation of such history. For Neil Bissoondath, his own experience of racism and exclusionary categorization brings him to the desire that citizens move beyond their ethnic and racial identities. His emphasis is on inclusion, and ultimately implicates a kind of national reimagination, but instead of following his argument to such a conclusion, he accepts the language of liberalism without acknowledging its contradictions.

As discussed in Chapter 1, Beiner's civic republicanism puts forth a similar argument. Beiner cites a 1992 report by Kymlicka, warning that 'if society accepts and encourages more and more diversity, in order to promote cultural inclusion, it seems that citizens will have less and less in common.' Kymlicka seems to suggest that 'society', whoever that might be, has the ability to choose to accept or reject, encourage or discourage diversity. In what industrial, democratic society is this possible? Diversity must be understood as a social reality, not an option. Even more troubling to Kymlicka and Beiner is that in the face of such diversity, 'there may cease to be a common culture.' Ultimately Beiner seeks to reassert the sovereignty of the individual; he calls 'groupism' no less than a 'threat to the idea of citizenship'. The hope springs eternal for a universal answer to the problems of diversity within a 'common culture'. This is the trademark of the 'homogenizers'. Those who call for a common culture through individualism reveal the suppression of diversity that the prevention of collectivism achieves; individualism clearly is intended to make one not singular and unique, but invisible and powerless.

This call to and for a common culture is deceptive and dangerous. To begin with, there is no common culture that 'may cease to be'. What exists is the attempts of the dominant class to homogenize all groups, to impose its own political and social values on them and to ignore or forcefully suppress those who disagree. There never was a common culture of which citizenship was an expression; there are dominated and dominant groups between which citizenship is a mediating institution and a contested field. The advocates of an imagined 'unity' deserve to be exposed for the *group* they are: a group with its own vested and *particular* interests, a group which benefits from the continued privileging of the white, male-dominated class. Those who fear the 'ghettoization' of the nation, a fragmentation of ethnic and racial identities that undermines the collective, ignore the role of the dominant classes in creating such ghettoes—economic and social as well as rhetorical—in the first place. Beiner's line of argument would in practice *ensure* the preservation of existing ghettoes, as it makes no allowance for their current existence. There is no recognition of existing power structures, of current hierarchies—political and material—of ethnicity and race. It is a reasonable-sounding argument that serves to perpetuate racial, ethnic, gender and sexual divides (not just differences) and hierarchies. As such, it contradicts its own liberal faith in equality and the meaning of citizenship (Beiner, 1995).

Decentring the Nation-State: First Nations and Aboriginal Rights

The identities of immigrants are not the only disruption of the nation-state's homogeneous narrative. Unquestionably, there is a real challenge to the authority and sovereignty of the nation-state posed by Aboriginal peoples. Australia, the United States and Canada all became nation-states at the expense of, not with the cooperation of, Native nations already inhabiting those territories. Through wars, land grabs (with and without treaty), disease and starvation, Europeans pushed Native peoples out of the way of their settlement. Actual face-to-face encounters were often unnecessary. In many instances, North American lands changed hands between European powers in situations that had no connection to that land or its inhabitants. This political practice, in its oblivion, was the beginning of a long history of silencing and rendering invisible Native peoples. We now turn to a consideration of the cultural and territorial dislocation of Native peoples under 'aboriginal citizenship' (see also Churchill, 1996).

Kymlicka has noted the central importance of land rights in Aboriginal cultural politics: 'the single largest cause of ethnic conflict in the world today is the struggle by indigenous peoples for the protection of their land rights' (Kymlicka, 1995: 30). Further, '[t]he survival of indigenous cultures throughout the world is heavily dependent on protection of their land base, and indigenous peoples have fought tenaciously to maintain their land' (43). We might note here that they have fought no less tenaciously than white capitalists—who are, of course, the reason Natives have had to fight. Kymlicka recognizes that 'this land base is vulnerable to the greater economic and political power of the larger society.' He then makes the problematic assertion that '[h]istory has shown that the most effective way to protect indigenous communities from this external power is to establish reserves where the land is held in common and/or in trust, and cannot be alienated without the consent of the community as a whole' (43). But common land title is worth nothing if the invaders choose to ignore it. Then he suggests that we avoid this whole individual versus collective ownership mess by judging issues according to his internal/external restrictions framework, which is his way of saying that if we just apply the 'objective' standards of liberalism's twin powers, freedom and equality, we can work out the problems. In practice, those are not the powers liberals have exercised.

The Australian state took one of the strongest stances against its Native population through its policy of '*terra nullius*', which denied Aboriginals title to land based on the assumption that they had no connection to their land (because they had not developed a Western property system). *Terra nullius* was implemented even though nothing under British nor international law at the time gave the colonial governments of 1788–1901 the right to alienate Native title. Progress in Aboriginal rights has been slight and very recent. *Terra nullius* was first overturned in 1992 by the Mabo decision, which led, not without controversy, to the creation of the Native Title Act in 1993. This act has yet to grant any land title to any Native community.

A more recent court decision has taken the further step of articulating Native claims. In December 1996, the Australian High Court established in *The Wik Peoples* v. *State of Queensland* that pastoral leases on Crown land did not inherently extinguish Native claims to that territory. The Wik decision does not remove pastoral rights to lease Crown land; indeed, in situations where there is conflict between pastoralists and Natives, pastoral rights supersede Native title. The Australian government, under Prime Minister John Howard, responded with legislation passed in mid-1998 that effectively returns the rights to pastoral land to agriculturalists, the majority of whom are large corporations with large-scale land holdings. Those pastoralists who had previous arrangements with the Crown to lease land for grazing will be granted exclusive rights, regardless of Native claims. More disturbingly, they will also be thus given the ability to rent the land to Aboriginals or evict them entirely. The government plans are tinged with scandalous self-interest: at least thirty of the current Members of Parliament and Senators, plus several other political insiders, are landowners who stand to gain personally from this programme. Under the plan, Natives who successfully assert their territorial claims in court will not actually be able to reclaim their land. The plan provides only for financial compensation, and acceptance of such compensation would nullify any further claims to the land. Such compensation is also a thorn in the side of some pastoralists, who desire exclusive occupancy and do not believe they should have to negotiate or pay for land they already use.

Similarly, a recent Canadian court decision (after thirteen years in the system) regarding Delgamuukw land not covered by treaty asserted that land claims must be negotiated (rather than extinguished) and that oral history may be considered appropriate testimony in the determination of continuous Native residence. This is perhaps the beginning of a small turnaround from the legal and social persecution of Natives in Canada. In addition to issues of land title, the state has a history of misrecognizing Native identity. The creation of 'status Indian' established a model whereby women were stripped of their status as Natives, in the eyes of the law, by marrying non-Natives, while Native men in mixed marriages could maintain their status and even extend it to their wives. This represents a systematic attempt to define for Aboriginals who they are and how they should relate to the nation and to their communities (Richardson, 1993).

Again, the question is not how much does this history matter, but how does this history get addressed in terms of political realities and issues of citizenship. As with racial and ethnic minorities, it must be acknowledged that the situation that Natives find themselves in is a product of a particular history, one that cannot be ignored if their situation is to be understood and justly addressed. Moreover, land title disputes are not always a case of 'ancient history' coming back to haunt the present, but are often long-standing claims. In July 1998, the Nisga'a people negotiated a treaty with the Canadian province of British Columbia and thus ended a legal battle that had been ongoing for more than a hundred years. If the treaty, which included financial compensation, land and some self-government rights, is imitated, it may change dramatically the political structure of the nation-state. The immediate response from neoliberals has been telling: in the name of freedom and equality, they have declared the treaty unjust, without a second glance at the history of inequality and systemic injustice Natives have endured.

Historically, Natives in Canada, the United States and Australia have not been given equal civic, social or political rights as citizens, nor have they been invited to participate fully in the polity. Natives demand the right to identification with a group, have this right legally recognized, and have a political capacity to influence the way in which such recognition manifests itself materially. In Canada and the United States, Natives now have the lawyers and politicians to be able to articulate and fight for their goals. Paramount is the demand for some form of self-governance. But this demand is always attached to the actual territory of nationhood. Whether this constitutes the only answer remains to be seen. It is hard to imagine that liberal regimes of government will find a solution, for it entails the undoing of liberalism, whose premise victimized the Natives in the first place.

Kymlicka discusses the efforts of Natives in Canada to be exempt from the Charter of Rights and Freedoms, and places their campaigns in the context of the internal/external group-differentiated rights framework discussed earlier. He suggests that governance from the non-Aboriginals in the application of the Charter is appropriate in the event of, say, internal, tribal councils not defending the rights of women. He further asserts that we should not see allowing such internal restrictions as respectful, or 'the 'logical' extension of current 'multiculturalism' policies' (41), and that members of minority groups do not support such internal restrictions. (Does that necessarily mean that they support the intervention of others?) This is not really the way federalism is supposed to work, that whichever level of government is 'right' gets to make the decisions. It would be interesting if Kymlicka would consider the reverse situation, say where a tribal council affords the political participation or social rights of Native women in a way that non-Aboriginal society does not. Given that Native women were until recently forced under Canadian law to forfeit their citizenship if they married non-Native men, this question merits investigation. Certainly, though, this issue of which level of government has ultimate authority is a fundamental problem: 'What they object to is the claim that their self-governing decisions should be subject to the federal courts of the dominant society—courts which, historically, have accepted and legitimized the colonization and dispossession of Indian peoples and lands' (40). We hope Kymlicka will explore this more thoroughly, because we believe it is at the heart of Native issues.

What also deserves further exploration is the lack of opportunities afforded Natives in Canada, the US and Australia to participate in the process of the development or amendment of policies or laws that apply to them. It isn't just that Natives are subject to what may be biased or unsympathetic courts; the legal context of such court decisions is also imposed. Natives have not been invited to participate in the formation of policy and legislation that affects them—which is supposed to be the basis of justice in a democracy, that citizens participate in at least the selection of their legislative representatives. In Canada, Natives have only been voting since 1960. Moreover, a case could reasonably be made for their lack of political voice (such as participation in debates, inclusion in high-level meetings, like the premiers' conferences, media coverage, inclusion in the machinations of party organizations), not because they are not politically organized, but because they are excluded.

If we examine what various groups are actually trying to achieve, we see that it is neither to dismantle the nation nor to be accommodated nor recognized but to reinvent it as a postnational state. This is not the divisiveness and tribalism of which many critics accuse the groups and their identity politics. Neither is it an idle threat. Liberals are right to sense an undermining of their power, for the collective nation previously excluded groups demand is a fundamental challenge to the nation-state as it is currently manifested. Social justice (both recognition and distribution) calls for the reorganization of the political system, the judicial system—the very social fabric itself. It would undermine basic property rights as the West currently understands them. In other words, group rights cannot really be conceived of without imagining a postnational state.

The Postnational State and Group Rights

It is not the nation-state as a collective that needs liberalism and its supposed individual rights; it is modern (and advanced) capitalism that needs to exclude collective rights. It is capitalism that needs hierarchies of imperialism to naturalize the inequalities that markets produce and entrench. It is capitalism that needs the façade of citizenship, no deeper than rhetoric, to buy the loyalty of workers. As Immanuel Wallerstein has articulated, the two faces of liberalism are integral to its success. Arguing that liberalism 'became the geoculture of the modern world-system in the nineteenth and twentieth centuries', Wallerstein asserts that this geoculture 'is not only logically self-contradictory, but the insurmountable contradiction it presents is itself an essential part of the geoculture' (Wallerstein, 1995: 1162). Wallerstein seems to appreciate the way in which postmodernism is implicit in, or at least the inevitable outcome of modernism. As he argues, the democratic principles established by the French Revolution had implications that, if realized, could seriously challenge the capitalist world-economy which had, of course, worked without democracy for a couple of centuries. 'Far from ensuring the legitimacy of the capitalist world-economy', he writes, '[these principles] threatened to delegitimate it in the long run' (1163).

Wallerstein, however, considers liberalism as an ideology rather than a regime of government with technologies of power. To illustrate the alleged logical contradictions of liberalism is not adequate to address its practical inequalities. To accommodate this economy, the state had to address democratic ideals and practices in a controlled fashion. Human rights had to be seen to be practised more than they were. For in fact, as Wallerstein explicitly demonstrates, human rights were not understood to be the possession of every human. From the 'almost universally agreed' denial of rights to infants, who do not possess 'the mental capacity to exercise them wisely' (1166), it has been too short a step to deny liberalism's 'fundamental human rights' to socially and economically marginalized groups, particularly ethnic and racial minorities, as illustrated earlier.

These restrictions were given their best articulation within the spatial framework of the nation-state. As noted earlier in this chapter, citizenship starts with location. The measurement of location changed with the political geography of the modern era: 'The modern world-system created a legal and moral structure that was radically different, one in which the sovereign states, located within and constrained by an interstate system, asserted *exclusive* jurisdiction over all persons falling within their territory. Furthermore, all these territories were bounded geographically, that is, by surveyors' measurements, and were thus rendered distinct from other territories; in addition, no area within the interstate system was left unassigned to some particular state. Thus when 'subjects were transformed into "citizens," the current inhabitants of an area were immediately divided into "citizens" and "non-citizens" (or aliens)' (1167). Immediately there was a means by which to justifiably allocate rights to some and to deny rights to others, by virtue of the spatial determination of citizenship. The controlling valve came in the distinction between the fundamental rights themselves and 'the politics of implementing them' (1163). It was through the process of implementation that liberals achieved the successful management of the contradiction between rhetoric and reality: the containment of the 'dangerous classes'. This implementation, this management, this containment, was achieved through the establishment of citizenship.

According to Wallerstein, 'liberalism needed a constraining force' to justify the selective nature of the allocation of citizenship, and '[t]hat force was racism. combined with sexism' (1170). Necessary as such a force may have been, it was equally necessary to disguise and deny such prejudice, 'since both racism and sexism were by definition anti-universal and anti-liberal'. The imperialist era gave liberals the mask of a saviour: their racist views of 'barbarous' peoples were articulated as a noble force of civilization, first religious, then political and economic (Holt, 1992; Said, 1993). Social scientists assisted the legitimation. But, as Said has astutely noted, the imperialists' 'liberality was no more than a form of oppression and mentalistic prejudice' (Said, 1978; Wallerstein, 1995).

To conclude, when we consider liberalism here not as a philosophy or ideology but as a regime of government which reveals the inadequacies of liberal political theory and its inherent inability to address inequality, its credo of individual rights appears as a façade for a particular group privilege; its half-hearted attempts to build a tolerant society are hindered by its grounding in hierarchical institutions and ideology; its desire to maintain the status quo of power relationships prevents the pursuit of social justice to those who have been discriminated against or exploited. While states have made progress in the area of civil rights through the gradual extension of certain privileges to an increasingly large portion of society, they have done little to amend the causes of injustice nor to create the conditions for a more egalitarian society, particularly as it pertains to interfering with the capitalist market. The liberal state has extended voting rights, legal citizenship rights and such, while rarely hampering the privileged position of capitalists to pursue trade. In fact, such government is careful to allocate only such rights as will enhance commercial practices or, at the very least, not disrupt them.

To articulate their challenge, minority groups and others are sometimes employing a universal language of 'human rights', rather than 'minority rights' as Kymlicka suggests, drawing on such articles of faith as the United Nations' Universal Declaration of Human Rights. This document emerged in November 1948 from a committee headed by Eleanor Roosevelt, which itself was careful not to mention ethnicity or race (Kymlicka, 1995) or religion (Weigel, 1995). Ultimately it is not a powerful document: no government or army backs it up and just about every major democracy's laws violate or fail to support some aspect of it. Nevertheless, it is an interesting use of a document that is a half-century old. New charters of rights created at all levels are in some way modelled on it. The focus is not on 'civil' rights, but 'human rights', as though membership in the *Homo sapiens* club came with guarantees. Rights are administered and protected by the state, which is currently installed in the nation. Without a nation-state's support of human rights, which are guaranteed through citizenship, the UN document is meaningless. It is of further interest to note that the UN Declaration does not singularly embrace individual rights. It provides not only for the rights of individual persons, but 'all members of the human family'. Its understanding of individuals is through the window of a collective. This approach is also expressed in the charter's endorsement of the family in Article 16 (3): 'The family is the natural and fundamental group unit of society and is entitled to protection by society and the State.'

As Kobayashi and others have argued, ethnic and racial minorities are not satisfied with the rhetoric of policies promising equality. Nice language may change the minds of a few, and may raise a new generation with more tolerance for difference. In the end, however, policies that are no more than rhetoric become empty promises, masking the ugly reality with good public relations (Kobayashi, 1993). Minority groups are instead interested in employing such policies in the pursuit of justice, to create real, lived equality. They demand a society that incorporates rather than accommodates their voices (Jacobs, 1996). The source of change needs to be the movement of power—away from the centre, the core to the margins, to encapsulate collectives. It is a new politics because it is a new strategy of politics: the difference is in the *how* of what happens. Through the use of processes that include all those affected, power, in some form, is redistributed to the local, to the marginal. Such a process will not splinter the collective, as critics will argue; such critics ignore the way in which exclusion has spawned alienation. Expansion is the only means to a new radical citizenship and perhaps the only way to invent a postnational and postnationalist state in which citizenship can become a product of diversity rather than an instrument of a dominant group, which uses it to 'accommodate' diversity.

Ethnicity and race are only two aspects of diversity. The modern nation-state is pressured not only by diasporic and Aboriginal identities, but also by sexual identities. Both women's groups and gay and lesbian social movements have protested their unequal status under modern capitalism, exposing its sexual order. Their identities and experiences are disjunctive to the master narratives and have bred a further challenge to liberalism's individualist citizenship.

4

SEXUAL CITIZENSHIP: IDENTITIES OF GENDER AND SEXUALITY

Introduction

This chapter focuses on the intersection between gender identities, including homosexuality, heterosexuality and transsexuality, and citizenship. While gender and sexuality are not the same thing, they are intimately linked and social movements along one line of identity have always implicated the other. Both the women's movement and the gay-rights movements have gone beyond their legal battles to challenge prevailing ideas of sexual roles on all fronts. However, the two movements, to the extent they are distinct, have not achieved equal measures of success in their battles for civil and social rights of citizenship. Women were initially the more explicitly excluded from political and social participation, but in the long run they have achieved a legitimacy in the public sphere for individual women and for women as a constituency. Despite the marginalization of many of their concerns as 'women's issues', their successful organization along gender lines has greatly enhanced their ability to mobilize women and lobby the state and other powers. Gay groups have not been able to accomplish the same. Often, as individuals, they remain oppressed (silenced, invisible or subject to harassment in public); as a group, the political legitimacy of their constituency and their claims of citizenship rights are regularly called into question.

These two constituencies have a mixed relationship with advanced capitalism. On the one hand, advertisers and other image-makers have responded to the criticism of the invisibility of women and gays. More images in more positive contexts have improved somewhat the representation of these groups in the media. Nonetheless, the reflexive accumulation that drives the consumerist economy resists the total inclusion of gays and women in public and corporate life. There are still severe limits to the public acceptance of gays and women in the technological spaces of consumption. For the time being, gay couples may advertise automobiles and 'girl power' may sell music, but the moment such images cease to appear profitable, they will fall by the wayside or even be reversed. Nor should we ignore the extent to which heterosexual stereotypes continue to flourish in all forms of the media. On the other hand, although the persistence of gender roles based on bourgeois family models in the home and their re-creation in the paid workplace have somewhat limited the employment opportunities of women and openly gay individuals, reflexive occupations ranging from advertising to design and services have been more open to women and gays than the masculine occupations of modern capitalism.

Exploring the rights of these groups and the issues of identity and citizenship they raise, this chapter benefits even more clearly from an analysis of the role public space, in metaphoric and material senses, plays in citizenship. In addition to the need for public space in order to participate fully in society, the spatial containment of both people and sexual practices adds another layer to the relationship between citizenship and geography. We argue that the landscapes of sexuality, for heterosexuals and homosexuals, are integral to their identity and the exercise of citizenship rights. This discussion also raises a further issue of the increasing privatization of space with advanced liberalism and the particular importance of this for women and gays. This last question will be addressed in still greater detail in light of consumer identities in Chapter 6.

Gender and Modernity: Moving from the National to the International

Sexist ideologies and practices are as old as any of the myths upon which Western civilization rests. However, the specifics of the gender ideologies that women in modern states still fight to change were entrenched during the industrial revolution and the establishment of the nation-state. Mainstream accounts of nationalism (e.g., Gellner, 1983; Hobsbawm, 1990) have neglected the central role of gender in the development of master narratives (Yuval-Davis, 1997). Fortunately, many others have taken up the slack to demonstrate that, while the roles and responsibilities of men and women did not originate with modernity, modern capitalism institutionalized these roles both spatially and economically. Moreover, the organization of society, politics and the paid workplace allocated power disproportionately to men. The removal of the paid workplace from the home and the assignment of men to public workplaces and women to the domestic workplace produced a spatial arrangement of gender identity that thus assisted in its reproduction. Women were female by virtue of *where* they were (or were 'supposed' to be) as much as any other characteristic. The gendered notions of these spaces were and are inextricable from the ideas of gender difference and hierarchy (Ardener, 1981; Blunt and Rose, 1994; Bondi, 1990; Mackenzie, 1986; Spain, 1992).

These ideas about women were strengthened by the construction of family narratives surrounding them. Robin Silbergleid has observed that the advent of the heterosexual 'family romance narrative' was coincident with 'the rise of industrial capitalism and the foundation of liberal citizenship', and suggests the patriarchal content of the family narrative, as it interacts with the economic and political, is what has maintained women's citizenship in a second-class position (Silbergleid, 1997). The state has not been a neutral arbiter in this process as liberalism would have us believe. David Evans, for example, argues in the context of late-twentieth-century Britain that 'the state has been active in constructing a fetishised family, one increasingly divorced from the complex varieties of the actual forms it has to sustain, and from the equally diverse roles of women within and without them' (Evans, 1993: 242). Others have illustrated governmental use of images and roles of women in patriotic rhetoric and propaganda, particularly the revered mother-figure who corrects declining birth rates and tempers the impact of immigrant populations (Offen, 1984).

The removal of the waged workplace from the family home also created the need for a separate support system for reproduction. The spatial segregation of production and reproduction along lines of sex produced a literal and mental map of gender, one which continues to guide socio-economic organization in the present. Even as advanced capitalism welcomes and accommodates women into the paid, public workplace, in many countries, women are still charged with raising pre-school-aged children without support. As many families rely on two incomes, and many men are apparently unwilling to return to the home to care for children even if they can afford to, pressures remain on women to continue to provide this service. Furthermore, with the improvements in health care, more people are living well into their senior years. There is considerable pressure on women to be caregivers to their parents and in-laws, and to keep this care in private homes rather than institutions at public expense. Advanced capitalism, then, rests on a tension between a desire to employ the best and the brightest, some of whom are women, and the identification of women as the caregivers of children and seniors, who will perform this work within the domestic sphere *for no pay*.

There are several such tensions, and they reveal the real limitations imposed on sexual citizenship by advanced capitalism. As Evans has noted, 'For women in modern first world economies, material, political and moral pressures are deeply ambiguous, devaluing procreation though enhancing motherhood, encouraging cheaper feminised forms of labour whilst also encouraging families (i.e., women) to re-assume responsibility for members in need of special care…, seeking to maximise private domestic commodification whilst developing women's access to public leisure and lifestyle consumption, all the while asserting traditional family values and the crucial role of the female in maintaining and retaining them' (Evans, 1993: 242).

These tensions originated with modern capitalism as it urbanized the countryside. The greater number of employment opportunities for women, both in factories and offices and in the private homes of middle-class families, brought them out of the private sphere and into public spaces. It gave them some measure of economic power and independence, and a subsequent desire to participate in the governance of society at all levels. Originally, working-class men excluded them from their unions, and, thus, women felt compelled to organize independently. For these workers, such organization reinforced the significance of their identity as women, and reproduced this identity with a component of social class (Briskin and McDermott, 1993; Chateauvert, 1998; Cook, Lorwin and Daniels, 1992; Jacoby, 1994). Although women were occupying public spaces with men, their experience of that shared space did not always lead to equality nor a sense of common weal, because they were not permitted, by the state, by corporations and by their male co-workers, to occupy that public space in the same manner (Stansell, 1986; Strange, 1995). Wherever possible, the domestic model was reproduced in the paid workplace: women were assigned to menial tasks similar to those performed in the home; they were paid lower wages; and they were frequently spatially segregated from male employees (Downs, 1995; Frances, 1993; John, 1986; Kwolek-Folland, 1994; Lowe, 1980; Steedman, 1997).

Particularly in the settler societies of Australia, Canada and the United States, the twentieth-century decentralization of residential neighbourhoods from central cities to the suburbs exacerbated the spatial component of this gender differentiation (Hayden, 1981; Jackson, 1985; Mackenzie, 1986; Rothblatt, Garr and Sprague, 1979; Strong-Boag, 1991). The home and the paid workplace were pushed farther apart, both literally and figuratively. Often left without transportation, suburban women managed households and raised children, isolated but for their neighbours who led similar lives. Their lives were thus removed from the centre of business and political activities, and they were encouraged to become professionals only in the roles of homemaker and consumer. The middle-class home of the city and suburb itself expanded in size and in usage. It became a support system for the wage-earning husband; in his home he was not only fed and clothed, but nurtured spiritually and sustained professionally. With the family man model as the corporate ideal, his wife was expected to seek and maintain relationships with other company wives, entertain the boss and other colleagues in the home, and even perform labour for the company's philanthropic projects (Friedan, 1970). This situation was not a little ironic, for the more devoted he was to his job, the less time the 'family man' could be with his family.

This home was also a site of middle-class upward mobility, displayed most concretely in the acquisition of consumer goods. As early as the nineteenth century, retail stores targeted women as consumers attached in some way to the patriarchal family model (Barth, 1982). Ever larger homes required appliances, furniture and decoration. Improvements in the area of housecleaning products and appliances motivated housewives to replace and renew the contents of their homes, and thereby demonstrate their husband's financial ability to own the very latest. Similarly, rapid changes in the fashion and style of furniture and items such as carpeting and curtains continually raised the standard for a middle-class modern home. This trend has only increased towards the end of the century, with big names in women's and men's fashion clothing, such as Ralph Lauren and Calvin Klein, expanding their industry into home decor.

The expansion of consumerism has affected sexual identities even more directly. Single and married women were and are encouraged to purchase romance and even their sexual identities through their consumption practices. The cosmetics industry frames its marketing almost entirely around heterosexual relationships. In this, her attractiveness is constituted of her intelligent selection and purchase of beauty products and clothes. More secretively, mother nature's work can be improved upon through the purchase of gym memberships, body-shaping garments and cosmetic surgery, while such products make such private spaces all the more public (see also Evans, 1993: 259–261). More recently men, too, have been invited to create their sexual identity through the purchase of clothing, cologne and supervised workouts. Romantic relationships and sexual identities have thus become in some measure engineered by the technologies of consumerism; as a consequence, any defiance of identities as defined by the market is rendered more difficult to legitimate (Miller, 1998).

While it has varied in degree and content, the unequal sexual division of labour at all class levels has been well documented for the United States (Blau, Ferber and Winkler, 1998; Kelly, 1991; Shelton, 1992), Canada (Parr, 1990; Pierson, 1986; Strange, 1995), Australia (Frances, 1993; Goodnow, 1994), Britain (Davidoff, 1995; Downs, 1995; Figes, 1994; Siltanen, 1994; Walby, 1986), France (Downs, 1995; Zylberberg-Hocquard, 1978, 1981), Germany (Franzoi, 1985) and other European countries (Frader and Rose, 1996). This gendered organization of production, reproduction and consumption has had real consequences for the meaning of citizenship for women (Walby, 1990). The allocation of citizenship rights under capitalism followed the gender map of public workplace and private home. As Marshall argued, such rights were extended for the specific purpose of facilitating capitalism; therefore, those who performed work that supported capitalism, but stood outside of it, were further weakened by the state. Women's work in the home was essential to their husbands, fathers and sons, and was related to their success in industry. But that work was not remunerated and, thus, not recognized in the manner that increasingly defined one's power and influence in Western society: material wealth and disposable income. It was on the basis of property and wealth that citizenship rights, voting in particular, were first determined.

While Marshall does not directly address this issue of gender, it in no way conflicts with his observations. In the early modern period, the state granted men rights of contract, property and suffrage, and explicitly denied the same to women. Until there was a shortage of male employees (such as during the World Wars), many Western states explicitly discouraged women from entering the paid workplace, through which they might gain social and political power on par with men. When large numbers of single women began working in offices and factories in the early twentieth century, their very presence in public urban spaces cast their character into suspicion in the eyes of men and upper-middle-class women (Stansell, 1986; Strange, 1995). Tellingly, during World War II, North American governments provided tax incentives, day-care for children and other accommodations for women who came to work in the war industries. These disappeared when the soldiers returned home (Milkman, 1987; Pierson, 1986).

What modern governments have explicitly demonstrated is that their preferred model of a professional-managerial class is composed of white men. The inclusion of women in the public, paid workplace is in many ways an ephemeral and tenuous arrangement, subject to reversal. Nor is the state merely cheering at the sidelines: the state itself is not a neutral arbiter but an active enforcer of gender roles, although human rights codes have made this more difficult.

The first wave of feminist activism was in the late nineteenth and early twentieth centuries and centred on gaining the right to vote. At the national level, Australian women won the franchise in 1902; Canadian women followed in 1918; their German and American sisters caught up the next year; British women waited until 1928; the French were denied until 1944. Many of the women who participated in this struggle were also active in other social reform movements, such as temperance. These activists were almost exclusively middle-class, white women, whose husbands, brothers and fathers possessed rights which they did not. Their challenge to the liberal state was minimal yet profound. By definition, their inclusion in the public world of politics disrupted the socio-economic, spatial order of modern capitalism. However, women were not, by and large, protesting liberalism and capitalism; they just wanted to be included. Their fight for citizenship rights, then, followed the framework described by Marshall and accommodated, rather than contested, the political and economic status quo. As they gradually left their middle-class homes for public employment, their own employment of non-whites and the working class enabled them to perpetuate the gendered, middle-class home, rather than make new demands of their husbands.

After World War II, feminists were inspired by the strategies and ideas of the African-American civil rights movement and began to take on new targets (Evans, 1979). Central to the cause of women's liberation at this point was an issue that introduced, if not in so many words, the idea of *sexual* citizenship: abortion. For many, 'feminist advocacy of women's right to absolute control of their own bodies and fertility, both necessary to the realization of waged careers and other public roles, turned abortion into *the* basic female civil right...' (Evans, 1993: 254; Friedan, 1991). These well-educated, often working women (or, at least, one group of them) were by this point aware that the extension of men's rights to women was insufficient. Their politics of sexual citizenship placed new forms of rights on the agenda for the public and governments.

In the so-called 'Second Wave' of feminism in the 1960s and 1970s, white middle-class women also began to be openly challenged by women of colour, working-class women and lesbians for the narrow vision of women's rights and issues. 'Because the models [of the women's liberation movement] usually focus exclusively on upon the effects of sexism', Diane Lewis argued, 'they have been of limited applicability to minority women subjected to the constraints of both racism and sexism' (Lewis, 1977). Margaret Simons agreed and decried the reluctance of white women to respond to minority women's concerns: 'This important challenge for feminism, to confront the problem of racism and ethnocentrism in the feminist movement, among its members and within its theory, has not generally been accepted by white feminists' (Simons, 1979).

Simons was particularly critical of a 1970 anthology edited by Robin Morgan, *Sisterhood is Powerful*. Simons pointed to the paucity of minority voices in the collection as well as their segregation from the other papers. They are prefaced with an introductory article, 'Resistances to Consciousness', implying that minority women are not interested in having or able to have their consciousness fully raised. These women's insistence on 'the importance of combating racism and capitalism along with sexism' made their feminism less than pure in the eyes of middle-class whites. Minority women complicated the picture even further for their white sisters by recognizing the impact of racism and capitalism on their fathers, brothers and husbands, and expressing 'solidarity with the men of their oppressed communities' (Simons, 1979).

Writing of the 1980s by feminists of colour brought this issue to the forefront (see hooks, 1981, 1989, 1990, 1992). The many layers of discrimination faced by women not just because of their sex, but also their race, ethnicity, ability, and so on, intersected, such that any understanding of gender inequality was incomplete without the inclusion of other hierarchies of identity. Furthermore, these writers insisted that the white second-wave feminists acknowledge the privilege their race afforded them. By the 1990s feminist scholars were recognizing the need to inform their understanding of gender with race, and to recognize that to be 'raced' was not only to be 'of colour'. In line with other studies of race and ethnicity (e.g., Ignatiev, 1995; Roediger, 1991), feminists began to address the construction of 'whiteness' (Frankenberg, 1993).

In many ways, what these scholars were doing was continuing along a path that was well worn with feminist critical interrogations of identity (see especially Butler, 1990; Nicholson, 1990; Riley, 1990). Initially feminist scholarship was preoccupied with uncovering and integrating the 'missing' studies of women. Scholarship in the social sciences and the humanities had been biased towards the male perspective, projecting it as an objective, universal, normative experience. This led to turning the discussion towards the idea of 'gender' (Nicholson, 1990; Scott, 1988) and the social construction of women's and men's roles, even their sexuality. These inquiries have now produced a deeper assessment of the nature of identity, its production and reproduction, and its cultural institutionalization in both time and, especially, space (Ardener, 1981; Blunt and Rose, 1994). Feminist scholarship on identity has necessarily included an examination of the technologies of power, and has thus influenced the study of other identities (Ardener, 1981; Blunt and Rose, 1994; G. Rose, 1993).

At the same time, feminist politics moved in another fruitful direction. In addition to re-examining their local and national organizations, their new racial sensitivity and the rise of postcolonial literature motivated some Western feminist scholars to look beyond Western capitalist states. The inclusion of voices from the non-Western countries broadened the scope of their thinking about the nature and situation of women on all fronts of cultural politics. In many ways some of this writing followed one path of feminist theory that universalizes the experience of women (an argument that is vulnerable to essentialism), but one which also opened the study of gender to incorporate critiques of capitalism.

In 1984, fourteen years after *Sisterhood is Powerful*, Morgan published another anthology whose title seemed to indicate the direction of the women's movement: *Sisterhood is Global*. In the preface to the 1996 re-issue, Morgan speaks assuredly of the 'global women's movement' and places the condition of women in a global context: 'Female human beings still comprise two-thirds of the world's illiterates (30 per cent of all women cannot read or write); we are now 80 to 90 per cent (an increase) of the world's 1.3 billion poor and, with our children, over 90 per cent of all refugee and displaced populations...' (Morgan, 1984, 1996). Even though these issues have not been anywhere near the agendas of Western nations' women's movements, under the umbrella of 'global sisterhood', they are presented as central issues, to be of concern to all women, including those in Western nations.

This global thinking, and meetings such as the United Nations conferences on the status of women, have brought about a change in the language (by some) of women's rights (Bahar, 1996). Women's rights are articulated as fundamental human rights. Part of this is to emphasize the centrality of women to society—that helping mothers helps children, helps families, helps the whole community—and focuses on the specific role mothers play in areas such as childhood education and health. Beyond even these, though, is also a more theoretical idea about women being truly equal to men, but in their way. There has been an increasing emphasis on the role of institutions such as the United Nations and Amnesty International protecting and promoting the rights of women and this emphasis has ushered the women's movement in an era of globalization of cultural politics (Bahar, 1996; Lister, 1997b; Yuval-Davis, 1997).

The idea of global sisterhood—women's rights as universal, human rights—opens up fresh possibilities but also embodies certain dangers (Yuval-Davis, 1997). While it can be one of the means by which capitalism's move from the national to the global is challenged, it can also dissipate energies across a variety of projects without having local effects. The extent to which the world is global is not in the spaces of these women; there is no global state or government for them to lobby. Moreover, removing the battle for women's rights from its local context can sever its apparent connections to economic structures and democratic processes that have a chance of success in the state. While these are general trajectories of the women's movements for citizenship rights, they have also articulated specific strategies and methods of struggle and politicized new domains, to which we now turn.

Space, Identity and Women

The selective allocation of citizenship rights along gender lines also reinforces the spatial nature of citizenship itself. If we consider the spaces within which citizenship rights were developed, it is clear that they were centred in non-domestic and, in this way, public spaces. Or, to look at it from the reverse view. citizenship rights were mapped in congruence with access to public space. The early modern nation-state was in many ways politically comprised only of its public spaces. The private sphere of the home, including women and children, was not problematized by the state to be an object of government. It was the responsibility of the patriarch to govern his home and family, and his actions in this regard were sanctioned by the state. The state's responsibilities were related only to the defence and preservation of non-domestic spaces, or what was considered the 'public sphere'. Through these spaces, state authorities also hoped to control the domestic space, but only gradually did they understand their role to include the protection of women's or children's rights, particularly in any of the ways that might conflict with what white men considered their rights, especially (but not exclusively) the smooth running of the free market (Foucault, 1998a).

Bahar has identified a parallel phenomenon in international human rights. These were defined, she argues, 'in terms of the interests of those who first promoted it, Western-educated, propertied men. It therefore focused primarily on the state's infringement of public civil rights, including the right to free expression, to political association, and to a fair trial. It ignored or refused to intervene, however, when violations occurred within the private sphere of the home and when not directly caused by the state.' It has further been argued that the state's support of the patriarchal family sanctions and protects even violence when it happens within the family (Bahar, 1996; Evans, 1993). The state has granted rights and protected its citizens only when such action benefited its order and wealth. To make any progress, women needed to demonstrate a vested interest in the public sphere. The rise of women as a constituency of voters and their participation in the public workforce were key to authorities taking their issues related to the so-called 'private sphere' seriously. Until women gained some measure of public influence, their situation in the domestic sphere remained marginal.

The spatial significance of the public sphere is re-emphasized by the necessity of actual public space—space that is visible, accessible and participatory—for the continued existence of democratic citizenship. As we shall see, under advanced capitalism and the rise of the new, professional-managerial groups, the public sphere is increasingly claimed by private space, that is, space that is privately rather than publicly owned and regulated. With the rise of neoliberalism as a regime of government, public space is on the decline and the defensive (Faulks, 1998; N. Smith, 1992). The spaces of public services, from transit vehicles to public schools, have been privatized. The encroachment of the private into the public in this way effectively disarms the latter of its most potent weapon: the power, authority and ability to author and claim space. Through reclaiming space, a group constitutes its identity and its attachment to place becomes a relatively durable disposition—group habitus.

Activism is for groups a significant means to participate in the formation of government policy that affects them. To be physically present in the public eye enables a group to reach a broader, and significantly more arbitrary, audience, rather than closed meetings where leaders are likely to be preaching to the converted. Moreover, this audience is likely to include the news media. Using multiple bodies and voices to become a body politic and thus claiming public space and attention is often a means to geographically and socially larger publics via newsprint, radio and television. For many groups, the use of public space, and, frequently, the disruption of the everyday life of that space, has been the *only* way to access the media and claim a public presence (S.G. Davis, 1986; Ryan, 1990, 1997; Stansell, 1986). As a counterbalance to the ability of more powerful interests, such as business and government, to access and perhaps control the media, the existence and availability of public space is crucial to the formation of identities and groups and articulating their rights.

These are crucial lessons that the new social movements have taught us in the past three decades. The use of space by rendering it public and embodying and investing it with meaning, using tactics of appropriating spaces and claiming media attention have become symbolic and material practices. This, in turn, also questioned the constitution of spaces as natural and regular. The women's movement, for example, illustrated that the attempt to restrict women to domestic space was part of a larger effort to keep women out of politics, and their interests out of the discussion of political rights (Marston, 1990). When women fought for the vote, which was a gain in public space, they won the right to participate in a gender-neutral way. What women are fighting for now, in many instances, is their right to participate *as women*, to allow their differences to be recognized as relevant and as integral to the constitution of sociality. While women are fighting to assert their right to be different, they are also simultaneously fighting for the legitimate recognition of this difference. Hence the extension of Marshall's citizenship rights to include such entities as reproductive rights and 'the right to participate in decision-making in a range of spheres' (Lister, 1997a; Massey, 1995).

The question of space and identity also raises one of the most significant challenges that social movements pose to modern thought: the dichotomy between the public and the private. As Evans puts it: '"equal" formal citizenship in public faces not only unequal public citizenship practice but also private patriarchal dominance...' (Evans, 1993: 246). Even when they have entered into the paid labour force, 'women have neither structurally nor ideologically been allowed to leave the family...[and] essential gender and sexual differences have been reconstituted rather than questioned...' (Evans, 1993: 250). We would argue that this is because the public/private divide has not been sufficiently challenged. Feminists are critical of this divide. Marston (1990), for example, suggests that we need to think in terms of both public *and* private; Lister argues that '[t]he rearticulation of this public–private divide provides one of the keys to challenging women's exclusion at the level of both theory and practice' and central to this rearticulation would be 'the disruption of the divide's gendered meaning...' (Lister, 1997b: 22). The personal may be political, but making all that is private public invites state intervention. Women may seek legal protection from violence in the home, but draw the line at permitting a legislature to codify other activities in that same place. Designating spaces exclusively as either public or private for the purposes of citizenship rights denies the complexity and reality of women's and men's everyday lives. Yet, the search for a definitive meaning of female sexuality is not the answer. Evans, for example, searches for such a definition and laments its absence. He observes the assertions of sexual independence and innate sexual knowledge of some, but then asks, 'is the "real" here natural or a social construct?' (Evans, 1993: 268). Invoking Foucault's claim that 'no one's sexuality is ever their own', he then misses the point that the search for sexual citizenship should lie in the process, not the specificity of laws and rights. In other words, the crux of the matter here is not *what* is female sexuality, but *who* has the authority to define (and regulate) it (and its contexts).

Gay and Lesbian Rights

Perhaps the group most subject to restrictions with respect to access to public space today is homosexuals. Within this group, it may be further argued that gay men are persecuted to a greater extent than lesbian women (Gallagher and Bull, 1996). Gays face various forms of oppression on several fronts: laws against public activities, even just handholding; protection in the workplace; the use of AIDS to criminalize their bodies as gay men and to try to push them back into the closet, out of public space; the attempt to bring AIDS into the public sphere in a sexuality-neutral, but really heterosexual, way.

The struggle for gay rights has not moved to the global stage to the same extent that the battle for women's rights has. Although AIDS has attained an international stature and there is some degree of international cooperation in fighting it, at that level it is framed no longer as a 'gay-rights issue', but as one of public health. Otherwise, gay-rights battles largely remain local. They are restricted to the local level for the basic reason that gays do not possess basic civil rights in many states. Gay-rights groups struggle to maintain public notice of the impact of this disease on gays, but neoliberalism and its emphasis on the individual as the author of his or her destiny stigmatizes AIDS as a result of individual choice. At its most homophobic, neoliberalism has conflated the disease with the gay man's body itself (Brown, 1995).

AIDS therefore has been a crucial aspect of identity formation for gay groups from within and without. Yingling asserts that 'the AIDS epidemic has been inscribed in dominant culture in a way that preserves the seeming autonomy of such fields as the scientific, the moral, and the aesthetic...' (1997: 18). He suggests that the state plays a role, if only in its acceptance of such autonomy and its lack of action. In the state's response to AIDS and his own experience living with the disease, Yingling finds evidence, in a Kafkaesque way, of 'the legislation of identity', in that identity is defined irreversibly by the disease (1997: 16). Yingling argues that early on gay-rights groups recognized that 'to effectively intervene in ignorant response to AIDS, the institutional homophobia (particularly of America and Britain) had to be addressed and exposed....' In other words, 'it is not enough to change the meaning of AIDS; we must begin to change that culture in which AIDS takes its meaning' (22).

Yingling has clarified the existence of 'a national feeling for the body that has to do with how our culture reads corporeality, physical competence, and health in general [and] that national identity requires an ideal conception of the body and a rejection of accommodation to Otherness' (25). His examination of 'how the American feeling for the body inscribes disease as foreign and allows AIDS to be read therefore as anti-American' is one of the most innovating discussions of AIDS, nationality and citizenship. It is further revealing that AIDS is considered as a subversion of the nation when it intersects with homosexuality and/or criminal drug use, but not with heterosexuality.

Similarly, AIDS and the role of the state and capitalism also intersect. Both Yingling and Shilts argue that 'the history of AIDS...would have followed a far different trajectory in a world not structured by competitive national economies that had in turn spawned competitive national economies and practices in supposed transnational areas such as scientific research...' (Shilts, 1987; Yingling, 1997: 41). Yingling argues that the state has largely abdicated its responsibility to identify and intervene in the spread of AIDS. Noting the strong participation of lesbians in gay-rights struggles for AIDS, Yingling recognizes the critical nature played by the spectre of AIDS in the identity politics of male and female homosexual citizens. Yingling asserts that 'gay and lesbian rhetoric links the fight against AIDS to Stonewall and to the entire question of gay and lesbian history...' (Yingling, 1997: 44). 'AIDS has required a continual vigilance against secrecy, shame, and repression, the hallmarks of that same (perhaps bourgeois) privacy that polices homoerotic desire...' (51).

While no Western state denies the right to vote to homosexuals, the public life of gay men and women is nevertheless severely constrained by laws and social norms. Indeed, in many places, homosexuality itself is illegal (Kaplan, 1996; Peddicord, 1996). It is instructive to cite a few cases. In Australia, the Victorian Crimes Act (1958) provides for punishing male homosexual acts by up to twenty years' of imprisonment. The law does not recognize the existence of same-sex relations between women. Italy punishes homosexual acts, considered offences against the common sense of decency in the Criminal Code, with jail terms ranging from three months to three years. In the United States, while some states have no restrictions on adult consensual sexual acts, in many states, sodomy, oral–genital sex and/or 'unnatural sex acts' are illegal; in some states sodomy is a felony.

Such outright legal banning prevents the public and free expression of gay identity. The modern state defines the citizen as a heterosexual person (Corvino, 1997). It is, moreover, the state that constitutes the heterosexual person as a criminal, endangering or explicitly threatening public order. This oppression on the basis of sexuality is, however, the most superficial denial of sexual citizenship. The absence of citizenship rights extends far into the social and spatial realms (Vaid, 1995).

The United States and Britain have both routinely discharged gay men and women from the military. In Australia, lesbianism has been considered legal grounds for divorce and for granting custody of children to the husband. In 1980, an Italian man who shot a lesbian claimed self-defence, arguing that she inherently threatened him; he was acquitted. In the United States, only a handful of states and municipalities protect the civil rights of homosexuals, in terms of public and private employment, public accommodations, housing, education and so forth. In contrast, Domestic Partner registration now exists for same-sex couples in the Netherlands, as it has in Denmark since 1989, Norway since 1993, Sweden since 1995 and Iceland since 1996. These cases have sparked consideration of similar policies in France, Spain and Finland. In 1998, the Netherlands began debating the institution of same-sex marriage.

In the United States, the state of Hawaii brought the issue of same-sex marriage to the forefront of national politics and revealed how little space there is in the country's public identity for homosexuality (Nava and Dawidoff, 1994). In December 1996, Hawaii Circuit Court Judge Kevin Chang ruled that the state constitution provided no grounds for the prevention of same-sex marriage, creating the possibility for its introduction. The ruling was stayed pending an appeal to Hawaii's Supreme Court, but is expected to be upheld. Twenty-three other states quickly introduced legislation that allowed them not to recognize such marriages performed in Hawaii. The US Congress has taken the even more dramatic step of passing a Defence of Marriage Act (DOMA), which explicitly does not recognize same-sex marriage and denies same-sex couples the right to file joint tax returns or for a person to collect any of a gay partner's government benefits. The Gay and Lesbian Network argues that this law is unconstitutional, but until an individual state sanctions same-sex marriage, there are no grounds on which to mount a court challenge. In November 1998, the Hawaiian legislature forestalled the state's Supreme Court decision by winning the support of almost 70 per cent of the electorate to amend the state constitution to define legal marriage as only between a man and a woman.

In Canada, one province launched a similar court battle against gay rights. Alberta passed its Individual's Rights Protection Act (IRPA) in 1973. Since its inception it has been renamed the Human Rights, Citizenship and Multiculturalism Act, and has been updated so that its list of protected categories now covers race, religious beliefs, colour, gender, physical disability, mental disability, age, ancestry, place of origin, marital status, source of income, and family status. On more than one occasion the Alberta Human Rights Commission requested the addition of sexual orientation to the list; each time, the provincial legislature voted against such a move. In 1989, the Supreme Court of Canada ruled that the list of prohibited grounds of discrimination such as race, national or ethnic origin, colour, religion, sex, age or mental or physical disability is not exhaustive and that analogous grounds of discrimination are implicitly prohibited by the Charter of Rights (Peterson, 1996: 35). This ruling left open the possibility of adding sexual orientation to the list.

In 1991, Delwin Vriend was fired from an Alberta college where he worked as a laboratory coordinator. The stated reason was Vriend's refusal to comply with the college's newly adopted policy forbidding homosexual practices among its faculty and staff. Vriend, who had previously admitted his homosexuality to the college's president, challenged his termination and sought legal protection under Alberta's human rights code. When Vriend first brought his case of discriminatory firing to the commission, he was told it was powerless to assist him. Vriend was successful in his first trial, where the judge cited the Charter and ruled the provincial legislation implicitly discriminated against gay men and lesbians. The government appealed the decision, bringing the case all the way to the Supreme Court. In 1998, the Supreme Court reasserted its 1989 ruling and explicitly instructed the province of Alberta to include sexual orientation in its human rights legislation. Although the authors of the Charter, including (the then Justice Minister and now Prime Minister) Jean Chrétien, had purposely elected not to bring sexual orientation under its protection, the Court chose to include it. The higher court's ruling in favour of reading gay rights into the Canadian Charter of Rights and Freedoms was met with much resistance in Alberta and a call to invoke the notwithstanding clause of the Constitution, which would allow the provincial government to override the Charter for a period of five years. This resistance came on two fronts. The first, homophobic sentiments often associated with religion, was not given much credibility by politicians and the media. The second, however, raised issues of governance, questioning the ability of the appointed court to supersede the voice of the people's elected legislature.

Eventually, the government relented and decided not to proceed. This legal victory notwithstanding, gays face an uphill battle in Alberta. Despite the Premier's assurance that his government would abide by the court's decision, it is still not certain that sexual orientation will be included in Alberta legislation.

In many ways, therefore, gays are still in the closet of private space. The AIDS crisis assisted conservatives who wanted to keep them there. The consumption of gay identities, particularly in television, movies and advertising, might lead one to believe that there is greater acceptance of homosexuality than there is in legal, social, political and spatial realms. It is, however, important to distinguish between these realms, particularly the legal realm from the others. To put it simply, the consumption of an identity does not grant it citizenship rights. It has, in some cases, even increased reactionary political pressure to deny such rights. As Evans rightly emphasizes, 'The inherent individualism and amoralism of the consumerist market inevitably leads us to the commodification of that which is most "personal", "private", "individual" and "natural". Capitalism encourages us to purchase our sexual identities and lifestyles and impels us to conclude that we are right to do so. In response the state is not a passive actor. It neither simply resists nor retreats. Rather it concedes relative and partial rights to "deviant" sexual minorities, investing them with particular, limited forms of gender/consumer power, i.e. sexual citizenship' (Evans, 1993). With reference to Marshall, among others, Evans recognizes the nature of citizenship rights development in the West: 'it is...clear', he writes, 'that in the first world economies of the global chain citizenship has increasingly focused on the rights of citizens as consumers' (Evans, 1993: 2). The consequences for sexual identities has been the exploitation of private pleasures for corporate profit and the ironic exploitation of the secrecy of sexuality (Evans, 1993). This irony is magnified in the case of homosexuality: capitalism profits both from its repression of gays and from the acknowledgement of that repression.

Yet, we should also recognize the increasing power of consumer spaces and the decline of the significance of public places for the acquisition of wealth, status and power. As corporate spaces maintain and entrench their power in social and political realms, those public spaces in which citizens attempt to engage the state become increasingly impotent. As will be further discussed in Chapters 5 and 6, we must distinguish between a consumer ethic and consumer citizenship: while the former urges individuals to invest private meaning in commodities they consume, the latter enables them to invest social meaning (see also Berlant, 1997). The acceptance or rejection of various groups by consumers in general, and by the advertising gurus or corporate bosses who may hire and fire employees based on their sexual orientation, does matter. All of these may facilitate the everyday, public life of gays, rendering them visible and active citizens. It may directly or indirectly grant gay individuals better access to the acquisition of wealth and status. But their success will always be subject to the dictates of the market, turning sexual identity into a commodity. The representations of persons marked as gay are not identities themselves, and it is important to consider that these representations are not always generated, either directly or indirectly, by gays themselves. Nonetheless, these images are part of the battleground for citizenship rights.

Sexual citizenship is about allowing gay men and women to participate fully in the political, economic, social, cultural and spatial life of the postnational state. It would include the social rights of citizenship granted to heterosexuals such as the right to marry, to adopt, to retain custody of biological children, and so on. More profoundly, sexual citizenship would include the rights deemed necessary by the gay groups—even if they are particular to homosexuals and irrelevant to heterosexuals. Or, at least, there should be a process whereby such issues may be publicly discussed and such rights not withheld arbitrarily without consultation with gay groups.

Space, Identity and Gays

Once again, understanding of the relationship between space and citizenship is crucial. On the surface, gay rights appear to be about the right to the privacy of sexuality and the body, and the rights of consenting adults to conduct themselves as they choose behind closed doors. Discrimination against gays is all the more unfair for the apparent intrusion of the state into the bedrooms of the nation. However, gay rights are also about access to public space. As discussed earlier, public space is about visibility and access for the citizenry and central to the idea and the *performance* and *practice* of democracy (Berlant, 1997; Grube, 1997). This access to public space concerns not the performance of sexual acts in public, but the right to participate in public processes *as a sexual person*, even if that sexuality is homosexuality. The right to privacy is implicit in this concept in that we should not have to defend private practices in public. But for gays, privacy has often gone hand in hand with silence and invisibility. Privacy has meant not protection, but rather a forced responsibility of secrecy (Waaldijk and Clapham, 1993). This secrecy has often been justified in the defence of the public, keeping the 'freaks' away from the general, 'normal' population. The closet has not been sanctuary as much as containment.

In light of this expulsion from public space, gay cultural politics is somewhat ironic, if not contradictory, for homosexuality is the first identity addressed so far in this book that is, on the *face* of it, invisible (Button, Rienzo and Wald, 1997). Gays' occupation of space, however, is not invisible; but more generally, finding spaces within the city to claim for their own has become a means through which gays constituted themselves as groups. These spaces are mostly social, but are not limited to places of leisure. West Hollywood, California, is a large-scale example of the same phenomenon; through municipal incorporation, gays sought to claim an entire city to create a political identity of homosexuality that epitomized middle-class stability (Forest, 1995). These spaces also span economic, political organizations, networks of business, housing and communication. In other words, the significance of space to the formation of gay and lesbian identities cannot be underestimated. It is worth exploring briefly why this is so.

Foucault's identification of the spatial containment of sexuality to the heterosexual, family home, and, more specifically, the bedroom with modern power has been crucial in understanding the relationship between space and sexuality (Foucault, 1978). His specific concern was to understand, among other things, how space was strategically used to mark out identities and to divide the pathological from the normal. Arguing against the hypothesis that sex was repressed in the modern era, he aimed to illustrate that, far from being repressed, sex was incited and encouraged when it took place in the right 'place'. The confining of 'illegitimate sexualities' to the brothel and the mental hospital allowed the state to bring sexuality, among other things, into the realm of regulation. 'Only in those places would untrammelled sex have a right to (safely insularized) forms of reality, and only to clandestine, circumscribed, and coded types of discourse' (4). Foucault also emphasized how modern discourse on sex announced the liberation of sex and declared the early modern period as the 'age of repression'. In his words, 'By placing the advent of the age of repression in the seventeenth century, after hundreds of years of open spaces and free expression, one adjusts it to coincide with the development of capitalism: it becomes an integral part of the bourgeois order' (5). The repression of sex was, he argues, not so much based in morality as economics: 'if sex is so rigorously repressed, this is because it is incompatible with a general and intensive work imperative. At a time when labour capacity was being systematically exploited, how could this capacity be allowed to dissipate itself in pleasurable pursuits, except in those—reduced to a minimum—that enabled it to reproduce itself?' (6).

Nonetheless, according to Foucault 'the essential thing is not this economic factor, but rather the existence in our era of a discourse in which sex, the revelation of truth, the overturning of global laws, the proclamation of a new day to come, and the promise of a certain felicity are linked together. Today it is sex that serves as a support for the ancient form...of preaching' (7). In other words, for Foucault, '[t]he notion of repressed sex is not, therefore, only a theoretical matter. The affirmation of a sexuality that has never been more rigorously subjugated than during the age of the hypocritical, bustling, and responsible bourgeoisie is coupled with the grandiloquence of a discourse purporting to reveal the truth about sex, modify its economy within reality, subvert the law that governs it, and change its future' (8). While Foucault questions the repression, he also asserts that 'it is not a matter of saying that sexuality, far from being repressed in capitalist and bourgeois societies, has on the contrary benefited from a regime of unchanging liberty...' (10). 'The object, in short, is to define the regime of power-knowledge-pleasure that sustains the discourse on human sexuality in our part of the world' (11). Foucault sought to illustrate that this regime could not be understood without recognizing how space became a tactical element in its articulation.

Following Foucault, Evans (1993) notes the increased sexualization of modern society, but rejects this as evidence of sexual liberation or equality of sexual minorities. Instead, as modern capitalism expanded, the policing of workers' sexuality rose commensurably. As he summarizes: 'capitalism required an efficiently exploitable, reproductive, malleable, undistracted labour-force with non-procreative "wasteful" sexuality repressed, the mode of production dictating a particular mode of reproduction in turn dependent upon a culture of silence about the sexual' (15–16). Evans then builds upon Foucault to emphasize the *material* and to propose that while the '*apparent* fundamental shifts in social structure' by late capitalism undermine the sense of class consciousness, they do nothing to reduce or slow the material production of class inequality. Accordingly, says Evans, 'sexually differentiated populations take up their place amongst numerous other alternative sources of individual and group reference' (24).

In other words, locating gay identities in their lived spaces reasserts the importance of the material context of sexuality: 'The sexual is inextricably, though in a complex and not necessarily obvious way, tied to the material' (242). As Evans has made clear, divorcing the sexual from its material consequences, as rampant individualism and consumerism attempt to do by framing it as an intimate, personal, natural and individual experience, denies the role of 'material structures and power relations' in the construction of sexual identities. Sexuality is not 'a private escape from the alienation of the public material world,…it is formally and customarily institutionalised and incorporated within [it]' (2).

Brown (1997) has also made a contribution to our understanding of the relationship between space and sexuality in the practice of citizenship. As Patton notes, Brown 'retains the notion of citizenship—the prescriptive and resistant practices that relate body to nation through rights, duties, responsibilities, and membership—but asks us to notice that the backdrop at which we see citizenship at play—the state, civil society, and family—is also fragmenting, acting incoherently, and constantly re-appearing in new hybrid forms (Brown, 1997: xii). Brown does not introduce a new theory of citizenship, but rather reasserts the citizen, as an active and activist individual (see also Sparks, 1997). Brown's individual, again according to Patton, goes beyond 'the well-formed, willing ego who speaks well (or at least without "interference")' of liberal theorists (Brown, 1997: xiii). Brown allies himself with the radical democracy of Mouffe and responds to her call to discover new spaces of citizenship. He finds them in what Wolch (1989) has termed the 'shadow state': places which are funded and minimally overseen by the state (and, importantly, could not exist without it) but which operate with volunteers within the spaces of the communities they serve.

Brown's strongest contribution to the scholarship on cultural politics is his insistence on and careful articulation of the spatial realities of identity and citizenship (see also Forest, 1995; Massey, 1995). He contends that Mouffe's and others' use of 'space' is metaphorical at best, and does not attempt to investigate material places. While such scholars may demonstrate 'a more geographic sensitivity to citizenship', they fail to 'consider that citizens are always engaging in politics in actual locations' (Brown, 1995: 13–14). A materially spatial exploration of radical democracy is Brown's starting point, and, thus, he bridges geography and political theory quite fruitfully. Moreover, the location of Brown's 'new spaces' of radical citizenship somewhere between the traditional public and private renews the criticism of feminists that such categorization is increasingly ineffectual, and responds to their call to move beyond this liberal dichotomy that confines more than it defines sexual identities.

Brown emphasizes identity through actual experience rather than the passive reception of information, recalling Judith Butler's articulation of (gender) identity as performative rather than substantive (Butler, 1990). Such experience is found in expression that is neither for profit nor beauty; 'for Brown, "just being there" for a sick buddy or at the moveable AIDS Quilt can express a deep and radical democracy ...' (Brown, 1997: xiii). An approach such as Butler's is of limited use, however; in the case of AIDS, there is an inescapable aspect of one's body that brands that body and hence the whole person as a 'Person With AIDS' (PWA). The presence of AIDS may or may not be derived from one's sexual practices, but the disease necessarily implicates sexuality by virtue of one means by which it may be transmitted. Thus, one's sexual identity in terms of self-understanding, self-expression and the policing of one's own desires—in other words, the performative aspect of gender and sexual orientation—is altered by the substantive reality of the disease (see Brown, 1997; Yingling, 1997). The position from which PWAs address the state is in these ways fractured and hybrid: their ability to conduct relationships is broken; their identity is woven through dangerous discourses of sexuality and disease, even criminality. The state's failure to appropriately respond and assist them is directly related to the state's identification of PWAs as gays, as criminal drug users, as non-citizens who are not part of the 'general population'. As Yingling writes, 'Myths of identity *have framed* the interpretation of AIDS, and it remains a disease that attaches—rightly or wrongly—to identities ...' (Yingling, 1997: 49). The integration of this particular illness and its politics (which are inseparable) in the rights battles of gay men and women is understandable.

The desired international cooperation on the part of scientists and governments has come at a cost. Despite the centrality of AIDS to gay identity politics, as the disease has moved through political frames, it has been distanced from such 'fringe' groups and their specific issues. The existence of laws is one thing but the ability to enforce them is another. As Patton says: 'in a more general sense, this body is not in the state because it cannot make the law work' (Brown, 1997: xix). Appropriately, Brown describes AIDS as 'a modern holocaust that conjoins issues of identity with political rights and obligations' (3). The challenge that the gay rights pose to modern legal, political and cultural forms of thought and practice is formidable. To meet this challenge—to articulate an adequate conception and practice of sexual citizenship—constitutes a measure of democracy.

Sexual Citizenship and Transgendered Identities

Norms of gender and sexuality were and are central to capitalism and the practice of liberalism. They have been spatially codified and institutionalized. Disruptions of these norms thus challenge the ability of authorities to exercise power and regulate markets. The state demonstrates the importance of sexual norms through its legal restrictions on such activities, and through the selective allocation of social rights based on gender and/or sexual orientation.

Those who refuse to accommodate themselves to even the biological limitations of gender frustrate the governing authority of gendered social norms even further. By doing so, transvestitism and transsexuality raise fundamental questions of citizenship (Foley and Wilkinson, 1994). This discussion of sexual citizenship would therefore be incomplete without the inclusion of the progression of 'queer theory' to a place beyond the 'hetero/homo binary' of sexuality. By adopting all who have been marked as perverse, queer, odd, outcast, different and deviant, queer theory has reconceptualized sexual categories, spaces and boundaries (Boone, 1996). Given the material construction of sexuality and its connections to capitalism in terms of both labour and consumption, the breakdown of the categories of gender/sexual orientation is a potential dislodging of the liberal regimes of government. As these categories form the basis of the traditional, heterosexual family and its oppositional Other of homosexuality, both gay and straight are challenged by their absence (Spahr, 1995). Without clear articulations of heterosexuality as identity, not simply practice or activities, the heterosexual family loses its claim to the moral and economic centre of the community. Similarly, as liberal democratic politics are currently constituted, gays cannot challenge the state for their citizenship rights without the ability to claim an identity and community that will mesh with and deserve equal treatment to those of heterosexuals. Witness the Tasmanian Gay and Lesbian Rights Group's objection to a state law that used the term 'lawful sexual activity' rather than 'sexual orientation'; as they see it, '[b]eing lesbian, gay or bisexual is an identity not an activity. It is dehumanising for lesbians, gay men and bisexual people to be considered only worthy of protection because of the activities in which we engage rather than because we are human beings deserving of respect' (Tasmanian Gay and Lesbian Rights Group, 1998).

Yet those who define themselves outside of the hetero/homo binary or even the male/female binary have claims to citizenship. These rights include the right to non-discriminatory treatment before the law, but they may also incorporate rights that do not parallel those already in existence. For example, does a transsexual person have the right to refuse to claim a sex or gender, or to claim both male and female? The consequences for legislation regarding marriage are already being observed in British Columbia, where a man and a woman married as a heterosexual couple, but afterwards the man had a sex-change operation. Current definitions of marriage insist we recognize the transsexual as a man, but such categorization clearly violates her claim to identify herself as a female and fails to acknowledge the lesbian relationship with her partner. The situation is not resolved by naming the transsexual exclusively as a female, for to do so would symbolically erase her history as a man. Such examples may be rare, but their reality is not lessened by their infrequency.

Although such examples appear to many to be on the outer edges of sexual politics, they raise basic issues of citizenship and identity, perhaps even better than those identities to which we have become accustomed. This applies to everyone—in terms of the right of self-determination in one's expression of gender identity and sexuality—reference to the state, particularly with regard to the institution of marriage, is an issue of recognition. But it is also the material consequences and rights that are granted through that institution (taxes, government and private benefits, custody rights, adoption). Again, this raises the issue of diversity of gender and sexuality. As with the discussion of constructivism and essentialism, these categories are neither fixed, immutable and natural nor are they trivial, arbitrary and immaterial. Rather, they are forms of identification with which men and women choose to conduct their lives and establish new forms of attachment, loyalty and identity.

5
COSMOPOLITAN CITIZENSHIP: CONTESTED SOVEREIGNTIES

Introduction

The key concept in examining the contemporary transformations of advanced capitalism is sovereignty. Earlier it was argued that the two sovereignties of modernity—state and individual—are challenged by the rising claims for group rights. Indeed, a central argument of this book is that modern citizenship needs radical transformation in theory and practice because of these new group rights (Shapiro and Kymlicka, 1997). The emphasis so far has been on specific groups based on ethnic, racial, gender and sexual identities and their struggle for recognition *and* redistribution within Western nation-states. In this and the next chapter, we shift our emphasis from these identities to identities that primarily form across national borders and create new transnational and transversal spaces. Of course, we do not wish to imply here that ethnic, sexual and racial identities are only formed within national borders. As we argued, such identities are formed within as well as across states, building new political networks. But the rise of new classes, the new identities they form and the new spaces they foster challenge the sovereignty of the modern nation-state in a novel way. In other words, the new transnational political spaces are not as 'contained' by modern nation-states as grantors of rights and imposers of obligations. Rather, new rights and obligations are emerging across borders (Jacobson, 1996). The rise of multinational corporations that produce commodities across boundaries, the flow of capital and labour across nations, the rise of organizations that operate beyond the reach of the state, new international regimes of governance, and the global flow of ideas, images and symbols are examples of rising political spaces that pressure the boundaries of the state and its institutions.

A familiar term to describe these new spaces of flows has been 'globalization'. Some theorists note that the general effect of globalization has been to weaken or undermine national forms of cultural identity. They argue that there is evidence of a loosening of strong identifications with the national culture, and a strengthening of other cultural ties and allegiances, 'above' and 'below' the level of the nation-state. Others, however, argue that national identities remain strong, especially with respect to legal citizenship rights, but that local, regional and community identities have become equally significant. They argue that above the level of the national culture, 'global' identifications begin to displace, and sometime override, national allegiances such as environmental concerns (Amin and Thrift, 1995; Falk, 1994; Hannerz, 1990; Held, 1995; Rosenau and Czempiel, 1992; Waters, 1995). The debate over 'globalization', its precise nature and its impact on the modern state is by no means settled. While at a general level globalization can be described as the intensification of global interconnectedness, the causes and consequences of such an interconnectedness, let alone the new political arrangements and kinds of democracy—cosmopolitan, realist, liberal, radical—that should respond to globalization are debated and contested. Moreover, the spatial metaphors used in the debate, such as 'above', 'below', 'local', 'global', mask more than they reveal. As Featherstone (1990, 1993, 1995) has argued, constituting these dichotomies builds an image of a master–slave dialectic, which is inappropriate. With these current metaphors the struggle appears between and among spaces rather than groups and classes, which use, produce and reproduce various spaces of domination, oppression and resistance.

The debate over globalization is, therefore, complex and an adequate discussion of cosmopolitan citizenship would have to come to terms with that complexity. This chapter focuses on the changing nature of citizenship because of the challenges to state sovereignty arising from the new spaces of flows. It first examines 'globalism' as a form of discourse and the questions of rights, accountability and representation in these new spaces. It then reviews the new transformations of advanced capitalism, focusing specifically on the rise of new classes and groups. Then it turns to three different fields where new forms of citizenship are beginning to emerge: the 'global city' as a specific concentration of the flows of different forms of capital and labour and the issue of rights of its citizens; the increasing role of the computer-mediated communications in constituting identities; and the rising tide of ecological citizenship, where loyalty and belonging are defined in new ecumenical and generational terms. These three forms of citizenship—urban, technological and ecological—arise from the challenges of globalization to the sovereignty of the nation-state. At first, by focusing on these three contested fields of cosmopolitan citizenship, we leave aside a debate over the type of democracy that is most appropriate for the global era. However, this debate will have consequences for conceptualizing cosmopolitan citizenship and we will briefly revisit it at the end of the chapter.

Advanced Capitalism, Class, Globalism

Of particular concern in this section is an account of advanced capitalism and the classes and groups it engenders, and an exploration of globalism as a new outlook or mentality that arises from these new groupings. Much has been written about globalization in the last decade but very little on 'globalism' as a discourse that constitutes globalization as an object (Albrow, 1996; Featherstone, 1990, 1995; Waters, 1995).

As mentioned earlier, 'globalization' has become a dangerously overused concept describing the intensified interconnectedness and mobility across space and time. A reason for this concern is that globalization dramatically alters the international system of states that has been the hallmark of modernity at least since the late seventeenth century. At stake is the principle of the sovereignty of the modern state as a polity. We shall underline three aspects of sovereignty. First, *territoriality*: the states that make up the system claim fixed and exclusive territorial boundaries that define the extent of their political and legal authority. Second, *autonomy*: states are entitled to conduct their own internal and external affairs free from external intervention or control. Third, *legality*: the relations between sovereign states may be subject to international law but only in so far as each state consents to being bound. These three aspects of sovereignty have come to constitute it as a code of supremacy, a claim of undisputed and exclusive right to rule over a territory with an indivisible authority (Bartelson, 1995; Hinsley, 1986). Although the sovereignty principle emerged in the seventeenth century, the growth of nationalism in the nineteenth and twentieth centuries contributed significantly to the consolidation of modern *nation*-states. As we have discussed earlier, nationalism reconstituted the state as an expression of 'national' sovereignty. It transformed subjects into peoples and coupled citizenship and nationality (Oommen, 1997). Each modern nation-state emerged within a system of states with its own self-contained, self-governing and territorially limited polity, claiming nationality as its founding principle. Of course, the modern nation-state did not evolve in an uncontested way, either internally or externally. The consolidation of modern nation-states occurred at the expense of the lives of millions of men and women, quashing an oppositional movement here, an uprising there, and waging bloody wars against the slightest perceived encroachment to its boundaries or authority.

But globalization has provided a fierce challenge to the sovereignty of the modern nation-state. In the last thirty years, information, pollution, migrants, arms, ideas, images, news, crime, narcotics and drugs, disease, amongst other things, have been readily and frequently flowing across national boundaries. One might immediately react to this statement by claiming such things have always flowed across national boundaries. That is true. But two things make such flows decisively different. First, the intensity of such flows is such that their consequences are experienced by a large number of people across national boundaries. Transactions in exchange markets, the Internet (the international network of computers originating in the American military and research networks in the 1960s), global tourism and travel, and the global media generate 'time–space- compressed' flows that are experienced simultaneously, instantaneously and massively. Second, as much as these flows define relations between states they also express new types of relation not between states but between transnational organizations, associations, corporations as well as between individuals, movements, regions and cities. The rise of postcolonial identities we examined in Chapter 3 is directly related to this new interconnectedness and mobility. These flows define new spaces in the sense that they are neither describable nor governable from the perspective of the fixed and self-contained territorial boundaries of the nation-state.

We shall draw attention to a few important points that have arisen from the literature on 'globalization'. First, 'globalization' should not be equated with either modernization or Westernization. Many argue that it is too simplistic to assume that, while the West's influence is significant, globalization is leading towards a Western-led homogenization. Rather, there is a degree of cultural interpenetration, hybridity and fluidity across different localities around the globe. The 'global' and the 'local' are not opposing but mutually constituting elements of globalization (Barber, 1995). Second, there is not one but several globalizations. That is, the rising forms of hybridity and interpenetration arise from and make possible a variety of levels and forms of globalization. While there is an increasing transnational migration of labour that results in new claims for group rights in the receiving states, the 'sending states' find themselves in a situation where the loyalty of their citizens needs to be regained at a distance. While multinational corporations intensify competition among different localities for attracting investment, certain localities intensify competition among multinational corporations to invest there. While there emerge organizations operating on variety of scales from local to global, discrete and hierarchical territorial polities from local to international criss-cross them. While some localities oppose globalization, protecting their interests, multinational corporations define their activities as 'localization'. There is no one pure form of globalization. All these flows are happening simultaneously but with multiple rationalities, rather than according to a single and uniform rationality that one might call 'globalization'. Third, it is more useful to conceptualize globalization as a concept that describes an intensified network of flows rather than a fixed geography such as a core–periphery model. The many dimensions of globalization point to the inherent fluidity, indeterminacy and plurality of globalizations. Fourth, several commentators have noted that Western academics should be reflexive in their descriptions of 'globalization' since their interpretations are embedded in a specific culture of seeing and experiencing and hence display a particular perspective (A.D. King, 1991; Lash and Urry, 1994; Massey, 1991, 1995). This is very important because many of these theorists are actually located in the cosmopolitan centres of knowledge production and distribution. Some even go further and argue that 'the Westernization of the planet' is perhaps a better description of the changes underway than a reciprocal global interconnectedness (Zolo, 1997: 134–138). As we suggested earlier, this view of globalization is too simplistic.

Whatever the disagreements about 'globalization'—over its definition, causes. consequences and responses—there is no doubt that there is a discourse that constitutes globalization as an object. In other words, even those who disagree about its importance or even its existence belong to a field of discourse in which such disagreements are possible. We would rather focus on globalism not as a process or a set of realities independent from researchers but as a discourse in which the very idea of 'globalization' is articulated, disseminated, justified, debated, in short, constituted as an object of reflection and analysis. Various groups participate in constituting 'globalization' as an object of discourse, ranging from journalists, corporate executives, government officials, professionals to academics, environmentalists, novelists and artists. In other words, globalism is an outlook that allows individuals and groups to participate in this discourse on globalization (Nederveen Pieterse, 1995).

To understand globalism two conceptual anchors are required. First, we need to develop an appreciation of the changing nature of capitalism as a dominant mode of production. Second, we need to develop a sense of the class restructuring under advanced capitalism and how the changing nature of capitalism places new demands and engenders changes in the state as a polity. These assertions may be interpreted as a form of economic determinism, where we will hinge our interpretation on a mode of production. Such an interpretation would be misguided. As we shall see, the emerging literature on the new political economy urges us not to make such simplistic and broad distinctions between economy and culture or economy and ideology. To define capitalism simply as an economic structure on which legal, cultural and ideological superstructures hinge has been widely discredited. Rather, capitalism is a mode of production where various forms of capital—social, symbolic, economic, cultural, political—are produced, reproduced and accumulated.

Modern capitalism has changed dramatically in the late twentieth century. This change was captured tentatively in the 1970s by discussions of 'deindustrialization' and 'postindustrial society' (Bell, 1973). The popular media focused on the changing character of work, the rise in the service sector, the decline of full-time jobs and the growing cadres of part-time workers, and, finally, the rise of 'information economy'. By the 1980s the literature increasingly converged on a bundle of concepts such as flexible accumulation and postfordism to describe advanced capitalism. Although it is not our aim to discuss in any detail this literature on 'late', 'informational' or 'postmodern' capitalism, it is important to briefly summarize its salient features (Castells, 1989, 1996; Harvey, 1989; Jameson, 1991; Lash and Urry, 1994).

Although theorists diverge in terms of the emphasis they place on each, four major changes can be identified as decisive (Lash and Urry, 1994; Slater, 1997). First, advanced capitalism is *informational* in the sense that the productivity and competitiveness of firms, regions, nations, have come to depend upon their capacity to generate, process and apply knowledge-based information. This is as much driven by new information technologies (which Castells rightly emphasizes) as it is a major factor in the invention of such technologies in the first place (which Castells fails to recognize). What this means is that to consider information technology as a causal variable in explaining advanced capitalism overlooks the fact that the very changes it seeks to describe have been factors in the invention of information technologies. Nevertheless, both as cause and consequence, the information technologies are an integral part of production of various forms of capital. Second, advanced capitalism is *global* in the sense that the core activities of production, consumption and circulation, as well as their components (capital, labour, raw materials, management, markets), are organized on a global scale. Many corporations now operate in many different markets and such multinational corporations account for an important segment of world trade. Third, advanced capitalism is *reflexive* not only in the sense that it depends upon knowledge but also because it defines new spheres as objects of production such as symbols, signs, images and sounds. New, non-material products such as producer and consumer services, including design, advertising and consulting, are increasingly involved in the reflexive economy. Many corporations pay vast sums of money not only to advertising firms, which is well known, but also to research companies to tell them about market trends and 'cool' products. Fourth, advanced capitalism is *flexible* because it depends upon the capacity of firms and individuals to be reflexive producers and consumers on an ongoing basis, incessantly adjusting to shifting and fluid capital and labour markets.

That advanced capitalism is informational, global, reflexive and flexible has significant consequences. Lash and Urry (1994: 122–123) make, in our view, a crucial point when they declare that manufacturing industries have now become more and more like the production of culture. To discuss the conditions under which such a transformation has been possible, since the 1970s, is beyond our scope. But it is important to mention in passing that this transformation is not a mechanical reaction or adjustment, but a structural change. In modern capitalism the way labour is reproduced—the level and nature of its consumption habits, its skills, competence and discipline—is central to the reproduction of economic capital. Wages and demand are related in determining the size of markets. There is always a tension between wages and consumer demand because they depend on each other to determine the size of markets: while capitalists incessantly pressure down the wages, this also means the shrinking of markets. In short, consumption and production are tightly knit in a cycle of reproduction. The regulation of this cycle—setting of minimum wages, labour laws, competition rules—is an object of struggle, which permeates not only economic but social relations from education to advertising and other modes of representation. In other words, while articulation of consumption with production is a functional necessity for capitalism, it is not automatically secured. The mode of regulation of capitalism—the way in which consumption is articulated to production—is therefore a significant aspect of its continuing success. 'Fordism' and postfordism are labels for two different modes of regulation that correspond to different regimes of accumulation that characterized capitalism in the last century. Until the 1970s, mass production was linked to mass consumption under a Fordist mode of regulation. Since then, however, to respond to the falling rate of profit due to the saturation of markets, modern capitalism has, on the one hand, pushed various automation and communications technologies to increase productivity, and, on the other, relentlessly expanded markets and production sites on a global scale. In other words, while it created new markets, it has also created new pools of cheaper labour. This has disrupted the Fordist mode of regulation in the sense that the postwar balance between wages and demands was tilted in favour of capital. Within three decades, via globalization of its production and markets, change in regimes of its accumulation, and massive change from the type of production, capitalism has been transformed into advanced capitalism, as briefly described above.

The importance of understanding the dynamics of advanced capitalism for citizenship and identity can hardly be underestimated (Lash and Urry, 1994: 309; Slater, 1997: 191). First, advanced capitalism has engendered new types of social differentiation, new types of occupation and the formation of new groups and classes. Understanding these new forms of differentiation is key to the development of a new conception of citizenship. As we discussed earlier, the relationship between class and citizenship is vital to understand. Yet, to understand the changing classes and groups in advanced capitalism is fraught with difficulties. In a sense a basic difficulty arises, of course, from the fact that, as discussed earlier, the description of a group or a class itself is a politically charged practice. As Bourdieu (1987) argued, classification struggles to claim the existence of absence of group or class are part of practices that make or unmake groups and classes. Second, advanced capitalism engenders a new work ethic and links it with an ethic of consumption that radically alters the idea of citizen. Advanced liberalism as a regime of governance under advanced capitalism has created a new image of self as an autonomous agent. We shall return to both of these themes in Chapter 6. But in this chapter we shall introduce these transformations with a focus on their interrelated but distinct empirical fields in which new practices of citizenship have emerged in the past three decades: urban, ecology and technology.

Urban Citizenship: Rights to the City

As we have seen in Chapter 2, Émile Durkheim argued a century ago that the modern nation could not survive without finding an order of meaningful solidarity between the state and the individual. He argued that, for the purposes of socialization, the state was too remote from individuals and its connections with individuals were too superficial, irregular and tenuous. He believed that this was the reason why, when the state is the only form of association, it inevitably disintegrates. In his view, a nation as a political association cannot be sustained unless between the state and individuals, a whole range of secondary groups exists with which individuals associate and identify. These groups must be close enough to the individual to cultivate loyalty and engage them in everyday practices, in so doing, to absorb them in everyday social and political life (Durkheim, 1984: liv). The question for Durkheim was how to encourage the formation of such groups (Durkheim, 1992: 96).

On the basis of historical experience Durkheim thought that there are only two kinds of group that fulfil such needs. Groups based on regional association, such as cities, villages and towns, organized as self-governing municipalities, constituted the traditional basis of European states, political representation and social engagement. Durkheim argued, however, that regional groups no longer had the importance that they once had because individuals were mobile and lacked loyalties to place. The ties which had united the members of self-governing municipalities were external and not permanent. There was something artificial about such groups. By contrast, Durkheim believed that the permanent groups, those to which individuals devote their whole life regardless of their place, those for which they may have the strongest attachment, were increasingly the professional groups. At the turn of the twentieth century, then, Durkheim envisaged that the professions would become the basis of political representation as well as of social structure in the future (Durkheim, 1992: 96–97).

Although the professions did not evolve entirely the way Durkheim envisaged, the prescience of his insight is remarkable. After he offered his analysis, the modern city as a corporation has steadily declined in importance and the professions gained a new political importance. What Durkheim could not see was that the city would emerge as a place not of loyalty but where the new professions organized themselves and their markets. The global city is different from the modern city in that its power does not derive from its corporate status within state law. Rather, it is a node within a network of cities across the world that organizes markets for professional expertise and services.

As mentioned earlier, telecommunications technologies have been among the driving forces in advanced capitalism. Many key activities in the global economy such as advanced producer services, including finance, insurance, real estate, consulting, legal services, advertising, design, marketing, public relations, security, research and development, and management information systems, rely upon telecommunications technologies for production and marketing. Given that these new key activities of advanced capitalism require these technologies, it is perhaps logical to conclude that advanced capitalism would tend to use space more extensively than intensively. As a result, dense, concentrated cities of modern capitalism would gradually give way to a geography of sprawling, low-density agglomerations. To an extent, the developments in North America and Europe have borne out this expectation. Major cities such as New York, Los Angeles, London, Amsterdam, Toronto, Frankfurt, Zurich and Milan have spread out in the last two decades. Recently, Soja (1992, 1997), Gottdiener (1991) and Fishman (1995) have argued that the concentric urban form of the twentieth-century metropolis with its bedroom suburbs and office-dominated central business district has been superseded by a polycentric, multinucleated urban form where several centres or 'edge cities' combine to form a vast, sprawling urban region. This urban form is neither a megalopolis, in the sense of obliterating the distinction between the city and countryside and extending to combine several metropolises, nor a metropolis, in the sense of having a well-defined centre around which the metropolitan economic, cultural and social life of the nation revolves (Isin, 1996a, 1996b). Rather, the new urban form is fragmented and disjointed, which symbolizes the contradictory global flows that brought it into being. If the modern metropolis was of the nation, the global city is of the world. The geography of the global city represents neither a large city, nor a metropolis with a dominant core city surrounded by suburbs. Rather, it is defined by multiple nodes of concentration (towns, villages and cities) interconnected in a space of flows and dispersed across an urban region (Castells, 1989, 1996; Gottdiener and Kephart, 1991).

It is difficult to gauge the impact of telecommunications technologies on this form as other factors such as automobile suburbanization were also at work (Graham and Marvin, 1996). More recently, Castells (1996: 379) has argued that a decade of research has shown that the dominant spatial pattern has been the simultaneous dispersion and concentration of new economic activities. While there has been some dispersion of activities, there has also been a concentration of advanced services in major global cities.

The term 'global city' aims to combine several ideas. It allows us to take into account the debate on the global city as a strategic space of globalization. In what new sense the city has become global is critical (P.J. Taylor, 1995). Friedmann (1995) has used five criteria to define the global city: that the global city is an organizing node of a global economic system; that 'global' does not mean it encompasses the entire world; that the global city is an urbanized space of intense economic and social interaction; that global cities are arranged hierarchically; and that the global city is controlled by a transnational class (Friedmann, 1995: 25–26). In a sense, these characteristics define the city in general, for we can argue that the city always incorporated these characteristics. Mumford (1938, 1961), for example, often emphasized that the city has been an organizing node of not only the accumulation but also the control and dissemination of ideas. Similarly, Weber (1958) and Pirenne (1925), despite differences in emphasis and approach, argued rather persuasively that the city was always situated within larger systems of cities encompassing large spaces.

The global city engenders new forms of capital (financial, cultural, social and symbolic) and is a strategic space for new classes and professions. For example, Sassen (1991) has described the rise of new professions in New York, London and Tokyo. Knox (1993a) has described the new 'middle' classes and their habitus in the global city. What appears to be new about the 'global city' is the rise of a new political economy driven by new forms of capital that are transferable across the globe, the rise of new classes that appropriate these forms of capital, and the new modes through which these classes organize power and engage in politics (Lash and Urry, 1994: 220–222).

As argued in Chapter 4, space is a constitutive object of group struggle. Harvey (1994) illustrated well that spatial practices—how individuals and groups overcome, appropriate and dominate space—are a crucial aspect of accumulation of different forms of capital and reproduction of class relations. Similarly, although Bourdieu uses space mostly as a metaphoric category, he also argued that:

> To account more fully for the differences in life-style between the different fractions—especially as regards culture—one would have to take account of their distribution in a *socially ranked geographical space*. A group's chances of appropriating any given class of rare assets (as measured by mathematical probability of access) depend partly on its capacity for the specific appropriation, defined by the economic, cultural and social capital it can deploy in order to appropriate materially or symbolically the assets in question, that is, its position in social space, and partly on the relationship between its distribution in geographical space, and partly on the relationship between its distribution of the scarce assets in that space. (Bourdieu, 1984: 124)

With the rise of flexible accumulation and the new groups and classes, advanced capitalism has intensified the city as a place of production, consumption and exchange. In the last two decades a few cities across the globe have emerged as concentrated nodes in a network of flows of information, ideas, images, labour and capital, specializing to attract specific flows. As Michael Smith (1997) argues, it is not appropriate to associate global cities only with those that command power, such as New York, London and Tokyo, but with all those that receive and send such flows. The global city is not a site where a new class struggle 'takes place' but is a space whose strategic control and regulation is an important leverage in the struggle (Sassen, 1996b). Although it shares a lineage with the polis and metropolis in the sense of being linked to a system of cities forming an economy, it is distinguished by virtue of being a new space for the accumulation of cultural capital and the new classes it engenders and breeds.

There are two aspects of the global city that require analysis in terms of citizenship and identity: the increasing hegemony of transnational classes over the city as a strategic space and the rise of new groups to service its production, consumption and exchange needs. The new professions dominate the global city with major fields of production such as business, advertisement, arts, science, media and journalism, politics, religion, sports administration, law and new types of medicine. As Peter Hall states: 'In the global cities, clustered around the major banks and headquarters offices, is a huge array of service industries: advertising, accounting, legal services, business services, certain types of banking, engineering and architectural services, which increasingly work for firms engaged in international transactions' (P. Hall, 1996: 404). In fact, these fields reproduce professionals because entry into them requires acquired skills, competence and accreditation, usually from institutions of higher education, technical colleges and universities. Unlike the aristocracy (land), labour (wage) or bourgeoisie (economic capital), the new professional-managerial groups are made up of career hierarchies of specialized members ostensibly selected by merit and based on accreditation, expertise, competence and skills (cultural capital). The members of the new professional-managerial groups receive a monetary compensation in the form of a salary, yet the salary is not measured like a wage in terms of work done, but according to the status and position of the member, determined by rank (Weber, 1978: 963). Markets for professional services involve some of the most difficult and complex arrangements to determine value (Bok, 1993). In advanced capitalism, except for those who inherit capital or land, the only legitimate avenue open to wealth, status and power is to become a member of the new professional groups (Gouldner, 1979).

Since the accumulation of cultural capital in the form of skills, reputation, fame, honour, knowledge, competence and the practical mastery of various fields is quite flexible and transferable from one milieu to another, the boundaries of the modern state and its regulatory regimes restrict the life chances of professional-managerial groups. As argued elsewhere, this contemporary shift has parallels to the 'decline' of medieval cities where the mercantile bourgeoisie found the cities, which it grew from, restrictive for its expansion needs. Instead, it entered into contracts with kings and princes to secure wider rights and protections than that possible in cities (J. Anderson, 1996; Isin, 1992). With this new shift, the new professional-managerial groups have become less concerned about their national interests and turned their back on the nation-state: they display cosmopolitan tendencies. The rise of neoliberalism as a dominant ideology can be seen as a consequence of the increasing secession of the new professional-managerial groups from the nation (Reich, 1992) and their shift to a global outlook (Perkin, 1996).

As we shall see in Chapter 6, although there has been considerable debate over the changing classes and the new professions, the focus has been, using Erik Olin Wright's (1997) phrase, on class counts, privileging classification over analyses of lifestyles and practices of class habitus. Bourdieu's work on taste and class (1984), academics (1988) and bureaucrats (1996), Brint's (1994) study on the role of professionals in public life and Kellner and Berger's (1992) study on lifestyle engineering are exceptions. The recently revived field of the sociology of the professions is promising in that it shows how class analysis can benefit from it and vice versa (Freidson, 1994; Macdonald, 1995).

A useful analytical concept that emerges from this literature is 'professional project'. The professions establish their legitimacy by controlling the circulation and dissemination of ideas and ideals through knowledge and thus achieving 'social closure.' Every year literally thousands of conferences, workshops, symposia and colloquia ('professional assemblages') take place in global cities that bring together members of the new class to frame 'issues' (Mayhew, 1997). The members of the new class assemble in these events to socialize, network, habituate and emulate certain practices and exchange knowledge. The global city is therefore not only a space of production and consumption of producer and consumer services but also a space of reproduction of the new professional class and its habitus. To break into this market, whose primary clientele is other new professional class members, they must create a niche for their knowledge products in order to establish their distinction as expertise in an intense competition. An enormous volume of reports, papers, documents and films come out of these events. A symbolic economy of signs and images has been formed, the most visible evidence of which is the sheer number of knowledge products (Heuberger, 1992; Lash and Urry, 1994).

This brings us to the second aspect of the global city in terms of the politics of citizenship and identity. The importance of the professional project is that non-professional groups are neither active producers of these products nor participants in their use. Rather, the citizen is increasingly constituted only as a consumer, who makes choices among these knowledge products. Various professionals, journalists, intellectuals and academics in turn offer their *paid* services to excluded groups to make these choices and to help them become conscientious opinion consumers. As Bourdieu (1991b) observed, various marginal groups are caught in a spiral: while the social world becomes less accessible as a sphere of power, they become increasingly more dependent upon the professionals and their language to interpret that very social world which is slipping out from under them.

Various groups in the global city, such as ethnic and racial minorities, immigrants, youth, unskilled workers, 'flexible' workers, semi-skilled clerical workers and technicians, and a permanent underclass, constitute the other side of the professional and managerial groups (Beall, 1997). But this should not be seen as the rise of a dual city with polar opposites. In fact, the new groups and classes depend on the postcolonial identities for a variety of producer and consumer services (Sorkin, 1992). The widening gap between the owners of cultural capital and the rest in global cities signals an inequality not merely in wealth but also in the spheres of influence of these groups and of the professional-managerial groups. The marginalization and exclusion of these groups from professional assemblages is a structural aspect of the global city. Instead, the official framing and representing by the professionals usually converge on the breakdown of the legitimacy of politics in the public mind. To counteract this trend, professionals often organize such stage acts as 'town hall meetings' and other spectator events where the public is asked for 'input'. These events, while generating more income for professional managers, make the subaltern groups more questioning of their real usefulness. To counteract 'the breakdown of law and order', the new classes and groups also urge the building up of a new kinds of state and corporation surveillance where hitherto unregulated areas of private life come under scrutiny (Ericson and Haggerty, 1997).

While the new groups and classes establish their rights to the global city with its distinct styles of life, there are those who invent new forms of citizenship by practising new forms of politics, often outside established lifestyles, and sometimes in defiance of them. These new citizens, as they may be considered, by refusing to appropriate the imposed language of journalists, intellectuals, professionals, managers, academics (in short, the new class), create and invent new languages and dialects, and hence are involved in counterhegemonic practices, which are practices of insurgence, refusal and resistance. Inventing these new practices is not an end but a means to establish new spheres of influence through which they create new political spaces. 'Homeless' citizens assemble together to create new forms of housing for themselves as in Toronto's Street City, bypassing the official language that establishes them as the 'underclass' and the institutions that condemn them to that status (Beall, 1997). The new diasporas discussed in Chapter 3 are mostly concentrated in global cities and advance new claims for citizenship understood as the rights to the city itself (Flores and Benmayor, 1997; Rocco, 1996). Across the globe, new networks are emerging, which, once again, are passing through the tight network of regulations and impositions and creating their own rather loosely defined, fluid, inventive and *cosmopolitan* associations. There are new practices of expression where poetry, literature, film and theatre are wrested from the shackles of large public and private bureaucracies and circulated outside their control and regulation. A new cultural politics has encouraged inventive practices in using new information technologies to create new modes of political expression outside and against the market (S. Hall, 1997).

Whether these practices can create effective political spaces and define new rights and responsibilities is an open question (Sassen, 1996b). But while the new classes and groups struggle for physical and symbolic spaces in the cosmopolis, there are two new emerging conflicts (Sandercock, 1998). The first is a widening gap between the cosmopolis and its hinterland. The cosmopolitanism engendered by the cosmopolis has created a new provincialism in its surrounding areas. As cosmopolises around the globe such as Tokyo, London, New York, Toronto, Montreal and Vancouver increasingly resemble one another in terms of the struggles they breed, the classes they host, the types of capital they invest, there is a widening gap between them and their provinciaı hinterlands, cities and towns, which are inhabited and controlled by different groups and classes. Therefore, a political conflict has been brewing between these cities, towns and villages and the cosmopolis. The francophone separatist elite in Quebec, for example, which is based on a provincial ideology, tried to wrest power from the Canadian government in a 1995 referendum; it found, much to its chagrin, that the cosmopolites in Montreal feel much more loyal to a cosmopolitan culture than either to Quebec or even a Canadian nationalism. Montreal voted against independence, while the rest of Quebec voted for sovereignty. Montreal is but one example of how the cosmopolis has become, with all the fractures, contradictions, dangers and possibilities it implies, a world in itself—having rejected the provincial separatists, it is now considering municipal independence.

The rise of the new professions in global cities raises two further significant issues for citizenship. First, for professionals their rights and obligations do not necessarily consist in their citizenship but in their professional occupation and practices. The professionals gain wealth, status and power through their occupation (Brint, 1994). Although this regulation and control through occupational association is more visible and successful in older professions such as law and medicine, the new professions such as journalism, planning, architecture, administration, consultancy, marketing, accounting, business management and advertising have achieved varying degrees of success in organizing themselves. In addition to the mastery of discourse, these professions struggle through their associations for legitimacy and resources. Professional associations enter negotiations with governments and corporations on behalf of their members. They also regulate the qualifications of entry and the size of the market. The rivalry among the professions and their claims to legitimacy and resources is one of the marks of the new class struggle. Their occupational status brings considerable rewards in terms of protection from the market. Hence, professionals are more loyal to their occupation than to abstract notions of the state or public. They are professional-citizens.

The second issue is the influence of the new class on 'representation' and 'discourse'. By virtue of its mastery of discourse, the new professions shift the primary locus of power and debate from the parliaments as public spheres to other forums: the mass media, events, symposia and other spectacles (Brint, 1994; Hannerz, 1996; Macdonald, 1995). Unlike the parliamentary assemblies, these new assemblages are not open to the modern citizenry except as passive spectators. In other words, the shift of power in the global age is from the modern public sphere centred on state assemblies to a new sphere dominated by consumption, production and exchange of knowledge centred on professional assemblages, the majority of which takes place in global cities. In other words, at present 'cosmopolitan citizenship' means less a membership in a global polity than a membership in the new professions that qualify one to deliberate and participate in its assemblages. The new symbol of politics and citizenship is neither the agora nor the council chamber nor the commons: it has become the convention centre.

Under such conditions it is imperative that an alternative, active conception of urban citizenship becomes a part of rethinking a multilayered conception of citizenship. The concept of the right to the city proposed by French philosopher Henri Lefebvre is useful. He suggested that '[t]he right to the city manifests itself as a superior form of rights: right to freedom, to individualization and socialization, to habitat and to inhabit' (Lefebvre, 1996: 173). He argued that '[t]he right to the *oeuvre* [as a collective product], to participation and *appropriation* (clearly distinct from the right to property), are implied in the right to the city' (174).

Neither a natural nor a contractual right, the right to the city 'signifies the rights of citizens and city dwellers, and of groups they (on the basis of social relations) constitute, to appear on all the networks and circuits of communication, information and exchange' (194–195). Accordingly, '[t]o exclude the *urban* from groups, classes, individuals, is also to exclude them from civilization, if from not society itself. The *right* to the city legitimates the refusal to allow oneself to be removed from urban reality by a discriminatory and segregative organization. This right of the citizen...proclaims the inevitable crisis of city centres based upon segregation and establishing it: centres of decision-making, wealth, power, of information and knowledge, which reject towards peripheral spaces all those who do not participate in political privileges. Equally, it stipulates the right to meetings and gathering...' (195).

To constitute the global city as a field of citizenship means investigating these class conflicts and the changes they bring about in the content and extent of citizenship, and how they condition the city, which has become the political space where new rights of citizenship to the city are being negotiated. At the same time, it means to avoid a primordial or rooted conception of community by reifying the global city as strictly a place. In this vein, Featherstone's reminder about the dangers of constituting the city as a community is very important.

Featherstone has argued that the binary dichotomies of the local and the global mask more than they reveal because the processes of globalization and localization are inextricably bound together (Featherstone, 1995: 103). He suggests that a nostalgic notion of community is dangerous and that 'we should be careful not to presume an integrated community' (107). With reference to Ernest Gellner, Benedict Anderson and Anthony Smith, he underlines the imagined or invented character of such communities, constructed by images, symbols and stories but argues that such constructs are not created out of nothing but are based on specific histories. Because of the invented or imagined character of nations as communities, they may appear more integrated and coherent than they are. The images and symbols can serve to mask internal differentiations. The presence of the mask of a community 'does not mean that inside the locality social differentiation has been eliminated and relationships are necessarily more egalitarian, simple and homogenous; rather, its internal differences and discourses may very well be complex. Internally we may be able to consider the community as incorporating all sorts of interdependencies, rivalries, power struggles and conflicts' (110). He adds:

> If globalization refers to the process, whereby the world increasingly becomes seen as 'one place' and the ways in which we are made conscious of this process, then the cultural changes which are thematized under the banner of the postmodern seem to point in the opposite direction by directing us to consider the local. Yet this is to misunderstand the nature of the process of globalization. It should not be taken to imply that there is, or will be, a unified world society or culture–something akin to the social structure of a nation-state and its national culture, only writ large. (114)

Featherstone argues that the rise of new professionals and their concentration in global cities have brought about increased transactions among the members of these professions (115). He refers to the cultures of these professions as 'deterritorialized cultures'. He calls into question the homogenization thesis, arguing that globalization often results in indigenization and syncretization of global symbols and hybridization of various local symbols. The result is an increased diversification of meaning and thus '[a] global conception of the modern is required, which, rather than being preoccupied with the historical sequences of transitions from tradition to modernity and postmodernity, instead focuses upon the spatial dimension, the geographical relationship between the centre and the periphery in which the first multiracial and multi-cultural societies were on the periphery not the core' (119). Featherstone, therefore, defines global culture as 'the sense of heaps, congeries and aggregates of cultural particularities juxtaposed together on the same field, the same bounded space, in which the fact that they are different and do not fit together, or want to fit together, becomes noticeable and a source of practical problems' (123–124). This sense of global culture captures the sense in which we think the global city has become a new political space (Magnusson, 1996).

Technological Citizenship

Technological citizenship, in the way we want to define it, raises two broad issues. First is the rise of computer-mediated communications and the new space of flows it has engendered (Calhoun, 1994b; Featherstone and Burrows, 1995; Morley and Robins, 1995; Turkle, 1995). Here we wish to raise some critical concerns about the hype that has been generated around the idea of cyberspace and its ostensible democratic potential. Second, we want to draw attention to technologies of identification, which are rapidly proliferating different forms of cybernetic control which modulate behaviour.

Traditionally, most discussion of media and citizenship has focused on mass communications involving centralized, one-to-many broadcasting, and we do not propose to engage that literature here. But it is important to make a few brief remarks about the ways in which the problem has been framed have shifted from earlier hypotheses of mass society to a more nuanced understanding of media and citizenship. It is very well known that television and radio in the postwar era have become the symbols of 'mass communication'. Initially, the analysis of the impact of radio and television focused on the decline of the public sphere thesis exemplified by Marcuse (1964), Habermas (1989) and Sennett (1974). The argument was that the public sphere—defined as a domain where citizens form themselves into publics of opinion and action—was dramatically curtailed by the rise of mass communications because the reflexivity and interactivity of the traditional print media were rendered ineffective by television and radio. The mass media in effect had become constitutive of citizenry as a mass, subject to manipulation, persuasion and alienation. By barraging the masses with a multitude of images and signs via advertising, shows and news, television and radio were assumed to have made a major impact on social behaviour and thought. The result was that the citizenry began to develop a cynical if not outright nihilist attitude towards democracy because it saw that the power wielders in the democratic process were the brokers of opinion, ideas, images and signs. The citizenry was thus reduced to a consumer of these media products rather than an active producer of them.

Raymond Williams (1990) offered the most compelling alternative interpretation of the social and political conditions that generated television. He was concerned with the way in which culture was produced, transmitted and reproduced. For Williams, television as a means of social control and communication was a response to the need for a mechanism of social integration created by the development of modern capitalism that uprooted much of the population, divided work from home, and isolated individuals from each other by privatizing ways of life. While everyday lives of the masses were fragmented and privatized, television broadcasting offered culturally unified experiences and even substituted relations to itself for some aspects of everyday life. For Williams, therefore, the allure of television had deep roots in the need for contact and the maintenance of identity and for a sense of belonging to a shared culture, the very aspects of life that modern capitalism undermined (Morse, 1998: 3–4). Williams was much more nuanced and subtle in his critique of television culture than Marcuse, Habermas, Sennett or even Adorno's (1991) critique of mass communications in that rather than seeing television culture as a means of manipulation and control, he saw it as filling a void generated by modern capitalism.

Nonetheless, the argument that the television was a symptom of the decline of the public sphere formed the backbone of critical media studies until the 1980s, when a new picture began to emerge. First, new studies began to shift the emphasis from the media to audience and argued that it was not as massive or passive as was assumed earlier. Neuman (1991), for example, concluded that the mass media audience was not helpless and passive, but an active participant in producing its own subjectivities and identities. Moreover, these subjectivities depended upon specific contexts in which audiences received mass media images, and therefore what was previously thought to be a mass was much more differentiated and segmented. By the 1990s, the prevailing view was that a mass culture does not exist. As Castells puts it: 'It is one of the ironies of intellectual history that it is precisely those thinkers who advocate social change who often view people as passive receptacles of ideological manipulation...' (1996: 335). Yet as Curran argued, to emphasize the autonomy of agents in producing their own subjectivities did not imply that the mass media were neutral institutions or that their effects were negligible (Curran 1991; Dahlgren, 1995: 120–121).

Second, the media conglomerates and monopolies were the first to draw the lesson from these studies in actively segmenting, customizing and individualizing the delivery of content. In the 1980s, the print media, television and radio became increasingly localized in the sense that centrally produced content was locally customized, taking into account the local taste, preferences and demand. The new media, although massive in terms of numbers, no longer reached a mass audience in terms of simultaneity and uniformity. This allowed the possibility of rethinking the media as a public sphere. Rather than seeing the mass media as a form of manipulation, critical media studies have begun exploring the ways in which television, radio and print can serve the citizenry in forming publics of thought and action (Curran, 1991). There is currently considerable tension between those who focus on the production of media images (who tend to lean towards the mass persuasion thesis) and those who focus on the consumption of such images (who tend to see oppositional and subversive ways in which images are consumed as well as means of persuasion).

This is an ongoing debate and struggle whose directions are far from clear, but, judging from the increasing globalization of production and localization of distribution, it seems like a tall order to expect that the mass media will serve democracy and a renewed citizenship (Dahlgren, 1995; Dahlgren and Sparks, 1991). While some, such as Thelen (1996), argue that televised committee hearings and debates provide remarkable opportunities for opening real conversation among citizens and with lawmakers, others, such as Dahlgren (1995) and Morse (1998), are more sceptical. Thelen believes that by taking issues from the hearings, committee rooms and assemblies and making them part of everyday conversation, citizens take back from politicians and journalists the capacity to define and manipulate the issue or promote partisan agendas. This view is naïve. The majority of viewers still rely on news to interpret the meaning and consequences of such debates and hearings. Morse (1998) has argued, for example, that the news format is a very restrictive rather than inclusive discursive type that both legitimates and severely limits the subjects produced by the news: 'This format of news delivery cloaks what is, after all, an impersonal transmission with the impression of discourse across a desk with the quasi-subjects or personalities in the machine. Far from confronting us with social reality, instrumental and impersonal relations are given their most disguised and utopian expression by simulating the paramount reality of speaking subjects exchanging conversation in a shared space and time' (38). Morse concludes that '[t]he effect of American news conventions is to extremely constrain, if not actually deny members of the public the opportunity to speak as subjects, to shift the agenda under discussion, or to govern the length or context of a statement'

(39). Such structure of television is not designed to satisfy the desire of the ordinary individual to become 'someone', let alone a citizen.

Recently, Bourdieu (1998) has expanded his general sociology of fields to focus on television as part of what he calls the journalistic field. He argues that while it is important to understand the ownership of media and its effect on content, it is not adequate to focus on ownership because television operates within a journalistic field with its own principles and modes of operation. Bourdieu points out a contradiction in the structure of the field. On the one hand, '[a]t stake today in local as well as global political struggles is the capacity to impose a way of seeing the world, of making people wear "glasses" that force them to see the world divided up in certain ways (the young and the old, foreigners and the French...). These divisions create groups that can be mobilized, and that mobilization makes it possible for them to convince everyone else that they exist, to exert pressure and obtain privileges and so forth. Television plays a determining role in all such struggles today' (22). On the other hand, television operates with an invisible censorship principle whereby, as Morse argued, this potential power is contained, neutralized and depoliticized. In this field journalists play a peculiarly powerful role despite the fact that they occupy an inferior, dominated position in the field of cultural production by virtue of their control of the means of public expression. 'With their permanent access to public visibility, broad circulation, and mass diffusion—an access that was completely unthinkable for any cultural producer until television came into the picture—these journalists can impose on the whole of society their vision of the world, their conception of problems, and their point of view' (47). While Bourdieu may be criticized here for exaggerating the power of journalists, the innovative and promising aspect of his analysis is, consistent with his sociology of fields, to shift the focus to cultural producers and the means by which they carry out this production. It is beyond the scope of this book to further explore the political consequences of television culture on democracy and citizenship, but from the point of view of technological citizenship, the issue is as much the content of television programming as cultural producers. We shall return to this theme when we discuss cultural citizenship and the rise of new classes in Chapter 6.

As the debate over the political role of television intensified, a whole new medium emerged in the 1990s that radically altered the discussions not only of media but also of citizenship. The Internet enjoined by personal computer technologies, with its emphasis on many-to-many communications, interactivity and anti-monopoly, provided a novel medium of communications. Initially restricted to military and research domains, the Internet has grown exponentially since the 1980s and by the late 1990s has become a network connecting hundreds of thousands of local networks and millions of computers world-wide. By the standards of mass media, however, the Internet remains relatively small in terms of the numbers of individuals using it, and the hype surrounding it by far exceeds its size: while global spectacles such as sports events are watched by billions of television viewers around the world, the Internet promoters—and there are many—can only boast that there are only about 35 millions of users.

When broken down by types of users, the active users are probably much smaller than that number. Moreover, Internet networks and computers are still very much concentrated in the northern hemisphere, particularly in cities—global cities—as we shall see. Nonetheless, the Internet has been catapulted into the public imagination and its faithful users claim that it ushers us in a new era of electronic democracy and technological citizenship. It is this claim that we critically examine in this section.

Without going into the origins of the Internet or even different protocols that constitute it, such as the user groups, list servers or the world wide web (Castells, 1996; Rheingold, 1993; Turkle, 1995), we will immediately focus on the challenges that computer-mediated communications pose to modern forms of citizenship and the new types of citizenship it possibly engenders. Then we will examine distinct but related set of technologies of identification and surveillance.

In terms of modern forms of citizenship—civil, political and social—computer-mediated communications pose several challenges (Tambini, 1998). Those regarding civil rights, privacy and censorship have received the most attention. The first reaction of many regularity authorities was to control content in this many-to-many form of communication. But these authorities learned two quick lessons: first, that, unlike the mass media, it was impossible to control content because where content originates and where it is used was beyond the technological means of control; and, second, that many users of the Internet had developed a distinct frontier culture in which the civil right of freedom of expression was taken very seriously (Poster, 1997). In several countries, such as the US and Germany, the attempts to regulate Internet content by governments proved very difficult and somewhat embarrassing.

With respect to political rights, the Internet defies political boundaries. For particular rights to exist for groups and individuals the prerequisite is a polity with boundaries or territory as content for those rights. The Internet poses major challenges not only to authoritarian regimes that restrict such political rights as public criticism, but also to democratic regimes where legitimacy of the state is called into question via information provided on the Internet for refugees, aliens and others. The formation of civic networks that transverse political boundaries, while promising, also raises questions about the durability of political rights gained via such fluid networks since these rights may prove just as fluid and ephemeral as these networks (Tsagarousianou, Tambini and Bryan, 1998). The Internet has, therefore, vividly illustrated that computer-mediated communications cut across territorial borders, creating a new realm and undermining not only the feasibility but also the legitimacy of allocating rights based on geographic boundaries (Johnson and Post, 1997). The Internet also raises the issue of whether solidarity and allegiance can be formed at a distance as its spatial structure is dispersed and asymmetrical (Breslow, 1997).

Perhaps social rights are the least discussed aspect of the Internet. Many commentators assume that to have access to the Internet all that is required is a cheap computer and a telephone line. Leaving aside for the moment the fact that many individuals cannot afford telephone lines let alone computers in much of the world, that statement underestimates the volume of social and cultural capital that one requires to 'get wired'. What we mean here is that to get wired to the Internet and become an active user requires a certain disposition that arises only from particular class, gender, ethnic and racial experiences. In other words, economic capital is not the only barrier to access. The Internet displays, on the one hand, its university origins where fairly well-educated and sophisticated groups created its protocols in their own image, and, on the other, a counterculture, also very well educated and sophisticated, which shaped the culture of the Internet. If we add the fact that the Internet has become increasingly commercialized and now offers outlets where one can purchase mutual funds and book international flights, the picture of the Internet is hardly one of ordinary folks eagerly sharing their life experiences (although that happens to a limited extent). The point that emerges from limited sociological studies on the Internet is that, despite the hype, it is a limited medium in terms of its scope and users and it remains an exclusive domain of an educated segment of the population in the most advanced countries. In fact, the Internet currently reinforces, as Castells (1996: 364) puts it, 'the cosmopolitanism of the new professional and managerial classes living symbolically in a global frame of reference, unlike most of the population in any country'. Perhaps it is not surprising that the Internet has received such attention disproportionate to its size or scope: the classes and groups that dominate its use also dominate the production, consumption and distribution of symbolic signs on a global scale. The experiences of a class that dominates discourse get magnified.

We believe that too much emphasis has been placed on the 'crisis of boundaries' that the Internet has supposedly created between the real and the virtual, between time zones and between spaces, near and distant (Shields, 1996). Other technologies such as the telegraph, telephone, radio and television had already created such a dislocation between the real and virtual. What is novel about the Internet is that it has created a real-time interconnectedness among nodes that serve as relatively permanent storage of information. The Internet has become the source of a networked intelligence that is available to anyone with resources to have access to it. The Internet can perhaps best be defined as a new form of culture in the sense of the sum total of ways of knowing built up by a group of human beings and transmitted from one generation to another. Unlike the telegraph, telephone and other mass communications technologies, the Internet, like a giant, unorganized library, serves as a depository of all that is produced, consumed and exchanged across boundaries. Moreover, to argue that the Internet has somehow blurred the boundaries between the real and the virtual is to assume that such clear boundaries already existed and that reality was once accessible (Erni, 1996). Only a naïve, objectivist philosophy would have us believe that such a correspondence existed.

In the light of these reflections, it might be thought that we are arguing against the possibility of the Internet engendering a new form of politics and citizenship, technological citizenship. On the contrary, consistent with other forms of identity that we include in a deep conception of citizenship, access to the

Internet in the way we have defined it must be taken seriously. Otherwise, it remains the exclusive domain of specific groups and classes that shape it according to their own image. In that sense technological citizenship can possibly have two meanings. First, it can mean a method of enhancing the existing forms of citizenship in civil, political and social spheres. For example, pressuring politicians for accountability or disseminating information about decisions made in political assemblies ranging from the municipal to the international are potentially significant uses of the Internet. Rheingold, for example, provides several examples, including an electronic citizen participation in San Francisco (1993) or how the Internet is used cleverly to gather public information to make it possible for citizens to match specific votes and specific stock ownership (1996). Similarly, e-mail campaigns and list servers are used very effectively to raise issues and rapidly mobilize large numbers of citizens to form publics. Recently, the failure to reach an international agreement on investment (MAI) has been largely attributed to the mobilization of labour and environmental groups via the Internet (*Economist*, 1998). As well, the world-wide attention the Zapatistas received in their fight against the Mexican government has been attributed, in part, to their effective use of the Internet (Riberio, 1998).

The second meaning of technological citizenship is less developed but by no means insignificant: the Internet has evolved into a culture where its many-to-many principle is cherished and protected vociferously by various groups and individuals. In other words, while encouraging difference and diversity, the Internet has managed to develop a culture where individuality lives side by side with sharing, giving and a form of egalitarianism. While the commercialization of the Internet has probably been the greatest threat to this experimental and egalitarian culture, there is considerable potential here for a genuinely new form of citizenship. Unfortunately, television culture is already appropriating the Internet and pushing for increased integration between them. There is a growing presence of television as a structuring metaphor on the Internet, which is becoming more and more like television not only in its graphics and visuals but also in its corporate-owned and commercially oriented mass-culture and one-way communication (Morse, 1998: 66). While the Internet is not yet dominated by journalists or professional content-providers, its integration with television understood both as a structuring metaphor and as a field of cultural production is an immediate danger to its potential use as a free public medium of many-to-many communication and hence as a form of technological citizenship (Loader, 1997).

Another set of technologies to which attention should be drawn are those of surveillance and identification. Surveillance technologies typically rely on recording digital data about events, spaces and domains and feed these data into databases that organize, analyse and classify (Ericson and Haggerty, 1997). The human body lies at the heart of identification technologies (A. Davis, 1997). According to those who promote new identification technologies, driver's licences, credit cards and office keys are obsolete; the age of the body-password, or *biometric*, has arrived. Unique biological characteristics—hand geometry, eye structure, fingerprints, voice patterns, even smell—are being mapped and digitized as part of a booming new industry. Biometric technology operates much like the gadgets in spy films: computerized scanners confirm a person's identity by examining a biological feature, then matching it with a digital file containing those exact characteristics. Identifiable traits can be physical, such as hand contours or retina patterns. They can be behavioural, such as voice modulation or keystroke typing rhythms. The possibility is open for this information to be stored in central databases and traded like commodities by direct marketers, insurance companies and government agencies. The smartcard and financial services industries are already promoting biometrics as privacy's friend, and experts say biometric IDs are unmatched for security. Body parts already are used as passwords in various systems, public and private: inmates must submit to retinal scanning in Cook County, Illinois, coming and going from jail to court appearances. Connecticut and Pennsylvania are two of several American states that now use digitized finger imaging to match welfare records with recipients. Frequent travellers crossing into Canada from Montana can zip through an automated voice verification system run by the US Immigration and Naturalization Service. This is an example of technology firms driving immigration policy, which has also expanded to social policy by urging the use of identification technologies ostensibly to combat welfare fraud. In the private sector, Lotus employees pass through a hand-geometry scanner to pick up their children from in-house day care. Coca-Cola is using hand geometry at the time clock to prevent workers from 'buddy punching' a late colleague's time card (A. Davis, 1997).

So far the attention to these technologies has been in terms of their impact on privacy, projecting an Orwellian world or a global Panopticon (Lyon, 1994). As frightening as these technologies are, their real use and impact may lie elsewhere. Deleuze argues that there was a shift from disciplinary societies, which Foucault analysed, to societies of control, which Deleuze offers up for analysis (Deleuze, 1995: 177–182). He suggests that while sites of confinement such as schools, hospitals, prisons, factories, are moulds in which individuals are shaped and habituated, controls such as performance audits are a modulation, which is a system of continuous adjustment with which individuals control themselves. Of course, control here refers not to social control, which assumes external authorities imposing constraints and extracting acquiescence, but to forces that are immanent in social relations that regulate movement: cybernetic control rather than social control. Deleuze cites the proliferation of new technologies of government such as telematics and informatics, computer models of flows of finance, water, traffic, monitoring of accounts, auditing and the rise of new contractual relations as instances of this shift from disciplinary techniques to societies of cybernetic control. Under advanced capitalism, the individual—not so much his or her moral and legal rights and obligations but his or her movements—becomes a field of control. While disciplines have two poles (individuals and masses), societies of control develop codes which condition the life chances of individuals as in access to certain concrete assemblages such as banks, databases and information sources. In societies of control the polarity of the mass versus the individual disappears; individuals are continuously confronted with individuating symbolic and real codes: 'disciplinary man produced energy in discrete amounts, while control man undulates, moving among a continuous range of orbits' (Deleuze, 1995: 180).

Deleuze sees this change associated with advanced capitalism. He notes that while modern capitalism was directed towards concentrated production requiring the factory as a site of confinement, advanced capitalism is directed towards dispersive production directed towards assemblages across space-time. The significant point about this shift is that the target of societies of control is no longer the individual in context, as it was in disciplinary societies, but the individual itself. As such, the sites of resistance shift from sites of confinement to the very identity of the individual. Such thoughts raise serious concerns about the technologies of identification, which are much more sinister and invasive than the technologies of surveillance precisely because they aim not to discipline and regulate but to modulate the behaviour of consenting individuals in the name of risk reduction. At a time when many discredit essentialism as an epistemological and political approach, the technologies of identification raise the worst fears about identifying humans with essential and individual biological characteristics. These technologies are, of course, also technologies of classification in which individuals are assigned to certain categories of modulation according to their essential characteristics. Technological citizenship is therefore not simply about how to harness new technologies for new forms of political enactment or about how to limit the uses of technology that encroach upon civil and political rights, but also about limiting the cybernetic use of modulating behaviour and defining identity.

Ecological Citizenship

Environmentalism has emerged in the last three decades as a specific 'ethic of care' towards nature. Following the early efforts of preservation and conservation of natural habitats, environmentalism has spanned movements including animal rights, maintaining biodiversity, advocating renewable energy resources, responsible use of natural resources, raising issues regarding the obligations and responsibilities of humans within and towards nature. These movements resulted in not only a plethora of rules and regulations within specific states to protect the environment but also a complex and evolving array of international arrangements and regimes. As well, environmentalism has brought about a new awareness or consciousness of the dependency between human activities and the environment, causing a major shift in the behavioural patterns of millions of people. From environmentally conscious investment and consumption to recycling, reusing and reducing consumption, such ideas have become mantras of our age. From these diverse movements and discourses, including sustainability, ecofeminism, deep ecology and conservation, can we identify a form of citizenship, ecological citizenship?

In order to explore an adequate concept of ecological citizenship, we must first address some of the more perplexing and puzzling problems environmental movements have posed for our ways of thinking and modes of learning. It is true that environmental movements have led to a legitimation crisis of modern political arrangements. While they raised serious doubts about the state as a container of policy issues by demonstrating that bioregional and ecological boundaries did not respect such boundaries, they also raised fundamental questions about the ways in which modern societies dominate and appropriate nature for production, consumption and exchange. In other words, environmental movements have contested not only the sovereignty principle of the state but also the sovereignty of the modern individual, and its anthropocentrism, thus decentring the subject. In so doing environmental movements raised the question of identity in a new, perhaps fundamental, way in the sense that they questioned the very place of humans in the realm of 'nature'. Today, after three decades of proliferation, while environmental movements articulated fundamental questions of being, they also face a crisis of their own.

In the past decade, modern environmental movements have shifted their ground and grown from an ethic of care focusing on conservation of 'natural habitats' to a much more complex, contested and rugged terrain. Today environmental movements include a wide range of claims, including advocacy of the sacred earth, various forms of environmental managerialism in state and corporate bureaucracies claiming the ultimate controllability of the environment, communitarian localism believing in total self-sufficiency, and ecofeminism advocating the liberation of women and nature together. In such a rugged terrain, it is very difficult to articulate a concept of ecological citizenship that succumbs neither to so broad a description as to be meaningless nor to an essentialist conception of nature independent of our conception of it. In the language of rights, it is very difficult to advocate rights for nature without imposing certain regulations and obligations on particular social groups and liberating others. So what ostensibly begins as advocacy of 'natural' rights ends up being oppression of some social groups and liberation of others. In the name of the environment or nature, all kinds of restrictions can be placed upon the rights of 'others' while conferring rights on those who supposedly have the knowledge necessary to address the problem (Harvey, 1996: 182).

With the rise of poststructuralist forms of thinking, to which environmental movements contributed by decentring the subject, the question today is: 'What happens to environmentalist concerns when the object of those concerns, the thing for the sake of which one speaks—nature, wild lands, animals—begins to lose its status as an object, a given, already set thing to which we can refer as if we were not involved in its construction?' (Bennett and Chaloupka, 1993: xvi). Or, as Macnaghten and Urry (1998) argue, the question is how to avoid environmental idealism, environmental realism and environmental pragmatism. We would like to take up three issues of ecological citizenship that particularly highlight these problems: an ethic of care, intergenerational obligations and international governance issues.

The most important terrain of citizenship that arises from environmentalism is a responsibility towards nature. However, as Dizard (1993) has argued, there are two different strands of this contested terrain. The first strand evokes a moment in history when humans and nature lived in harmony and evolves along two trajectories: humans must care for nature because they are dependent on it (utilitarian) and because it is a moral responsibility (ethical). This notion of responsibility towards nature, however, often leads to forms of essentialism that construe nature as an independent entity with an intrinsic value (Macnaghten and Urry, 1998: 1–2). Nature appears as a pristine, pure and divine whereas humans appear greedy, dominant and exploitative. From environmental fundraising demands to green advertising, the pristine nature of the environment is invoked to establish an aesthetic sensibility towards nature. The problem with this trajectory is that the purity or divinity of nature is a social and cultural product not an unmediated 'fact' found in nature. As Jennings and Jennings (1993) have argued, essentialist advocacy for nature often comes up against other social groups and invokes issues of race. When considering the Amazonian rainforest, for example, Eric Katz argues that the current inhabitants of the rainforest cannot be made to pay for protectionist policies that arise from the West, which irresponsibly used its environmental resources for centuries. Instead, he believes that '[a] truly global ecological ethic will view the problem in terms of the entire planetary system, both human and natural. From this all-encompassing perspective, it becomes incumbent upon the richer nations of the world, who have previously gained the benefits of environmental destruction and economic development, to pay their fair share in the preservation of a diverse planetary environment' (E. Katz, 1997: 175). But his solution is equally problematic and raises political questions because the distribution of economic capital in the rich nations is not equal. In other words, if rich nations are to foot the bill for ecological justice, the question of *who* in those nations will pay for it must also be raised. Ecological justice and social justice here are closely linked. Just how such ecological justice can be possible and how nature could have inalienable rights remain unresolved and, perhaps, irresolvable dilemmas of environmentalism.

Faced with such dilemmas, some environmentalists turned towards science as the arbiter of the rights of nature. While environmentalism began its trajectory with a scepticism regarding modern science, today it wages its war often on the basis of its objectivity and scientificity. Of course, this is a very dangerous game which the opposing forces also engage in. More importantly, however, environmentalism, by using this strategy, forces itself to make claims of empirical objectivity, relying on a mechanistic model of nature to establish it as an independent, knowable and controllable object. 'The critique of science and an increasing dependence upon science turn out to be intertwined. With the rise of modern environmentalism, it has become obvious that science no longer controls the vision of the world' (Eder, 1996: 174). The scientists and experts claim objectivity and yet produce contradictory evidence, analysis and interpretations. While environmental movements constitute nature as an object of care, protection and conservation, the consequences or possibilities of such care are fraught with difficulties. When environmentalism slips into fundamentalism, it results in a form of naturalism. According to this view, which is shared among many environmentalists, the fundamental problem with the environment is that modern capitalism has exploited and destroyed it. This hubristic domination of nature thesis branches out into many variants and results in a mechanistic view of the distinction between nature and culture, failing to recognize that the very idea of nature is socially and culturally constructed and that we do not have access to nature without the mediating effects of social and cultural relations.

An alternative trajectory of an ethic of care towards the environment is to regard nature as a social construction and elaborate upon responsibilities of humans in their use of the environment. On this view, ecological citizenship is an ambiguous but worthy ideal in which various competing claims for rights intersect each other. There are no universal or essential grounds on which an ecological citizen can defend nature but contingent and unstable grounds on which she weighs her responsibilities towards the environment as well as her other sources of identification and loyalty (Dizard, 1993).

The second contested terrain of ecological citizenship is the issue of intergenerational responsibility (de-Shalit, 1995; Gower, 1995). As de-Shalit puts it, 'although future generations are by definition people who will live after our deaths, our obligations to them are a matter of *justice*, rather than of charity or supererogation. It is therefore our duty to consider them when we distribute access to resources and when we plan our financial policies and budgets. Our obligations, however, are not infinite or boundless. When obligations to future people conflict with genuine need to improve the welfare of contemporaries, a middle way has to be found' (de-Shalit, 1995: 11). The problem with intergenerational justice is that such a middle ground is often impossible to find. Once one argues on the basis of the immutable rights of future generations, it raises questions of social justice. Similar arguments have been made with respect to budget deficits. But is it socially just to withdraw services from the working classes and obliterate social rights in the name of future generations? Similarly, in the name of ecological justice, is it socially just to oppose specific types of development that would provide jobs for this generation? These are very difficult questions that cannot be answered in the abstract but only under specific and contingent conditions. Nevertheless, the issue of intergenerational justice raises significant matters for ecological citizenship.

The third contested terrain of ecological citizenship is the rise of international governance regimes that address endangered plants and animals, migratory species, airborne pollutants, marine pollution, hazardous wastes, ozone deletion and climate change (O.R. Young, 1994, 1997). These regimes, often composed of non-state and non-governmental agencies and actors as well as state organizations, deal with physical or biological systems that lie wholly or largely outside the jurisdiction of any individual state but that are of interest to two or more of them as valued resources. Examples include high seas fisheries, deep seabed minerals, the ozone layer and climatic change. Environmental regimes also deal with shared resources such as renewable resources (e.g., migratory stocks of wild animals), non-renewable resources (e.g., pools of oil that underlie two jurisdictions) or ecosystems that transcend national boundaries (e.g., shared river and lake basins). Finally, these regimes deal with transboundary consequences of environmental impacts such as acid rain or the loss of biological diversity (O.R. Young, 1997: 6–8). While quite effective in raising environmental issues in the international media and even resolving certain conflicts, the regimes raise two questions for ecological citizenship. First, these regimes lack accountability in terms of their day-to-day operations and negotiations. Citizens of states, although bound and affected by the decisions and negotiations of these regimes, are often not in a situation where they can practise their citizenship and deliberate upon these matters. In other words, the spaces in which these regimes form also reflect the interjurisdictional and transboundary spaces that they are trying to address. Second, the access to regimes is by and large restricted to professional and managerial groups in that many other groups are cut off from their deliberations by virtue of the lack of cultural, social and symbolic capital. How these regimes interact with those on whose lives they have major impact and how they become accountable to them are major unresolved issues of ecological citizenship.

These critical reflections on ecological citizenship raise more questions than they resolve. 'Ecological citizenship' politicizes the concept of ecology in a way that is more than an ethic of care towards the environment. 'Citizenship' refers not only to legal and political rights but also to various practices in which humans act as political and moral agents. In so far as 'ecological citizenship' is *not* understood as a political concept, it has a limited value for reconstructing an adequate concept of citizenship in our era. Ecological citizenship must mean ecological reason is inherently political not in the sense that it can be made into a political programme but in the sense that the bearers and claimants of rights are individuals and groups not nature or the environment. Ecological citizenship means that obligations and responsibilities of political agents are towards the socially constructed value of nature as much as towards each other. As Thomashow argues, 'Adding the word *ecological* substantially challenges the notion of identity. Ecological identity refers to all the different ways people construe themselves in relationship to the earth as manifested in personality, values, actions, and sense of self. Nature becomes an object of identification' (Thomashow, 1995: 3). Thomashow admits that this identification entails considerable ambiguity since the very object of identification is itself a produced subject: nature is a social construction. However, he provides a deeply problematic definition of ecological citizenship: 'The ecologically aware citizen takes responsibility for the place where he or she lives, understands the importance of making collective decisions regarding the commons, seeks to contribute to the common good, identifies with bioregions and ecosystems rather than obsolete nation-states or transnational corporations, considers the wider impact of his or her actions, is committed to mutual and collaborative community building, observes the flow of power in controversial issues, attends to the quality of interpersonal relationships in political discourse, and acts according to his or her convictions' (Thomashow, 1995: 139). As we argued, identification with bioregions and ecosystems is not possible *without* identification with political associations and is possible only from within them. To consider nation-states and corporations as obsolete misses the fact that coming to terms with these political arrangements, claiming rights through them and changing these arrangements is part of ecological citizenship.

Cosmopolitan Democracy

So far our discussion illustrates how the new political spaces opened up across boundaries contest the sovereignty of the modern nation-state in novel ways. How to allocate rights to groups that form across boundaries and how to impose obligations on them are vexing questions of cosmopolitan citizenship. The issue at stake is what kinds of *global* political arrangements are likely to engender citizenship understood not only as political and legal rights but also practices in these new spaces? As mentioned earlier, there is currently a debate over the most appropriate political arrangements in the global era, almost exclusively focused on international relations theory.

As Magnusson (1996) says, the underlying assumption of international relations theory is that world politics is to be conceived primarily in terms of relations within and between states. The state is considered so central that everything of consequence in world politics is forced through the system of states and inter-state relations. With the collapse of the bipolar world order and the emergence of a global economy and culture various scholars have challenged this assumption. The neat patterns of politics in the postwar liberal democracies have been disrupted, and the standard accounts no longer make much sense. More and more, theorists are putting the state at issue, that is, they are coming to see it as a historically, culturally and geographically specific form of political order; beginning to inquire into its conditions of possibility; and recognizing a wider field within which state formation, state policy-making and inter-state relations are seen as particular activities that do not encompass the whole. Some believe that the 'new' social movements have changed the conditions for political action and generated 'spaces' for politics that are incommensurate with the ones defined by the state system. As we have seen, to think of the global environmental movement, the international movements of human rights and women's movement as domestic pressure groups or as non-state actors in the international system misses much of what is significant about these new formations.

A multiplicity of global flows, from financial to ecological to symbolic, connect the fate of polities in one locale to the fate of polities in distant regions of the world. Although such flows become most visible during crisis situations such as war or economic recession, everyday lives of people are increasingly woven together in complex ways that go beyond the borders of nation-states of which they are members. As we have seen, in response to such complex flows various international regimes of governance and a multitude of arrangements, agreements and regulations have emerged that not only curtail the capacities of nation-states but also create new gaps in consent, accountability and legitimacy. Simultaneously, various groups based on ethnicity, race, language, lifestyle and age seek new rights for representation, recognition and redistribution. In short, the principle of the sovereignty of the state as an indivisible entity is called into question. And just as sovereignty is being divided under the pressures of globalization, so too is the idea of citizenship becoming group-differentiated (Linklater, 1996; McGrew, 1997). We end this chapter with a brief discussion of the models of democracy and citizenship that emerge from the debate in international relations theory.

Three normative models emerged in the past few years to precisely deal with the types of question raised by urban, technological and ecological forms of citizenship: liberal-democratic internationalism, radical communitarianism and cosmopolitanism (McGrew, 1997). These theories, as their proponents also claim, are normative not in the sense that they are utopian or unfeasible but because they give expression to immanent tendencies and latent directions. They claim their intellectual credibility, in the words a proponent, from 'where we are—the existing pattern of political relations and processes—and from an analysis of what might be: desirable political forms and principles' (Held, 1995: 286). McGrew argues that although these three models diverge widely, they share certain principles. They all agree that globalization is transforming the conditions of liberal democracy; that democracy needs to deepen and widen; that a world government modelled after the modern nation-state must be rejected; and that normative thought has a vital role to play under the current circumstances of globalization and fragmentation.

The report *Our Global Neighbourhood* (Commission on Global Governance, 1995) expresses liberal-democratic internationalism. Rejecting the prospects of a world government, it sets out to adapt the institutions and practices of global governance that have emerged in the past few decades, also known as the international regimes of governance (O.R. Young, 1994, 1997). It calls this a 'global civic ethic' that 'accelerates the merging of national civil societies into a broader global civil society' (Commission on Global Governance, 1995: 55). While urging the reform and adaptation of existing practices, liberal-democratic internationalism leaves intact major issues of accountability, legitimacy and consent that arise from the transformations of politics described in this chapter. As such, liberal-democratic internationalism is a status quo contract that legitimizes the current powerful interests in the world order: multinational corporations, non-governmental professional organizations and international professional networks and alliances. Moreover, it still assumes the indivisibility of state sovereignty and construes citizenship as a matter of nationality.

Radical communitarianism rejects existing structures of governance and any attempt to institutionalize them since they are conceived as privileging the interests of the wealthy and powerful and excluding the mass of citizens from the circuits of power. It therefore stresses the creation of alternative and radically different forms of global governance based upon a combination of direct democracy and new structures of representative governance. While ranging from Burnheim (1996), advocating functional organizations such as based upon trade, environment and health as opposed to territorial organizations, to Bookchin (1992) and his confederalism, radical communitarianism, nonetheless, takes the new social movements as its model of governance. Through a politics of resistance and empowerment, ecological, women's, peace and solidarity movements, among others, challenge the definition of the political and the conventional boundaries by bringing ever broader spheres into the orbit of politics. As R.B.J. Walker (1988: 147–148) suggests, critical social movements have defined a new progressive politics which involves 'explorations of new ways of acting, new ways of knowing and being in the world, and new ways of acting together through emerging solidarities'. However, although sceptical about the liberal-democratic vision of reformed regimes of global governance, radical communitarian models have not coalesced into a model of global democracy with a defensible conception of the global citizen. Sandel argues that '[s]ince the days of Aristotle's polis, the republican tradition has viewed self-government as an activity rooted in a particular place, carried out by citizens loyal to that place and the way of life it embodies. Self-government today, however, requires a politics that plays itself out in a multiplicity of settings, from neighbourhoods to nations to the world as a whole. Such a politics requires citizens who can think and act as multiply-situated selves' (Sandel, 1996: 351). But how such a conception can become practical has so far eluded the proponents. Radical communitarian models so far remain at the level of principles.

Recent years have witnessed the emergence of a third model of global democracy: cosmopolitanism. Forms of cosmopolitanism have been traced back to Greek stoics and Immanuel Kant, but its current revival, while building on an invented tradition, establishes new rules and expresses new sentiments (W.E. Connolly, 1991; Falk, 1994; Heater, 1996; Held, 1995, 1997; Linklater, 1996)

At the core of a cosmopolitan vision of democracy is a cosmopolitan democratic law. Cosmopolitan law, rather than imitating the existing international law as an expression of arrangements between sovereign states, would give an expression to a new transnational structure of political action in which law becomes the governing principle of a cosmopolitan community of communities. While initially such a cosmopolitan law would not necessarily coincide with the principles of each existing state, as more and more states begin to affiliate with it, it would inculcate an ethic of the cosmopolitan citizen with a growing loyalty to cosmopolitan principles. Therefore, 'individuals who composed the states and societies whose constitutions were formed in accordance with cosmopolitan law might be regarded as citizens, not just of their national communities or regions, but of a universal system of "cosmo-political" governance' (Held, 1995: 233). The idea of multiple citizenships would gain legitimate assent because cosmopolitan law would be a binding framework for the political practices of states, societies, regions, cities, but not a detailed regulative framework for the direction of their affairs. The principle of sovereignty would derive from cosmopolitan law rather than the nation-state as a territorially fixed polity. In fact, cosmopolitan law would strip sovereignty away from the idea of fixed borders and territories and establish it as malleable time-space clusters (Held, 1995: 234). In short, cosmopolitan law would demand the subordination of regional, national and local sovereignties to an overarching framework but within this framework associations (time-space clusters) may be self-governing. According to Held, this conception opens up a new way of thinking about old problems associated with sovereignty because 'the cosmopolitan model of democracy is the legal basis of a global and divided authority system—a system of diverse and overlapping power centres, shaped and delimited by democratic law' (Held, 1995: 234–235).

The cosmopolitan model of democracy is ambitious. The affinities between cosmopolitanism and radical communitarianism are obvious. However, while forms of communitarianism rely on a concept of confederalism in which a variety of levels of communities negotiate with one another, cosmopolitan democracy envisages a legal and political framework that is binding (McGrew, 1997: 251). Yet, it also refrains from going as far as to suggest a world government or world citizenship. While it is true that the type of multilayered or differentiated citizenship explored in this book is consonant with the principle of the necessity for establishing a cosmopolitan legal and political framework, there are also various difficulties with this concept that critics have been quick to point out. These difficulties can be seen in two groups.

First, globalization and its effects on democracy centred upon the nation-state may have been exaggerated. As argued earlier, some have suggested that globalization is still a very restricted phenomenon and at different levels (economic, cultural, environmental) means different things and has different consequences. The fact that the nation-state is being undermined by increasing global interconnectedness needs critical scrutiny. If that is the case, it can be argued that the advocates of cosmopolitan democracy have been too quick to dismiss the territorial forms of government and democratic norms that can be effectuated through the state in the international arena. On this view, which is advanced by neo-realists such as Krasner (1995), the emerging international regimes of governance based on various non-governmental organizations as well as states already provide a legal and political structure of action that needs critical commitment.

Second, there are inherent dangers in cosmopolitan law towards Westernization and even cultural imperialism. Although the advocates of cosmopolitan law are aware of these dangers, advocating a form of 'subsidiarity' principle, where appropriate levels of decision-making are clarified at the outset. does not solve it (Held, 1995: 235). While in criticizing cosmopolitan law, Zolo (1997) may have been at fault because he ascribed to it a desire to form a world government, nevertheless, his critical comments revolving around the dangers of cosmopolitan law have to be taken seriously. Zolo criticized the idea of a global civil society on the grounds that while it was a problematic conception to begin with, to extend the concept of civil society to a global level ignores that much of globalization has really been the Westernization of the planet. According to Zolo, terms such as 'global interdependence' or 'global interconnectedness' belie the fact that so much of the global flows in trade, finance, entertainment, arts, science and politics originate in the West and that other power brokers in the so-called 'global civil society' are mostly composed of Western-born or Western-cultivated individuals. Zolo contends that '[w]hat Western cosmopolitans call "global civil society" in fact goes no further than a network of connections and functional interdependencies which has developed within certain important sectors of the "global market"' (Zolo, 1997: 137). Zolo adds: 'Nor, moreover, does it go much beyond the optimistic expectation of affluent Westerners to be able to feel and be universally recognized as citizens of the world—citizens of a welcoming, peaceful, ordered and democratic "global village"—without for a moment or in any way ceasing to be "themselves", i.e., Western citizens' (Zolo, 1997: 137).

These critical remarks remind us of our earlier point that theories of globalization and global democracy are themselves produced by the possessors of cultural capital in major cosmopolitan centres of the West. Although these authors often make reference to a 'global elite', it seems that authors themselves are somehow excluded from that group. Of course, this is a problematic assumption that does not stand up to scrutiny. In other words, these critical comments by Zolo indicate that the issues of class differentiation of theorists as well as what they say are inadequately addressed in international relations theory. It has not been particularly attentive to issues of class (nor gender, race or ethnicity for that matter). This is a mistake. While rethinking democracy, it should be taken into account that advanced capitalism has changed dramatically and that the modern frame of thinking about rights in terms of individuals versus the state (or any other authority) misses this dramatic change. Cosmopolitan citizenship cannot be reduced to an exercise of a board game where states, regions and cities as actors and agents are placed in positions. The struggle for recognition and redistribution that is taking place is a struggle between not places but groups, and these groups are already making demands in their states that are not easily recognized elsewhere.

This chapter on contested sovereignties may have raised more questions than it answered regarding the possibilities of cosmopolitan citizenship. Significant political and theoretical struggles lie ahead in terms of inventing new forms of cosmopolitan citizenship that allocate group-differentiated citizenship while opening up global areas of governance to accountability, legitimacy and consent. While various visions for global democracy and citizenship struggle for dominance, for some time to come many rights will still be claimed at the level of the state. Even cosmopolitan rights and obligations, such as ecological, technological and urban, will be negotiated through the state. Perhaps in the future one of the ironies of globalization will be remembered as the invention of a new state without nationalism.

6
CULTURAL CITIZENSH
CONSUMING IDENTI

Introduction

This chapter discusses the rise of 'culture' as a field of production and consumption and barriers and opportunities in participating in it. In discussing cultural citizenship, the chapter works through two different arguments. First, Bourdieu (1984) and his influence especially in Britain via Featherstone (1991, 1995) and Lash and Urry (1987, 1994) making a crucial connection between consumerism, professional groups and distinction. Second, studies on governmentality and neoliberalism by Gordon (1987), Rose (1996a, 1996b, 1996c), Burchell (1995, 1996) and du Gay (1996) linking consumerism and regimes of government under advanced liberalism. Via these arguments, we establish cultural citizenship as a field in which the rights to access to production, distribution and consumption of culture become a field of struggle and conflict. We use 'culture' to mean a specific field in which symbols, ideas, knowledge, images and sounds are produced, exchanged and consumed. This narrow use of cultural citizenship differs from the usage that employs it as a synonym for 'multicultural' or 'ethno-racial' citizenship that we discussed earlier (Ong, 1996; Pakulski, 1997; Stevenson, 1997).

We shall first elaborate upon the discussion of class in general and the so-called 'new class' in particular, to both of which we have made several references, particularly in Chapter 5, but which so far have remained latent in our analysis. In other words, while so far we have focused on forms of citizenship urged upon us by various forms of the politics of recognition such as gays, lesbians, blacks and ethnic groups, we do not necessarily agree that such forms have somehow displaced class politics; rather, they have generated new forms of class politics, which require analysis.

Cultural Capital, Citizenship and Identity

There are, of course, those who claim that the concept of class can no longer capture the principles of social differentiation in advanced capitalism (Pakulski and Waters, 1996). They argue that other forms of identity such as gender, ethnicity and 'race' have come to dominate the everyday lives of people and class has lost its primacy. Thus, there is no reason to insist that it should occupy a dominant role in theory. Others are more sceptical about this thesis and search for a viable or workable conception of class (J.R. Hall, 1997; E.O. Wright,

97). Esping-Andersen (1993), for example, agrees that the concept of class inherited from nineteenth-century sociology cannot deal with the rising complexities of advanced capitalism. Nevertheless, that does not mean that class analysis needs to be abandoned. He states, 'The question is whether the emerging structure of employment, of life-chances and of inequality can be fruitfully understood with our inherited theories of class' (8). Similarly, as we have seen, Bourdieu (1987) argues that classes cannot be made to exist only objectively (occupation, income, status) or subjectively (identity, belief, loyalty) but do so at the interstices of both. The art and politics of group-making include practices of naming, organizing, struggling, truth-telling, identifying and structuring. But these practices can come into being only on the basis of real class positions that exist. Hence, while the significance of a class or social group cannot be established without reference to real class positions, the absence of practice that make such positions mobilize and palatable would hamper the existence of such a class or group. The existence of a class or group must emerge out of practices that include truth-telling. On this view, it is not reflexive sociology to declare the death or birth of this or that class without exposing the conditions under which such declarations are made.

Much attention in recent class analysis of advanced capitalism has focused on the increasing significance of professional and managerial occupations. It has been observed that since the 1940s the rise of professions has been quite dramatic: fields such as engineering, medicine, law, journalism, planning, marketing, policy, consulting, public relations, management, administration, adjudication, negotiation, advertisement, inspection, investigation and care-giving have become important means through which individuals seek to augment their wealth, gain status and exercise power. Castells (1996: 303), for example, estimates that of the total labour force the professional, managerial and technical occupations accounted for 29.7 per cent in the United States (1991), 30.6 per cent in Canada (1992), 32.08 per cent in Britain (1990), 25.9 per cent in France (1989), 26.7 per cent in West Germany (1987) and 14.9 per cent in Japan (1990). Although there is considerable diversity, he noted that there is a common trend towards the increase of the relative weight of the professional-managerial occupations (Castells, 1996: 218). Recent comparative studies confirm this trend in occupational structure (Clement and Myles, 1994; Esping-Andersen, 1993; E.O. Wright, 1997).

The change in occupational structure, of course, does not necessarily mean a change in class structure. A body of literature emerged in the last few decades on the existence of a 'new class' in advanced capitalism, taking into account the change in occupational structure under advanced capitalism but also how production, consumption and exchange of commodities have changed as well. This literature is complex and varied but fits well with Bourdieu's concept of 'classification struggles'. As some scholars struggled to generate a dominant interpretation of the 'new class' and debated over ontological, epistemological and methodological problems, the real class positions that are invoked to compose this class underwent significant change. Frow (1993, 1995) and Szelényi (1990) have provided recent reviews of this literature and we do not propose to repeat their analyses here. However, we provide a discussion of new class theories from the point of view of classification struggles and hope to develop a concept of cultural capital pertinent to cultural citizenship.

Classification Struggles: From the Power Elite to Cultural Intermediaries

The changing class structure of advanced capitalism has been a subject of debate since the 1940s (Burnham, 1941; Mills and Gerth, 1942). At issue is how to interpret the new classes and groups—cadres of professional and managerial occupations—which neither own the means of production nor are oppressed cogs in a production machine. Within Marxism the class position of salaried professionals and managers has been an issue of controversy even earlier then the 1940s (Burris, 1995). In the 1890s, a debate over 'revisionism' was centred on the question of 'mental workers' (Ross, 1978). Similarly, in the formerly communist states, the rise of the new class was first noted by Djilas (1957), who argued that a cadre of managers and officials were exercising considerable influence and power. Following Thorsten Veblen, C. Wright Mills was influential in raising the issue of the new class. Tracing theories of the new class to Germany before the rise of fascism, he claimed that 'the range of theory had been fairly well laid out by the middle 'twenties, and nothing really new has since been added' (Mills, 1951: 290). In the last two decades, however, studies by Bell (1973, 1979) and Gouldner (1979, 1985), albeit in different ways and for different purposes, have drawn considerable attention to the new class. Further, there have been two major edited works on the new class edited by Bruce-Briggs (1979) and Hansfried Kellner and Frank W. Heuberger (1992). More recently, an anthology was edited by Arthur J. Vidich (1995) on the new 'middle' class. Although often not considered as such, the studies by Bourdieu (1984, 1988, 1996) are among the most important contributions to the new class studies. Finally, Erik Olin Wright (1985, 1997), in his studies of class, accepted the challenge of coming to terms with the new middle classes. In view of this long history, as Heuberger (1992) has argued, new class is not so new anymore. But that does not mean that either the idea is uncontested or coherent or even its adherents agree on basic principles. That is why we turn to a brief history of the classification struggles revolving around the 'new class'.

Although Holton and Turner (1989) argue that '[t]he strong class idiom, with its increasingly polarized view of relations between the organic class communities of labour and capital has now been sharply revised. One prominent area of revision is to be found in New Class theory', there is no agreement on whether to constitute the professionals and managers as a new class. They add that '[w]hile earlier attempts to differentiate the capitalist class from a managerial class proved inconclusive, there is now a far greater weight of support for the need to differentiate between property-based and knowledge- or credential-based class positions and class strategies' (Holton and Turner, 1989: 177). They argue, however, that '[i]t is still too early...to accept New Class theory as a coherent extension of the repertoire of class analysis' (Holton and

Turner, 1989: 195). While, therefore, there is an agreement that the professions are equally widespread in both private and public sectors, there is little consensus on whether to constitute the new professions as a new class (Brint, 1994; Elliott, 1972; Macdonald, 1995). The difficulty partly stems from the fact that, as salaried professionals, most social and political theorists are themselves members of the new class, an issue that Bourdieu addressed persistently (Bourdieu and Wacquant, 1992). Bourdieu has also been most consistent with his insistence on situating the new class within a broad theory of fields as social practices and the role of different forms of capital (Bourdieu, 1991a). Apart from this are reasons that derive from the distinctive characteristics of the new class. The new class is heterogeneous and fluid, making it difficult to situate within advanced capitalism. Two problems are particularly pertinent here for cultural citizenship.

The first is the question of whether the new class is a status group between two opposing classes in modern capitalism or a new class on its own. Those who write in the Marxist tradition consider the members of the new class as those aspiring bourgeois whom Marx identified as the petty bourgeoisie (Marx and Engels, 1967). Marx essentially saw the petty bourgeoisie as 'a burden weighing heavily on the working base and increase the social security and power of the upper class' (Marx, 1967b: 573). Marx held this class in contempt and included in it 'the horde of flunkeys, the soldiers, sailors, police, lower officials and so on, mistresses, grooms, clowns and jugglers', as well as 'ill-paid artists, musicians, lawyers, physicians, scholars, schoolmasters, inventors, etc.' (Marx, 1967b: 218). Obviously, Marx was not very precise in his conception of the 'middle class' and he included in it anyone who was not a wage earner in factories, a proletarian, or an owner of the means of production, a bourgeois. Rather, he was more concerned with reducing the complexity of the class situation in the nineteenth century into two opposing classes waging a struggle against each other. As a result, he never attributed any political or economic significance to the new middle class (Burris, 1995: 20).

It is a matter of speculation whether Marx would have revised his view on the new class if he had finished his famous incomplete chapter on the classes in the third volume of *Capital*. It was precisely the problem of the new class that he was beginning to address at the point where the manuscript breaks off. Marx was aware that the class situation even in England was not as simple as he presented and he accepted that 'the stratification of classes does not appear in its pure form. Middle and intermediate strata even here obliterate lines of demarcation everywhere' (Marx, 1967a: 885). Nevertheless, Marx thought the important question was what constituted class: 'What makes wage-labourers, capitalists and landlords constitute the three great social classes?' (Marx, 1967a: 886). He argued that at first glance the sources of revenue would seem to differentiate these classes since the 'individuals forming them live on wages, profit and ground-rent respectively, on the realization of their labour-power, their capital, and their landed property' (Marx, 1967a: 886). But he raised the question of how to classify physicians and officials, or more broadly professionals and civil servants, because they would also constitute classes from the standpoint of revenue. Although the manuscript breaks off here, elsewhere Marx made it clear that the decisive element in determining class situation was not revenue but ownership of the means of production. As such he would have likely rejected the new class on the grounds that its members were either supported by or contributed to one of the three means of production in the modern economy: labour, money and land (Burris, 1995: 21). It must be noted, however, at the time when Marx was writing on capitalism in the 1860s and 1870s, neither the salaried managers in state or corporate bureaucracies nor the professions had reached the level and size they have reached in advanced capitalism.

Those who see the new class as a new middle class employed in large state and corporate bureaucracies consider it an intermediary class. Veblen and Mills certainly saw the white-collar workers as salaried workers in state and corporate bureaucracies. They occupied the 'middle' of the class structure of modern capitalism because of their income rank as well as their increasing numbers. James Burnham (1941), on the other hand, considered the rise of the new class as a managerial revolution where the bureaucracy and technocracy had become the new ruling class. Burnham was not concerned with precise classification or categories of the new class but its direction. His thesis was based on the assumption that function rather than ownership was the crucial category of power in technocratic society. He presented a simple theory of historical class succession so that just as the oppressed peasantry did not succeed the oppressive feudal lords but both were displaced by an entirely different class, the bourgeoisie, who remade society in their own image, so the working class would not succeed the capitalist, but both would be replaced by the managers, who would become a new ruling class, wielding power on the basis of their technical superiority. Burnham claimed that the managers were on their way to exercise control over the instruments of production through their control of the state. In Germany and Italy there already was a shift from capitalism to managerial society. In Russia, 'the nation most advanced towards managerial structure', the managers, who were the managers of factories and state agencies and state farms, were already getting the largest proportion of the national income (Bell, 1973: 92). From this observation, Burnham (1941) claimed that while the First World War was the last great war of capitalist society, the Second World War was waged by the new managerial class.

In 1951, Mills argued that between 1870 and 1940 there was a significant shift in the American class structure where a new middle class became prominent. A decade earlier he had criticized Burnham for exaggerating its prominence as a new ruling class (Mills and Gerth, 1942). Unlike the wage earners, land owners or capitalists, the members of the new middle class were defined by their occupation and profession. While in 1870 the new middle class comprised only 6 per cent of the labour force, by 1940 it was 25 per cent. Meanwhile, in the same period, wage workers declined from 61 per cent to 55 per cent and the old middle class, farmers, businessmen and free professionals, declined from 33 per cent to 20 per cent (Mills, 1995: 190). According to Mills the new middle class comprised the salaried managers and professionals, sales and service workers, and office workers (190–191). As a result of the trend towards this occupational shift, he argued that 'as a proportion of the labour force fewer individuals manipulate *things*, more handle *people* and *symbols*' (191). The observations Mills made regarding the trends towards white-collar jobs were prescient. He accurately observed that the increasing productivity of machinery used in manufacturing resulted in fewer workers producing more things in less time; that the increasing importance of distribution comprising marketing, circulation, advertising and trade engendered new occupations; and that as markets expanded with distribution of things, workers who move, store, finance, promote and sell goods are knitted into a vast network of enterprises and occupations of coordination.

Mills saw the main consequence of the rise of the new middle class as the expansion of corporate and government bureaucracies (195). He observed that managerial and professional employees formed links in chains of power and obedience in these bureaucracies. Associated with these occupations, to maintain the continuity of the chain of command, was a layer of clerks, supervisors and managers. Also associated with the new occupations was the rise of professional associations, which regulated standards and limited entrance into the occupation thereby creating a controlled market (196). The occupations ranked individuals in a system of hierarchies based on various types and levels of skill.

Mills, then, placed decisive emphasis on the occupations as the central aspect of the rise of the new class. He argued that 'as sources of income, occupations are connected with *class* position; and since they normally carry an expected quota of prestige, on and off the job, they are relevant to *status* position. They also involve certain degrees of *power* over other people directly in terms of the job, and indirectly in others social areas' (197). Occupations are thus tied to class, status and power as well as skills. In terms of class situation, Mills considered occupation to be more important than property in advanced capitalism since it has become the predominant source of income. By dealing with symbols, coordination, recording, promotion, supervision and distribution, the individuals in the new class fulfil their functions as dependent employees, and the skills they employ are sometimes similar in form to those of many wage workers. Yet the prestige and higher incomes as well as guidance power of occupations differentiate the new class sufficiently from that of the wage workers in manufacturing (201).

With the hindsight of writing in the late twentieth century, we can point out three problems in Mills' analysis of the new middle class. First, he saw managerial and professional workers merely as cogs in a bureaucratic machine, programmed to execute their orders in exacting detail and precision. The image of a professional worker caught in a machine is not new, and something certainly Weber gave considerable attention to in his discussion of bureaucracy. But this image of a 'cheerful robot', as Mills would later describe it, does not describe the ways in which professional occupations organize themselves (Mills, 1959: 169–173). One of the characteristic aspects of those employed in the professions is precisely their self-image as being in an independent work situation subject to their own control. As Gouldner (1979) and Perkin (1989) were to emphasize later, the image of a cheerful robot working as a salaried employee in a corporate or state bureaucracy is only a small and *declining* aspect of the professional sector. By and large professionals control their own work situation and enter into the labour market with greater freedom than a cheerful robot could. As we shall see later, this point has a direct bearing on the rise of advanced liberal views of government and neoliberal technologies of government.

The second problem concerns Mills' conception of property. By claiming that occupation replaced property as a source of wealth, Mills conflated occupation as a form of capital with occupation as a possession. Modern professional occupations are not held as hereditary offices. Rather, managers and professionals market their skills and education in search of positions which they then occupy. Many professionals are highly mobile, and accumulate not offices or occupations but skills, expertise, symbolic products, habits and education—in short, cultural capital. They use their cultural capital as leverage for mobility. In advanced capitalism, occupation is not a form of property but a form of realized capital. In different forms, property still plays a significant role. In fact, as Bourdieu (1986) emphasized, one of the crucial aspects of advanced capitalism is the ways in which one form of capital is transformed into another.

The third problem with Mills' analysis is his conflation of service and clerical workers with managerial and professional occupations. That service and clerical occupations allow very little chance for accumulation of cultural or other forms of capital and that they require little use of cultural capital as a requirement of entry into the market are decisive differences. The new class based on cultural capital should be kept separate from the clerical and service workers, who may be considered to constitute a new rising working class.

We believe Mills, as a reflexive sociologist, was aware of the pitfalls of his classification. He knew that developing a class analysis of advanced capitalism would be fraught with difficulties. He knew, too, that a classification struggle was being waged, variously announcing the emergence of a socialist revolution, or a revival of liberalism (Mills, 1995: 205). Mills was aware of the classification struggles of which he was a part. Thus, he strategically opted to leave the trajectory of the new class open to various alternatives. He did not rule out a trajectory in which the new class, or a crucial segment of it, could wrest power from the other classes and develop into a new ruling class. Alternatively, he also considered the possibility that the new class would continue to grow but remain as salaried, dependent employees of large bureaucracies. Another alternative he discussed was that the new class was really not new at all, but a faction of the bourgeoisie and would remain so for the foreseeable future. Lastly, he did not dismiss the Marxist alternative that the new class would become the new wage-earning class with political aspirations, a trajectory chronicled by Djilas (1957).

Within two decades after Mills, both Bell and Gouldner, albeit in different ways, were convinced that the first trajectory considered by Mills had become a reality: the new middle classes had developed into a new ruling class. In his well-known grand narrative, Bell's originality was to have interpreted the occupational shift documented by Mills as an indication of a broader shift to a postindustrial society. If, broadly speaking, industrial society was based on machine technology geared towards fabricating, postindustrial society was shaped by an intellectual technology, geared towards processing it strategically for the exchange of information and knowledge (Bell, 1973: xii–xiii). If capital and labour are the major structural features of industrial society, information and knowledge are those of the postindustrial society. According to Bell, then, the centrality of knowledge was a prominent aspect of the postindustrial society. Associated with it, he saw the rise of a new knowledge class as being the trend behind the occupational shift Mills had discussed. Underlying this class shift was a radical shift from an economy that produced goods to one which produced personal, financial and other services.

Bell argued that the fastest growing occupational group in postindustrial society was the technical and professional strata, constituting a knowledge class (Bell, 1973: xvi). As such, the postindustrial society awards status less on the basis of inheritance or property than on education and skill, which Bell called the rise of 'meritocracy'. Broadly speaking, the knowledge class is made up of individuals with some higher education who handle tasks that require some certified competence. The knowledge class includes intellectuals and knowledge workers concerned with the creation, evaluation, transmission and application of knowledge (scientists, scholars, mathematicians, economists, jurists); the creators and critics of culture (novelists, painters, musicians and critics); appliers and transmitters of knowledge (doctors, lawyers, engineers, social workers, planners and social service workers), who are often organized as professions or guilds and have controlled entry requirements into each field; managers and administrators in corporations and enterprises, state bureaucracies and non-profit organizations; news and entertainment workers (reporters, journalists and broadcasters in the print and electronic media, film makers, other entertainment professionals) (Bell, 1979: 183). Following the centrality of knowledge and status based on merit, Bell argued that the emphasis on class in analysis should shift to what he called estates and situses, a set of functional and institutional orders as loci of political and economic position (Bell, 1973: 374–375). The functional estates are scientific, technological, administrative and cultural strata, while the institutional situses are economic enterprises, government bureaux, universities and research complexes, social complexes and the military. In the postindustrial society major conflicts would take place between the situs groups rather than between classes or status groups.

Alvin Gouldner, on the other hand, believed that a new class struggle was rising in Europe, North America, Japan and the non-Western world, as well as in the formerly communist countries. He was convinced that the class struggle that characterized the modern era in the last two hundred years between industrial capital and the working class was no longer the characteristic struggle in advanced capitalism. In a grand narrative, he described the rise of the new class, comprising intellectuals and technical intelligentsia, through several critical historical episodes. First, the rise of the new class was marked by its independence from the church, an episode of secularization. A second episode was the development of a new language outside Latin as the vernacular mode of expression among the intellectuals and intelligentsia. Another episode was the breakdown of the feudal and old regime system of patronage of intellectual work and a corresponding growth of a market for the knowledge products and services of the new class. These developments allowed the intellectuals and intelligentsia to lead relatively autonomous lives without close supervision and control. The new class rose originally in Europe, where its multinational character allowed the new class members life opportunities in other than their state of birth. This gave the new class, along with the 'universal' character of their products and service, an international outlook and ideology.

The decline of the patriarchal family and the rise of the nuclear family, while being an effect of the rise of the new class, in turn accelerated the entry of women into ranks of the new class. As well, there is an increasing difficulty experienced by family authority in imposing and reproducing its values and ideals in its children. Another aspect of this development is the rise of a mass public education system, which increases the influence of the state on education and dramatically curtails the role of the family. The public education system has thus become more cosmopolitan and universal and less local and specific. The modes of thought and speech inculcated in the public system, allow its graduates to join in the ranks of the new class by rendering it possible to act without higher authorities but on the basis of universal ideals. This situation-free language, accelerated by publishing and information technologies makes possible the definition of the social world by geographically, culturally and socially distant people, and renders definitions of the social world by the local elites and authorities less credible and legitimate. Gouldner called this situation-free language game a culture of critical discourse.

As such the new class, Gouldner argued, is neither a class of benign technocrats nor is it a master new class. Nor is it an ally of the old class in that it furthers its interests only through the moneyed class. Nor is it a servant of power as a subservient class to the old class. Instead, he regarded the new class as a flawed universal class, which is 'elitist and self-seeking and uses its special knowledge to advance its own interests and power, and to control its own work situation' (Gouldner, 1979: 7).

According to Gouldner, the new class was new in that it was neither like what he called the 'old moneyed class', nor was it arising from the ashes of an old class such as the working class. Although Gouldner never elaborated his notion of the old moneyed class (whether it consists of industrial bourgeoisie or aristocracy or nobility or a mixture), he argued clearly that the new class is a new cultural bourgeoisie because it is based on ownership, production and reproduction of cultural capital. But Gouldner did not claim that the new class had established its hegemony over other classes, nor did he imply that other classes had dissipated. In fact, the new class often accepts a subordinate status because it is consistent with its ideal and material interests. He then added that '[t]he new class's capacity to pursue its own aggrandisement and overcome the resistance of the old (moneyed) class, is, however, considerably greater than other subordinated classes' (Gouldner, 1979: 12). Although the new class was not a ruling class, it could conceivably become so in time. The influence of the new class, Gouldner insisted, was rising through its management and ownership of the means of production of knowledge. As well, the new class, while not going to the barricades, waged wars against the privileges of the old classes, the aristocracy and bourgeoisie. An important contribution of Gouldner was to have linked the rise of new social movements such as the environmental movement, the women's movement, the movement for social rights, struggles for freedom of speech, and the gay and lesbian rights movement with the rise of the new class (Eder, 1993; Gouldner, 1979: 17–18). His point was that the rise of these movements was closely associated with the changing class structure of advanced capitalism in which modern political parties were unable to accommodate and give voice to new political demands articulated by new groups.

Gouldner believed that the new class was evolving into a ruling cultural bourgeoisie. The reason he insisted on retaining the designation 'bourgeoisie' for the new class was because he argued that the new class arose out of the industrial bourgeoisie by using knowledge to increase productivity and power. It was inherent in its structure that the old class should bring the new class into existence insofar as the new class was at first either trained or employed under the old class enterprises and firms (18). Soon, however, the new class developed a culture of occupational professionalism, claiming autonomy, superiority and legitimacy. The new class was, therefore, a cultural bourgeoisie whose capital was not its money but its control over valuable cultures. For a systematic analysis of the new class Gouldner said a general theory of capital was needed where different forms of capital would be investigated. His plea was that 'what is required for the understanding of culture as capital is nothing less than a political economy of culture' (21).

As such capital is 'any produced object used to make saleable utilities, thus providing its possessor with *incomes*, or claims to incomes defined as legitimate because of their imputed contribution to economic productivity; these claims to income are enforced normally by withholding, or threatening to withhold, the capital-object' (21). Thus, education and credentials are as much capital as are factories and machines. Gouldner also made a brilliant connection on the identity of the concepts of culture and capital. When discussing August Comte, he noted that Comte described the origins of capital in labour, in the human capacity to produce more than it can consume, the surplus product, thus permitting its accumulation over generations and transmission through time. He said 'but this is exactly what is entailed by the anthropological concept of "culture." Comte was at that early juncture between political economy and sociology where cultural and capital were interchangeable, and where one might say that either capital *or* culture was "the basis of social development"' (25). Culture, however, becomes capital when there is *private* appropriation of the goods it produces, when it is protected by law. Culture becomes capital when incomes are set aside for those possessing culture, while denying these incomes to those lacking it. 'The provision of special incomes for those possessing any culturally acquired skill through wages, royalties, patents, copyrights, or credentialling is the capitalization of skill' (25).

With its ideal of professionalism, the cultural bourgeoisie aims to control the supply and limit the production of its cultural capital, and to remove any restriction on the uses for which its culture may be purchased. The new class, therefore, establishes its distinction and transmits its cultural capital through its culture of critical discourse, which is a historically evolved grammar of discourse concerned with justifying its assertions not by invoking authorities but by eliciting the voluntary consent of those addressed solely on the basis of arguments adduced. At first, the radical nature of this proposition is not readily apparent. But when one recalls that for millennia humans exercised power over each other only with the authority of gods, traditions and kings, the recency of a relatively situation-free speech, without the burden of authority behind the speech, is remarkable. The culture of critical discourse dethrones all authority, while it authorizes itself as the standard of all serious speech (O'Neill, 1995). The utterances of people can now effectively conceal their class position, and utterance of statements becomes impersonal, decontextualized and self-grounded. In other words, no class is more interested in declaring the death of class than the new class. As such, the culture of critical discourse differentiates the new class from the industrial bourgeoisie but also from the bureaucrats, the cheerful robots of command and control (Gouldner, 1979: 30).

Gouldner was certainly an original thinker but his grand narrative contained several flaws. First, his insistence on identifying the intellectuals with revolutionary potential and intelligentsia with conservative, although understandable as a political strategy, is problematic. Gouldner was concerned with formulating a new radical programme for the left by revealing its class situation. In so doing, he was very careful to salvage something for the intellectuals to consider the culture of critical discourse as forward-looking and progressive, if not revolutionary. His faith in the revolutionary intellectuals was ultimately a value judgement that cannot be demonstrated as false or true. But his judgement was not sound on the face of evidence he adduced concerning the ideal and material interests of the intellectuals to rule. It was he who labelled the new class the universal flawed class because while it establishes a critique of domination and escapes from tradition, it also bears the seeds of a new domination (83–85). How could he have anticipated that the new class would overcome its 'Platonic Complex, the dream of the philosopher king with which Western philosophy begins, the deepest wish-fulfilling fantasy of the new class' (65)? Gouldner's view of the new class as 'the best card history may have dealt us' is too grand a narrative to have theoretical adequacy or political feasibility.

Second, Gouldner reified the new class in that he ascribed actions to it. He said that 'since Marx did little to define "class" formally and connotatively, I feel similarly free not to make a scholastic issue of the matter' (8). This, however, begs the question as to why one must be bound by Marx and his conception of class. If Gouldner had turned his attention from his 'left but not young Hegelianism' to Weber's discussion of class he would have found a more fertile ground, as did Harold Perkin and Pierre Bourdieu. It is not that he was unaware of the problem. He dealt with the issue of the coherence of the new class by arguing that for a class to be defined, *contra* Bell, it need not be a cohesive class with explicit solidarity. Still, he argued, there were historic occasions where the new class acted in solidarity, such as against the Vietnam war and against fascism in the 1930s. He also said, 'The denial that the new class can ever act in a solidary political way because of its internal differentiation, reminds one of similar claims once made about women's or blacks' capacity to form politically effective status groups.' However, he went on to repudiate himself by claiming that 'classes themselves do not enter into active political struggle; the active participants in political struggle are usually organizations, parties, associations, vanguards. Classes are cache areas in which these organizations mobilize, recruit, and conscript support and in whose name they legitimate their struggle. Classes as such are never united in struggle against others' (31). Gouldner conflated the objective and subjective states of class.

Gouldner's innovation was to see the new class as based not solely on occupation but on a form of capital: cultural capital. Gouldner argued that '[w]ith the growth of public education, the accumulation and distribution of cultural capital is now no longer so tightly correlated with moneyed capital. A new class of the culturally advantaged is now created that is not as integrated with, and not as dependent on, the old class of the moneyed rich as it once was historically. Indeed, cultural capital increasingly controls resources requisite for the reproduction of moneyed capital, but the latter decreasingly control the resources for the reproduction of cultural capital' (27). As we have argued in Chapter 5, the recognition of cultural capital as a principle of new differentiation under advanced capitalism has a direct bearing on the relationship between citizenship and class in our era. Another significant contribution by Gouldner was his emphasis on the relative autonomy of the members of the new class through the culture of critical discourse. Gouldner went beyond the image of a cheerful robot caught in the bureaucratic machine and described the members of the new class as controlling their own work situation and maintaining a culture of critical discourse, which is also crucial to understanding how the new class is forcing a new conception of citizenship, based on cultural property rights.

Although his study concerns the rise of the professional class only in Britain, Perkin's work is useful here because his account is also roughly applicable to the North American development of the new class. Perkin begins with the premise that we now live in a society dominated by the professional ideal: 'Modern Britain, as elsewhere in the developed world, is made up of career hierarchies of specialized occupations, selected by merit and based on trained expertise' (Perkin, 1989: 2). While pre-industrial society was based on land as property, and industrial society on industrial capital, professional society is based on human capital created by education and enhanced by strategies of closure and control of the market. Perkin insisted that professional society was not a society dominated by professionals, in that they have not become the ruling class, but it is a society permeated by the professional social ideal cutting across classes and occupations. 'A social ideal is a model of how society should be organized to suit a certain class or interest and of the ideal citizen and his contribution to it' (3).

According to Perkin, pre-industrial society was permeated by the aristocratic ideal based on property and patronage, while industrial society was permeated by the entrepreneurial ideal based on capital and competition. The rival ideal of the working class, never achieving dominance in industrial society, was the ideal of labour and cooperation. 'The professional ideal, based on trained expertise and selection by merit, differed from the other three in emphasising human capital rather than passive or active property, highly skilled and differentiated labour rather than the simple labour theory of value' (4). Perkin argued that in every type of society, individuals struggle to earn income, gain power and achieve status by using the available means to do so. In every type of society, there have been professionals turning their human capital, based on skill and expertise, into other forms of capital. 'But only in postindustrial society have the professions as a whole been able to establish human capital as the dominant form of wealth' (6).

Unlike Mills and Bell, Perkin argues that property is not an object or a credit instrument. Although it has a specific meaning as the right to immediate use of tangible objects like a car, property is a right to a flow of income: rent, interest, profits, labour service or goods in kind. The professions transform a service or symbolic product into income yielding property by controlling the market in which their goods and services are supplied. Perkin is critical of Alvin Gouldner and Pierre Bourdieu for their conception of cultural capital by which investment in acquired knowledge and expertise yields a rate of return commensurate with material capital. Perkin argues that professional goods and services would generate only earned income, which may fall below or above the market value, without the control of a market. The transforming method is professional control of the market. 'When a professional occupation has, by active persuasion of the public and the state, acquired sufficient control of the market in a particular service, it creates an artificial scarcity in the supply which has the effect of yielding rent' (7). The value of professional goods and services will always be proportionate to the scarcity of the good or the service. Since the essence of property is the right to the flow of income, cultural capital, which is even more tangible than stock or shares, less destructible than many forms of material property, and capable of renewal through upgrading of skills, is certainly a form of property (8). The importance of recognizing cultural capital as a form of property is that it allows us to understand the relative autonomy of the professional, and hence, using Gouldner's term, the culture of critical discourse. Cultural capital provides the professional with the right, security and confidence to criticize and change society because his or her authority and right to income flow neither from patronage nor directly from the state.

Ultimately, Perkin provides no less a grand narrative than Bell or Gouldner. He claims that the gradual triumph of the professional ideal between 1880 and 1980 paved the way for the hegemony of cultural capital and the emergence of professional society. Perkin insists, however, there was a crucial difference between the hegemony of aristocratic or entrepreneurial ideals and that of the professional ideal. Whereas in every type of society citizenship was limited to a particular group with the ownership of landed property, in professional society citizenship became dissociated from landed property. It is this potential extension of ideal citizenship to the whole that is the unique aspect of professional society. However, professional society is neither egalitarian and committed to equality nor devoid of hierarchy. 'It is not a class society in the traditional sense of a binary model with a small ruling class exploiting a large underclass, but a collection of parallel hierarchies of unequal height, each with its own ladder of many rungs. In this way the inequalities and rivalries of hierarchy come to predominate over those of class' (9). As a result, in postindustrial society citizenship as a political practice loses its meaning or political usefulness. Instead, a specific position in the new professional hierarchy determines different political, social and property rights.

Perkin thus considers professional society not merely as the old-class society fitted out with a new ruling class but as a society structured around a different principle. Since the principle of the new society is the vertical career hierarchy rather than the horizontal connection of class, conflict takes the form of rivalries between different interest groups competing for resources. Here Perkin is much closer to Bell's description of estates and situses as rival arenas of postindustrial society. Among these rivalries, the most dominant struggle for resources is between those who benefit directly from government expenditure and those who see themselves as the source of that expenditure. Consequently, the chief rivalry in postindustrial society is between the public sector professions, those funded directly or indirectly by the state, and the private sector professions, chiefly the managers of private corporations. 'As the struggle between lord and peasant was the master conflict in feudal society and the struggle between capitalist and wage earner the master conflict in industrial society, so the struggle between the public and private sector professions is the master conflict of professional society' (10). Of course, this division leaves out a large number of professionals employed by non-profit organizations such as the universities, research institutes and centres, charitable organizations, policy centres and advocacy outfits. Perkin says that '[w]hich side of the divide their officials will lean towards will depend on their perception of how their incomes are derived and where their interests lie' (11). As a result, the political landscape in postindustrial society is fundamentally different than that of industrial society. Advanced capitalism is run by professionals and managers who are salaried employees and whose status and income differ only in degree from their counterparts in other sectors. Besides, other professionals employed in large government bureaucracies may be as powerful as their private counterparts. Yet professionals, politicians, sociologists, journalists, talk as if society is still divided principally into a small employing class of individual capitalists and an undifferentiated mass of wage earners.

With this analytical framework, Perkin raises an interesting and significant question: if the political landscape and class situation of postindustrial society is so different from industrial society, why is the political discourse still dominated by the terms of industrial society such as the 'left' versus 'right' or 'capitalist' versus 'working class'? According to Perkin, 'The answer to the puzzle is that the old rhetoric of class happens to suit the protagonists of the master conflict of professional society. The ideology of the free market appeals to the professional managers of great corporations and their allies because it protects them from the accusation they most fear, that they themselves are the major threat to competition and the freedom of the citizen' (12). On the other hand, the rhetoric of the left suits the public sector professionals because doctors, lawyers, social workers, urban planners, professors and bureaucrats have a greater stake in maintaining and expanding government services than anyone else. As a result, once a service becomes professional under public auspices, there is a relentless pursuit and pressure to expand services into ever more minutely defined areas of everyday life. The rhetoric of left and right therefore effectively disguises what is happening in contemporary economy and society and helps to serve the professional ideal to legitimate its claim as though it were the universal social ideal (17).

In terms of the origins of the new class as Gouldner would describe it or the professional ideal as Perkin would define it, there is no disagreement between the two authors. Both see the origins of the professions in industrial production with its increasing division of labour and relentless pursuit of productivity by pressing knowledge into service (17–20). With respect to his criticism of Gouldner and Bourdieu on property, Perkin is unfair because both authors were keenly aware that the key to the accumulation of cultural capital is the control of the market. Perkin is in more agreement with Gouldner and Bourdieu than he acknowledges. However, where Perkin differs from both authors is in terms of seeing the postindustrial society beyond class divisions and permeated by the professional ideal as a new principle of division. Perkin carefully avoids entering the new class debate. As discussed earlier, this is a value judgement that cannot be interrogated.

To argue that in advanced capitalism all class struggles cease to exist and that the master struggle is between interest groups situated in different professional fields is certainly a plausible interpretation. But what Perkin considers as the master conflict in postindustrial society between public and private sector professionals can be considered as a struggle between two fractions of the new class, without slipping into a position where one must announce the disappearance of class conflict. There is plenty of evidence in Perkin's work to support such usage (455ff, 470ff).

This brief history of the classification struggles revolving around the 'new class' illustrates that there is considerable convergence on the need to recognize a radical change in the class relations engendered by advanced capitalism and that how to conceptualize this change is a contested terrain. We have particularly singled out a literature that has focused on the rise of a new class. Although, as Holton and Turner argued, it may be too early to constitute the professional-managerial groups as a new class and there are already signs of diverging interests, there is also evidence that the new class has consolidated itself in postcommunist societies (Eyal, Szelényi and Townsley, 1997).

Writing perhaps under the shadow of Marx, the 'new class theorists' have shown a tendency towards grand narratives. From the perspective of this book, in which our aim is to establish a relationship between new group identities and forms of citizenship, it is sufficient to accept that classes and groups based on cultural capital have become integral parts of production, consumption and exchange under advanced capitalism. At first assisted by the expansion of the welfare state, which was a response to the demands of the working class for social citizenship, in great state and corporate bureaucracies, a professional-managerial class with career hierarchies as its ideal has gained increasing influence and power. But, as we shall argue later, more recently, private sector professionals have been influential in instituting neoliberal regimes that dramatically reduced the welfare state. For the new professionals their political identity does not necessarily consist in their citizenship but in their professional engagement as a political practice. It is in their professional spheres that professionals pursue their political interests. This relationship between citizenship and the new class has been popularized by the Labor Secretary for the first Clinton administration, Robert Reich, and the management guru Peter Drucker. Reich (1992) argued that symbolic analysts (his term to designate the new class) constitute themselves as the 'information elite' and are highly deterritorialized and footloose. Their secession from specific cultures cultivates lifestyles of insulation and protection. Similarly, Drucker (1993) argues that the growing polarization between a 'knowledge class' and 'service class' and the increasing isolation and mobility of the former and exposure and immobility of the latter is creating new tensions. Among scholars it has become increasingly common to refer to a global elite, informational elite or knowledge elite (Castells, 1989, 1996; Cox, 1997; Sassen, 1991). More recently, Perkin (1996) also joined the global elite rhetoric.

We find this concept of a global power elite problematic. While highlighting an important feature of reflexive and flexible accumulation and globalization under advanced capitalism, the global elite theories are too concerned with concentration of power rather than its dispersal. By focusing only on the very powerful, on those whose overall volume of capital is the highest, the elite theories of power misrecognize the ways in which power is exercised by the less visible but perhaps more numerous agents of social change engendered by advanced capitalism. That is why the work of Bourdieu on specific modes in which cultural capital is linked with economic capital and the role of what he calls the cultural intermediaries has been an important contribution to studies of professional-managerial groups in advanced capitalism. The important role of cultural capital in circuits of production, reproduction and consumption highlights the rise of new class positions as objective possibilities rather than a homogeneous class with unified interests. This is nowhere more clear than in the field of consumption.

Consumption as Identity

With the advent of the argument that consumption has become a constitutive element of identity formation and of politics, some commentators have argued that citizenship should be freed from its exclusive connection with the state and associated with markets. An example of this argument was recently put forward by Saunders (1993), who tries to demonstrate that liberal citizenship governed by the market is inherently superior to state-centric models. He argues that a voucher system to allow citizens to become informed consumers would enhance their position as citizens rather than providing services directly for them. Similarly, albeit with a different political vision, Lash and Urry (1994: 309–310) have argued that a novel kind of 'consumer citizenship' is emerging whereby social agents increasingly constitute themselves as citizens by virtue of their ability to consume goods and services.

Within sociology until recently there was a dominant focus on production, with consumption accorded a secondary or subordinate status (Veblen being considered an exception). Consumption is thus considered somehow less important than the real world of production, industry, commerce and administration. While work is seen as noble and productive, consumption and leisure are commonly conceived—in the Protestant tradition—as less worthy, frivolous, even wasteful, indulgent or decadent (Weber, 1930). In addition to a moral judgement or moral worth, the passivity of consumers is congruent with notions of the passivity of women, and the traditionally male world of work privileged over the female domestic arena.

As we have seen earlier in our discussion of media and citizenship, this perspective is known as the 'mass culture critique' or the production of consumption perspective. Adorno and the Frankfurt School, writing in the inter-war period, argued that the expansion of mass production in the twentieth century had led to the commodification of culture, with the rise of culture industries. Consumption served the interests of manufacturers seeking greater profits, and citizens became the passive victims of advertisers. A materialistic culture emerged in which commodities lacked authenticity and instead merely met false or invented needs, which were generated by marketing and advertising strategies and increased the capacity for ideological domination. The shift came to be associated with the decline of the public sphere and the growing privatization of everyday lives. This perspective attributed to consumers a profoundly passive role, portraying them as manipulated, mindless dupes, rather than as active and creative beings.

As the story goes, sociology has now awakened from its slumber and no longer construes consumers as the passive victims of capitalism. While environmental movements questioned excessive consumption, sociology no longer sees consumption as evil or disempowering. Instead, in contrast with traditional approaches, the new perspective accords to consumers a more important and creative role. Rather than a passive, secondary, determined activity, consumption is seen increasingly as an activity with its own practices, tempo, significance and determination. Window-shopping becomes 'oppositional cultural practice', shopping becomes 'empowering and enhancing self-esteem', and consumption an instrument of 'subaltern empowerment'.

While this new perspective undoubtedly has strengths, it runs the risk of constituting consumers as free subjects in the sense of *sovereign* subjects with autonomous will. As we briefly discussed in Chapter 4, while it is important not to regard consumers as passive subjects, easily swayed by advertising and mass media, it is equally problematic to consider the consumer as a free subject who makes rational decisions in a competitive field without mediation of power relations. As Frank argues, the practitioners of this perspective 'often tend to limit their inquiries so rigorously to the consumption of culture-products that the equally important process of cultural production is virtually ignored' (Frank, 1997: 18–19). This view of the subject has been questioned in this book more than once. One of the major contributions of Foucault was precisely on this point: while he recognized subjects as active agents, he also stressed that subjects constituted themselves under constraints of power relations. The subject is always formed via two types of technologies: of power and of the self. This point has been usefully picked up by studies on governmentality, seeing the subject as neither a passive receptacle or bearer of structure nor a free and unmediated agent. Instead, technologies of government constitute subjects as active agents of their own destiny but implicate them in ever deeper and wider relations of power that constitute their habitus. We shall explore Bourdieu and studies on governmentality in more detail and focus on the relationship between identity and consumption.

Class and Consumption: Distinction

Bourdieu has had a major influence on the sociology of consumption. We have seen earlier how Bourdieu deploys the concepts of the four types of capital: social capital (family inheritance and networks), symbolic capital (reputation and honour), cultural capital (intellectual and educational qualifications) and economic capital (ownership of property, stocks and shares). We have added to this natural capital (renewable and non-renewable resources). The volume and combination of different forms of capital appropriated by individuals and groups place them in a specific class situation in social space. In Bourdieu's *Distinction*, these forms of capital—along with a battery of concepts he had worked out earlier such as habitus, fields and class—are brought to bear on the question of the production of consumption. His focus was specifically on the variation of consumption habitus across different classes and their fractions. Bourdieu attacked the pure or innate conception of cultural taste and illustrated its social and class origins by arguing that individuals literally learned to consume and that this learning was based upon membership in a particular class or fraction. He mapped out the legitimate cultural tastes and preferences in France in the 1960s and isolated their correspondence with class. By virtue of this mapping, he was able to argue, for example, that the working-class aesthetic was a dominated aesthetic, constantly obliged to define itself with reference to the dominant aesthetic. The working class was less able than the middle or upper classes to develop an autonomous aesthetic of judgement (Jenkins, 1992: 137–149). From the point of view of citizenship the significance of this argument is twofold. First, it opens up the sphere of cultural rights as a legitimate sphere of struggle and claim. The working classes are dominated not merely in the sphere of social rights but also in the cultural sphere, the latter perhaps determining the former. Bourdieu elaborated upon this point in his later work and made it clear that the symbolic universe of the working classes was dominated by professional groups and their interpretation of the world (Bourdieu, 1991a). Second, it allows us to make a new relationship between class and citizenship in a way anticipated by Marshall but never pursued and which remains latent in Bourdieu. That relationship is the significance of cultural capital in accessing citizenship rights.

Cultural capital is analysed by Bourdieu as existing in three different states. First, it refers to the cultivated dispositions that are internalized by the individual through socialization and that constitute schemes of appreciation and understanding. Cultural commodities differ from material commodities in that one can appropriate or consume them only by constructing their meaning. This means not only developing particular tastes and forms of recognition allowing one to classify and distinguish commodities, but also applying these categories to oneself by cultivating and incorporating certain manners, bodily movements, gestures and even specific ways of seeing, hearing and smelling. The embodiment of cultural capital, therefore, requires cultivation. The accumulation of cultural capital in its embodied form begins, therefore, in early childhood. It requires intervention and the investment of time by parents, other family members or professionals to make the child aware of cultural distinctions. The acquisition of cultivated dispositions presupposes distance from economic necessity and thus translates original class differences into cultural differences. The investment of inherited cultural capital returns dividends in school, rewarding those with large amounts of cultural capital and penalizing those without. This way of classifying the world becomes an instrument through which individuals also enact their tastes in the larger world than education such as in making spousal choices, hiring and being hired.

Second, cultural capital exists in an objectified form, referring to objects, such as books, works of art and scientific instruments, that require special cultural skills. Third, cultural capital exists in an institutionalized form, which is the educational credential system. Like Gouldner, Bourdieu places great importance upon the growth of the higher education system and the role it has come to play in the allocation of status in advanced capitalism. Expanded higher education has created massive credential markets that are decisive in reproducing the new class. Since educational credentials have become increasingly necessary for gaining access to job market, it become essential for parents to invest in a good education for their children so they can reap the profit on the job market. This process of investment involves the conversion of economic capital into cultural capital, which is a strategy more readily available to the more affluent. Bourdieu argues that the growth of the objectified and institutionalized forms of cultural capital has played a significant role in engendering new principles of class differentiation in advanced capitalism. As Swartz says, 'The unequal distribution of objectified and institutionalized cultural capital across social classes is for Bourdieu one of the key dimensions of social inequality in modern societies' (Swartz, 1997: 77).

The 'new petite bourgeoisie' or 'new intellectuals' are the class on which Bourdieu places particular emphasis. He argues that 'the new petite bourgeoisie comes into its own in all the occupations (sales, marketing, advertising, public relations, fashion, decoration and so forth) and in all the institutions providing symbolic goods and services. These include various jobs in medical and social assistance (marriage guidance, sex therapy, dietetics, vocational guidance, pediatric advice etc) and in cultural production and organization (youth leaders, tutors and monitors, radio and TV producers and presenters, magazine journalists) which have expanded considerably in recent years; but also some established occupations, such as art craftsmen and nurses' (Bourdieu, 1984: 359).

Here Bourdieu lumps various and diverse occupations into the category 'new petite bourgeoisie'. We have seen above that the 'new class' has been the subject of classification struggle since the 1940s, from Mills, who relied on even an earlier literature, to Gouldner, Bell and Wright, who tried to classify and describe the 'new middle class' (Szelényi and Martin, 1990; Vidich, 1995). Each successive wave has come up with a new label and description for occupational groups that compose this class, which gives a new meaning to 'classification struggles'—a term Bourdieu coined. We have also seen how the new class has been popularized as the new information or global elite, drawing upon elite theories. In more recent years, there has been a move away from defining these new groups as a new class and towards an analysis of various professions and para-professions that typically occupy the new middle-class positions. The new emphasis is on fractions and diversities in this class rather than commonalities (Longhurst and Savage, 1996). The emerging view is that the new middle class is sufficiently divided among different professions that it is more fruitful to analyse it in terms of its constituent fields than as one homogeneous class. Brint (1994), for example, argues that public sector professionals and private sector professionals (whom Bourdieu conflates in *Distinction*) have different conceptions of politics. Similarly, professional and para-professional occupations (which Bourdieu also conflates) or the old professions (law, medicine, academe) and the new professions (accountancy, brokerage, information technology specialists) have different habituses. Studies that focus on the professions as fields with distinct strategies for market closure, habitus and rationalities tend to be more useful in understanding the place of consumerism and politics in the mentalities of the agents in these professions than those that assume a homogeneous class (Ben-David, 1964; Freidson, 1994; Katz, 1972; Kellner and Heuberger, 1992; Macdonald, 1995; Parsons, 1939; Perkin, 1996).

Cultural capital and cultural intermediaries are crucial concepts to an understanding of why and how a cultural economy emerged in advanced capitalism such that even manufacturing is saturated with specific cultural practices. The new cultural economy has seen a proliferation of cultural intermediaries in advertising, design and marketing, perhaps as a consequence of the parallel rise of large multinational corporations that produce and distribute cultural commodities such as music, film, television, print media and computer software. As well, more and more commodities and services produced for consumers across a range of sectors can be conceived of as cultural commodities, in that they are deliberately inscribed with particular meanings and associations as they are produced and circulated in a conscious attempt to generate a desire for them amongst consumers. In other words, the cultural intermediaries link production to consumption and cultures of production to production of culture.

Liberalism, Advanced Liberalism and Governing Consumers

The term 'liberalism' is commonly used to describe a political philosophy that emerged in the nineteenth century. It refers to a set of distinctive features that exhibits its 'modernity' and marks it off from other modern intellectual doctrines and ideologies. These distinct features usually cluster around four elements: liberalism is individualist in that it asserts the moral primacy of the person against the claims of any social collectivity; it is democratic in that it confers on all citizens the same status before law; it is universalist in that it affirms the moral unity of human species and a secondary importance to specific historic associations and cultural forms; and it is progressive in that it affirms the corrigibility and improvability of all social institutions and political arrangements (Gray, 1995). Such a view is associated with diverse thinkers exhibiting branches of a common lineage but adhering to these four principles. Immanuel Kant, for example, may not be thought to have affinities with F.A. Hayek. Similarly, John Stuart Mill may be considered as an advocate of a very different liberalism than John Rawls. Nevertheless, liberalism adheres to a particular conception of a human being and a particular conception of polity where the demands of the latter are always in conflict with the former. Or, as in the work of Isaiah Berlin, this appears as a conflict between positive and negative forms of liberty. As we have seen, liberalism also is erroneously considered as the prevailing philosophy of government and politics in modern Western states—hence the term 'liberal democracies'.

As we have mentioned throughout the book, following Michel Foucault's work on governmentality, a number of authors have suggested a different usage of liberalism, emphasizing it as embodying various technologies of government. Foucault used the term 'technologies of power' to designate four types of technologies. First, *technologies of production*, which permit humans to produce, transform, or manipulate things. This usage parallels the conventional use of the term 'technology'. Second, technologies of sign systems, which permit humans to use signs, meaning, symbols or signification. Systems of writing, communication and advertising would be examples of these technologies. We can call this the *technologies of representation*. Third, *technologies of power*, which determine the conduct of individuals and submit them to certain ends or domination, an objectivizing of the subject. The disciplines which Foucault had analysed in *Discipline and Punish* would constitute such technologies of power. And, fourth, *technologies of the self,* which permit individuals to effect by their own means or with others a certain number of operations on their own bodies and souls, thoughts, conduct, so as to transform themselves in order to attain happiness, purity, wisdom, perfection or immortality (Foucault, 1988: 18).

Foucault argued that these four types do not function separately but each is associated with a particular type of domination and each implies certain modes of training in the sense of acquiring certain skills, attitudes and dispositions (Foucault, 1988: 19). Nevertheless, technologies of power and of the self constituted his main domain of research and he defined the contact between these two technologies as 'governmentality'. In a very well-known argument at the end of *The History of Sexuality* Foucault described the profound transformation in the West from old governmentality, which seized the right over death of subjects, to the liberal technologies of power, which seized the right over life of subjects (Foucault, 1978: 136–145). Or, in other words, 'the ancient right to *take* life or *let* live was replaced by a power to *foster* life or *disallow* it to the point of death' (Foucault, 1978: 138). More importantly, however, the power over life had evolved, according to Foucault, in two basic forms since the seventeenth century. First, it centred on the body as a machine: its disciplining, the optimization of its capabilities, the extortion of its forces, its usefulness and its docility. These procedures of power characterized the disciplines: a form of anatomo-politics of the body. The second, formed more clearly in the eighteenth century, focused on what Foucault called the species-body: its mortality, longevity, health and propagation. Foucault referred to the combination of these two foci as 'biopolitics' to describe the problems presented to ‘governmental practices by groups constituted on the basis of health, sanitation, birth-rate and race (Foucault, 1997: 73). Groups posed a significant challenge to nascent liberalism because '[i]n a system anxious to have the respect of legal subjects and to ensure the free enterprise of individuals, how can the "population" phenomenon, with its specific effects and problems, be taken into account? On behalf of what, and according to what rules, can it be managed?' (Foucault, 1997: 73). Foucault brilliantly articulated a tension in modern power that was both *individualizing* and *totalizing* at the same time. This meant an incessant tension between impulses for liberty and order, between technologies of power and technologies of the self, and governmentality as a constant incitement to govern in the sense of dealing with this tension.

The focus on liberalism as technologies of power is novel in that it construes individual liberty not as natural but as a product of 'government'. But the term 'government' here also follows Foucault in that it refers not simply to institutions and structures, and even less so to the party or regime in power, but to different modes through which individuals affect the conduct of other individuals: government as a general principle of conduct of conduct. In this view of government, the rules and principles that regulate a household, neighbourhood, municipality or state all embody government. Thus, individual liberty as defined in the nineteenth century is considered as an effect of a multiplicity of interventions concerned with the promotion of a specific form of bourgeois life. It exposes the nineteenth-century conception of liberty by specifying that it implies liberty of the male head of the household as responsible for less autonomous members, women and children. This was the bourgeois model of man that the young Marx (1977: 54) subjected to critique. The liberty of the individual is not a natural liberty but a particular form of responsibility towards governing the conduct of the self and others. Ultimately, then, liberalism refers not to a political philosophy but to the assemblage of techniques, rationalities, methods and instruments of government that constitutes individuals and influences their conduct (Burchell, 1996).

If we regard liberalism not as a philosophy but as an assemblage of practices of government, new possibilities for thought open up. Nikolas Rose (1996b) has suggested that liberalism was a response to a series of problems about the governability of individuals, families, markets and populations that arose out of the tension between the need to govern in the interests of order and in the interests of liberty in the nineteenth century. Associated with the rise of these problems was the rise of expertise in the sense of authority arising out of a claim to knowledge, to neutrality and efficacy, which came to provide a number of solutions to the tension between liberty and order. By a sheer explosion of statistical and other forms of knowledge, the governing authorities described in detail how the lifestyles of various groups (e.g., the working classes, the mentally ill, immigrants, hysterical women, unruly children) departed from expected and useful norms. The rise of sites for correcting such departures, such as hospitals, correctional facilities, prisons, housing projects and othei institutions, marked the characteristic form of government in the nineteenth century and the early twentieth century. What made liberalism governmental rather than theoretical, philosophical or moral was its wish to make itself practical, to connect itself up with various procedures and apparatuses of correction, inculcation and disposition.

Obviously, there is an affinity between liberalism as described and the rise of modern capitalism associated with the accumulation of 'private' wealth by self-interested individuals viewing the sovereignty of the state as an impediment to rather than an instrument for their pursuit. To see liberalism as an assemblage of governmental practices should not, however, lead one to assume a straightforward causal homology between liberalism and capitalism. As much as capitalism needed liberalism as a series of technologies of government, the rise of liberalism as a series of technics also made capitalism possible. Well before the rise of factories and factory discipline, for example, the early modern state practices of workhouse discipline made a major contribution to the discipline of the working classes. Labouring men and women were not found in cities looking for jobs; they were made into a class by various disciplines (Tilly, 1990).

As an array of technologies of government, the liberal form of rule relied on strategies, techniques and procedures through which different state authorities sought to enact programmes of government in relation to different groups and classes and the resistances and oppositions anticipated or encountered (Burchell, 1996; N. Rose, 1996a, 1996c). These technologies of government did not derive from a formula but were invented throughout the late eighteenth and nineteenth centuries in Europe and America. The more there was talk about the liberty of the 'bourgeois man', the more there was a proliferation of such techniques. The constitution of the self as an object of regulation, control and discipline was therefore the novel characteristic of liberal government. By constituting individuals as autonomous moral agents responsible for their destiny, liberalism invented self-government as a mode of regulation. At the centre of modern liberalism was the image, generated by a Protestant ethic, of a citizens as worker, whose identity was tied to his work (N. Rose, 1990: 102–103). The identity of the citizen-worker was firmly enshrined in production and derived its legitimacy from that realm.

Since the 1970s, however, the most powerful images of the economic function of the citizen have been decisively altered. From Sweden to New Zealand, we have experienced the rise of new mentalities of government. The primary focus of these mentalities has been to 're-engineer' the welfare state: the privatization of public utilities and welfare functions; the opening of health services, social insurance and pension schemes to markets; educational reforms to introduce competition between colleges and universities; the introduction of new forms of management into the civil service modelled upon an image of methods in the private sector; new contractual relations between agencies and service providers and between professionals and clients; and a new emphasis on the personal responsibilities of individuals, their families and their communities for their own future well-being and upon their own obligation to take active steps to secure this. In other words, we are seeing the emergence of a new 'governmentality'— the deliberations, strategies, tactics and devices employed by authorities for making up and acting upon a population and its constituents to ensure effective governance (N. Rose, 1996a).

The shift towards a new regime of governmentality has been called 'advanced liberalism' and its tactics, strategies and rationalities 'neoliberal' (N. Rose, 1996b, 1996c). Similarly, the much vaunted 'Protestant work ethic' has been gradually displaced with a consumption ethic. As Rose describes, this ethic cultivates a new image of the citizen: 'The primary image offered to the modern citizen is not that of the producer but of the consumer. Through consumption we are urged to shape our lives by the use of our purchasing power. We are obliged to make our lives meaningful by selecting our personal lifestyle from those offered to us in advertising, soap operas, and films, to make sense of our existence by exercising our freedom to choose in a market in which one simultaneously purchases products and services, and assembles, manages, and markets oneself. The image of the citizen as a choosing self entails a new image of the productive subject' (N. Rose, 1990: 102–103).

Thus, in the last decades of the twentieth century, a new programme of government has come to dominate liberal democracies. Consistent with the view that considers liberalism a political philosophy, neoliberalism has been defined by its fiscal conservatism, by the reduction of budget deficits that have been the hallmark of the activist welfare state and hence the reduction of the role of government in markets. The problem with this definition is that it focuses upon visible clues rather than broader shifts that envelop these specific instances. Some studies have shown, for example, that despite severe cutbacks in the public sector, government spending as a percentage of gross domestic product has actually continued to increase. From the perspective outlined above, if we consider neoliberalism as technologies of government, this apparently paradoxical empirical record may make more sense. In other words, it can be argued that neoliberalism has not been about less government but about shifting the techniques, focus and priorities of government.

Although various neo-conservative regimes have been elected in Britain, the United States, Canada and New Zealand since the 1970s, it would be misleading to suggest that these regimes had a clear political ideology or programme at the outset which they implemented. Rather, they initially sought to solve some perceived and real problems associated with finance, services and accumulation (Carpenter, 1995). But gradually, these diverse experiments were rationalized within a relatively coherent mentality of government that can be described as neoliberalism. Despite all the rhetoric of the reduction of government and the rollback of the state, neoliberalism has not abandoned its will to govern but merely shifted its focus, and, more importantly, rationalized some old techniques and invented new techniques of government. Therefore, the state in liberal democracies is perhaps stronger and more affective in more sectors than it was in the 1970s. And, yet, the image that persists is the decline of the state, if not its death. How can we account for this? What does it mean to govern in a neoliberal way?

Three characteristic shifts have been suggested with the rise of neoliberal technologies of government (N. Rose, 1996b, 1996c). The first shift concerns a new relationship between expertise and politics. While in liberalism knowledge had come to occupy a central role in government by virtue of its ability to raise claims to truth and validity in fields such as education, health and cities, the legitimacy and authority of new knowledges derive not from their truth and validity but from their ability to assess performance. Accordingly, there has been a shift from older occupations of law, medicine and academe to newer occupations of expert consultancy, accountancy and audit (Starr, 1987). If the modes of circulation of knowledges that animated liberal technologies of government were verity, validity and reliability, the new modes of circulation are enumeration, calculation, monitoring and evaluation. With this shift from older occupations to new ones, there is also a shift in the sites where education, training and certification take place (Stehr, 1994). Universities that traditionally educated and trained cadres of public sector professionals in law, medicine and administration are now pressured to shift to new occupations. As well, the new occupations shift their focus from the patient, the poor to the client and consumer, who are constituted as autonomous individuals capable of making the right choices (Brint, 1994). Risk reduction becomes an individual responsibility rather than a collective or state responsibility. Neoliberalism therefore constitutes the individual not as a subject of intervention but as an active agent of decision and choice. This is a significant shift in the production of subjectivities in that instead of disciplines, the field of choices and its structure becomes a contested arena of political struggle. This is partly why the new telecommunications media have come to play such a significant role in politics (Morley and Robins, 1995).

A second shift concerns the proliferation of new technologies of government. Evidenced by the rise of quasi-autonomous 'non-governmental' organizations, the new technologies arise out of the shifting of responsibilities from governmental agencies and authorities to organizations without electoral accountability and responsibility (e.g., the 'privatization' of 'public' utilities, the civil service, prisons, insurance and security). Again, with the proliferation of these technologies neither government nor its will to govern (nor its size) declines. Rather, this shift is about the manner in which individuals are constituted as subjects of government and the agents who are invested with the responsibility of governing.

A third shift concerns a new specification of the subject of government. The rise of the powers of the individual as client or customer of services specifies the subjects of government in a new way. Individuals are now constituted as active purchasers and enterprises in pursuit of their own choices: vouchers in education, housing and other services replace 'paternal' forms of distribution. As much as avoiding risk becomes the responsibility of individuals as authors of their own destiny, ill-fate and misfortune also become the responsibility of individuals: the unemployed, the homeless and the poor are constituted as responsible for their own condition.

Just as there were affinities with the rise of liberalism and capitalism, there are affinities with advanced liberalism and advanced capitalism. This has been associated with the rise of new classes variously described as the 'new class', the professional class or the information bourgeoisie (Clement and Myles, 1994; E.O. Wright, 1997). As we have seen, Gouldner and Bourdieu argued that the rise of new groups and classes based on the accumulation of cultural capital has changed the political arrangements and institutions in liberal democracies. The widespread adoption of neoliberal technologies of government undoubtedly favours private sector professionals. The point made by Perkin about the conflict between public sector and private sector professionals is relevant here (Perkin, 1989, 1996). Many aspects of the various neoliberal technologies shift responsibilities from the *paternalistic* state or public professions such as law, medicine and academe towards *entrepreneurial* professions that emphasize client and consumer control. Much of the move towards privatization does not really cost less in terms of delivering government services but shifts the control to these new professions. Brint has characterized this move as from 'social trustee professionals' to 'expert professionals' (Brint, 1994: 204). A similar homology can be construed between the rise of these new classes and groups and neoliberalism as a series of technologies of government.

Identities as Commodities: Consumer Culture or Citizenship?

With the fragmentation and proliferation of identities, is identity formation becoming a simulacrum where identities are consumed like commodities?

Especially with new identities emerging around groups of commodities and individuals being increasingly 'branded' by corporations, are cultural identities up for sale? Are neoliberalism, reflexive accumulation and the new cultural intermediaries different aspects of the process of globalization? This is where the postmodern analyses of consumption and identity run the risk of giving too much autonomy to the cultural sphere and to the autonomy of individuals. As du Gay argued: 'Having rescued consumption from the pessimism of the mass culture critique, certain forms of cultural analysis end up inverting the errors of earlier accounts. Instead of representing consumer behaviour through an exclusively productionist frame, these account project a vision of consumption practices as inherently democratic and implicitly "subversive"' (du Gay, 1996: 87). Or as Slater states: 'Being active in one's consumption—as opposed to being a manipulated mass cultural "dope"—does not mean being free (textually or socially) let alone oppositional' (Slater, 1997: 171). While not 'cheerful robots', individuals and their identities nevertheless are being formed under very complex and constraining conditions, ranging from reflexive accumulation to neoliberalism. To identify these constraints under which identities are formed is neither to condemn nor to condone but to specify dangers and possibilities. Citizenship, with its emphasis on rights and obligations centred on social struggles, can provide a corrective to such simple readings of consumption and identity.

In theorizing consumer culture, the notion of the postmodern, signifying an epochal shift, has become influential. The idea of a postmodern culture highlights some of the features of advanced capitalism such as the domination of knowledge-based production, media and signs, the disaggregation of social structure into lifestyles, the general priority of consumption over production in everyday life and the constitution of identities and interests. The postmodern culture thesis interprets the shift from manufacturing to service industries, the increasing importance of design, packaging and advertising in the production and consumption of commodities, the proliferation of an infusion of representations of commodities into everyday lives, and the increasing role of expertise in production and consumption as a shift towards a dematerialization of commodities (Slater, 1997: 193–194). In other words, the emphasis of the postmodern interpretation of culture is decisively upon the production and consumption of signs. The postmodern culture is then infused, on the one hand, with the circulation of non-material commodities ranging from advertising, information, databases to personnel and client relations management, producer services, planning and marketing functions and, on the other hand, with less labour being spent on transforming matter and more on imagineering. Business corporations now fancy themselves as purchasing not labour but commitment, personality, emotional warmth, personableness and sincerity, and selling not products but the fulfilment of desires, commitment, image and lifestyle. In fact, as du Gay (1996) argues, there is an increasing convergence between identity as worker and as consumer: workplaces cultivate an ethos of work and consumption at the same time.

Such analysis of postmodern consumer culture has been taken up by Featherstone (1991, 1995). While drawing upon elements of the Frankfurt School as well as Baudrillard, Featherstone arrives at an original account of consumerism. He uses Bourdieu to develop three distinct themes which earlier studies of consumerism neglected: that individuals are not passive consumers (in the way suggested by theorists of mass society) but are actively engaged in consumer practices; that such forms of activism could be seen as related to class strategies and habitus (and hence that they are not part of an undifferentiated 'mass'); and that the term 'lifestyle' could be used to understand the dynamics of consumer cultures (as individuals exercised agency to mould their consumer practices into distinctive patterns).

The dematerialization of commodities and the proliferation of identities as lifestyles have profound consequences for citizenship. The enormous speed-up in the circulation of different forms of capital and consumption in all phases and rates of investment and redeployment of capital, the rapid innovation and obsolescence of both producer and consumer goods, and style changes with 'hysterical velocities' have dislocated and disrupted stable identities. Many forms of instability, malleability and fluidity of identities are associated with the postmodern condition. It appears that in postmodern culture all modern identities such as based upon class, gender, race and ethnicity blur and disappear. As the new cultural economy becomes increasingly saturated with signs and their circulation, things lose their meaning as soon as they are invested with one and there can be nothing but endless choice among signs. The meaning of signs gets deterritorialized and disembodied from their context and circulate, hybridize, creolize and recirculate. In postmodern culture there emerges an irresolvable tension between sign and reality, or between signs and their referents. The signs can no longer be anchored in the finalities and realities of the world. As Slater puts it, 'as a result, contemporary experience is "depthless": there is nothing credible beneath or beyond the flat landscape of endless signification' (Slater, 1997: 197). As styles, references, images and objects circulate independently of their original context as signifiers, meanings become pastiches assembled and reassembled from different spaces and times with no immediate obligation to coherence or consistency.

Under such conditions the schizophrenic postmodern subject is unable to form a coherent and stable self and identity (Jameson, 1991). As a consumer, the postmodern subject experiences everyday life as a simultaneous and depthless surface composed of signs, the choice of which must happen without any reference. But at the same time, the postmodern consumer is ironic, knowing, reflexive and active. Therefore, the postmodern consumer, as Slater puts it, 'must have considerable cultural capital in order both to make sense of the wealth of mobile and detached signs and to be able to treat them as *just* signs; must obtain pleasure from the things themselves but form the experience of assembling and deconstructing images; must be free of obligations to finalities in order to keep in view the play of signs, and keep up with it' (Slater, 1997: 197–198).

In a society not only divided by wealth, status and power but also by gender, race, ethnicity and age, we would expect forms of culture and experience to be divided and differentiated too. Whose postmodern culture was the above account? Obviously, we do not believe that everyone living under advanced capitalism experiences culture in the way postmodern culture is described. The above account can be described as the self-image of the holders of cultural capital, the new class. Featherstone places a significant emphasis on the new class. However, instead of treating the new class as a homogeneous group, he singles out what Bourdieu calls the 'new cultural intermediaries' or the 'new intellectuals' (Featherstone, 1991: 44ff). These new cultural intermediaries are those artists and intellectuals who are engaged in providing symbolic goods and services in advertising, media, marketing and public relations. They are 'fascinated by identity, presentation, appearance, lifestyle, and the endless quest for new experiences. Indeed, their awareness of the range of experiences open to them, the frequent lack of anchoring in terms of a specific local or community, coupled with the self-consciousness of the autodidact, who always wishes to become more than he/she is, leads to a refusal to be classified, with the injunction to resist fixed codes as life is conceived as essentially open-ended' (Featherstone, 1991: 44). These broad currents were subsequently taken up by Lash and Urry (1994) and linked to advanced capitalism.

In accounts of postmodern culture, the producers of such accounts and interpretations, their material position in the social space, often disappear and we are led to believe that we are reading an account of postmodern culture without a perspective, without a position, seen with eyes from nowhere. But these eyes are located somewhere and their interpretation of culture is consistent with the rising classes in advanced capitalism. While it is argued that signs are no longer anchored in stabilities, finalities and consistencies, we are told that the postmodern culture is to be understood as 'post-responsibility'. There remains no possibility of citizenship, no right to make promises. Of course, this is the logical extreme or the opposite tendency of essentialism: identity becomes like a sign that can be chosen at will. Does such freedom really exist? While wishing to avoid the trap of determinism and essentialism, we would also argue that such freedom does not exist and identities are formed under very specific material conditions. Freedom consists not in imagining a hypothetical position, free from all constraints and conditions, but in recognizing, understanding and critically acting upon such constraints and conditions.

Cultural Citizenship

Let us draw together the key themes which have been developed through Chapters 5 and 6. We have now critically appropriated three distinct but in our view interrelated bodies of literature to analyse the types of citizenship advanced capitalism might engender and jeopardize. Theories of postfordism with their emphasis on flexible and reflexive modes of accumulation and regulation allow us to grasp the new structural dynamics of advanced capitalism and the dematerialization of production in the sense of a shift of emphasis from material production to images, sounds, symbols, information and signs. Theories of the new class, for all their tendencies towards grand narratives, nonetheless allow us to grasp better the new principles of class differentiation not only engendered by advanced capitalism as described by postfordist theories but also as conditioning factors for its rise. Theories of advanced liberalism allow us to recognize that transformations in advanced capitalism, particularly in methods of production and consumption, are accompanied by new technologies of government that make such transformations possible. In fact, these three perspectives—postfordism, cultural intermediaries and governmentality—allow us to see different but interrelated aspects of advanced capitalism. Under advanced capitalism the cultures of production and the production of culture are interwoven and the clear distinction between economy and culture may not be possible to sustain. The rise of 'culture' as a means of changing the way individuals relate to the work they perform and to their sense of self as consumer indicates that identity becomes a technology of government.

Cultural citizenship is not only about rights to produce and consume symbolic goods and services but also an intervention in this identity work. It is not only about redistributive justice concerning cultural capital but also about recognition and valorization of a plurality of meanings and representations. Moreover, as our discussions on technological citizenship and sexual citizenship have shown, individuals and groups are excluded from the cultural sphere on account of their lack of access not only to economic capital but also to cultural capital, which means much more than education but also includes competence, social and symbolic skills, and credentials. Although postmodernism can be said to have demolished the difference between high culture and low culture and may have established that consumers are more active in affirming their identities, this still does not mean that everyone has equal access to the means of production and consumption of culture. Following Perkin, Bauman noted that the professionals in many fields constitute subjects as passive recipients of their expert knowledge. In media, advertising, marketing, sports, politics, academe, arts, law and medicine the public is treated as a collection of objects to act upon (Bauman, 1995: 234). The aestheticization of everyday life that Featherstone describes as the habitus of the new cultural intermediaries is far from the lived experience of the working classes and other fractions of the middle classes in services, retail and manufacturing. Nonetheless, the new working classes cannot be reconstituted as victims when they have already been constituted as active agents of their destiny. Cultural citizenship is about becoming active producers of meaning and representation and knowledgeable consumers under advanced capitalism.

7

RADICAL CITIZENSHIP: FRAGMENTATION VERSUS PLURALIZATION

To breed an animal which is able to make promises. In order to have that degree of control over the future, man must first have learnt to distinguish between what happens by accident and by design, to think causally, to view the future as the present and anticipate it, to grasp with certainty what is end and what is means, in all, to be able to calculate, compute—and before he can do this, man himself will really have to become *reliable, regular, automatic,* even in his own self-image, so that he, as someone making a promise is, is answerable for his own *future*!

Nietzsche, *On the Genealogy of Morality*, II, 1

Introduction

We use the term 'radical citizenship' to describe the ethos of pluralization that underlies our approach in this book. While sympathetic to the expressed need for a deep or multilayered conception of citizenship, we hope that the political and theoretical difficulties of such a conception have also become obvious throughout this book. Can citizenship become an articulating principle to recognize group rights (Clarke, 1996; Mouffe, 1992c; Trend, 1996; Turner, 1994b)? A growing literature on radical democracy answers this question in the affirmative. But what are the dangers and possibilities of such a conception of citizenship? This chapter ends with a series of questions and openings towards rethinking the relationship between citizenship and identity. It recaps the debate over diasporic, consumer, sexual, technological, cultural, ecological and other identities, exploring the claim of a 'radical citizenship' and its ability to recognize such diverse identities.

Fragmentation, differentiation, dispersal and decentring of meaning and experience are recurring themes in this book. The late modern condition is interlaced with the structural transformations of modern capitalism that move us towards new forms of production, distribution, regulation and consumption. Scholars such as Harvey (1989), Lash and Urry (1994) and Jameson (1991) have investigated the fragmenting and disruptive effects of such transformations and they have called attention to the sensory overload resulting from massive proliferation of objects and signs in the sphere of consumption. Given these conditions, our experience has been described as disjunctive and jarring, disturbingly incongruous, and beset by multiplicity and fluidity. Others, such as Baudrillard (1987) and Lyotard (1984), have found such fragmentation to be potentially promising, even liberating. While having drawn our attention to structural changes, these analyses of contemporary social and cultural experience overlook two important issues. First, whether condoning or condemning such fragmentation in social and cultural experience, many neglect to recognize that these experiences are not universal but distinctive to particular groups or classes. It is remarkable that even those who argue against universals should assume that the experiences they describe are shared by everyone. Furthermore, experiences are not fragmented in a haphazard and accidental way but differentiated along the fractures of social space such as class, gender, ethnicity, sexuality, race, place and age. Second, these experiences have also engendered their own counter-tendencies of a search for origins and unitary identities.

There is, then, a crucial distinction to be made between fragmentation and pluralization. While such disruptive and disjunctive forms are present, we have argued in this book that the new social movements and the resultant cultural politics in the past three decades have propagated numerous social, political, cultural and social groups in search of new kinds of identification, politicization and solidarity. To recognize only *fragmentation* overlooks the resurgence of group *pluralization*. Robert Dunn refers to fragmentation and pluralization as two logics of postmodernity and argues that 'postmodernity generates both a sense of ephemerality and loss associated with cultural fragmentation *and* movements of cultural renewal as manifested in an expanded field of cultural and political practices' (Dunn, 1998: 144). To recognize only one logic at the expense of the other is to misrecognize the variety of experiences and subjectivities that arise under advanced capitalism. The late modern condition has, therefore, both destabilizing *and* restabilizing aspects. While academic and non-academic populism emphasizes fragmented identities, the new social movements can be seen as efforts to redefine and reconstitute identity through political and discursive struggles over group rights and values. As Dunn says, 'The frequent conflation of these distinct logics can be seen as a failure to adequately sort through the scattered democratizing tendencies of postmodern culture' (Dunn, 1998: 145).

The question facing us today, therefore, is not *whether* to recognize different ethnic identities or to protect 'nature' or to enable access to cultural capital or to eliminate discrimination against women and gays or to democratize computer-mediated communications, but *how* to do all and at the same time. Whether we like it or not, all this 'strange multiplicity' (Tully, 1995) is upon us, in all its forms at once. The question is how to imagine a postnational state in which sovereignty is intersecting, multiple and overlapping. Advanced capitalism, with its reflexive and flexible modes of production and regulation, is paradoxically the most important ally in raising the question. But it is also its most important impediment. The challenge we face today is to conceive of a new way of governing ourselves, a new way of being political under advanced capitalism. Both fragmentation and pluralization are inextricably associated with advanced capitalism. As Douglas Kellner observes, 'Capitalism must constantly multiply markets, styles, fads, and artifacts to keep absorbing consumers into its practices and lifestyles' (Kellner, 1995: 40). But, by doing so, advanced capitalism also disrupts older hierarchies and universalisms in favour of more particularistic appeals. In its relentless search for markets, it aims to fragment markets into segments for which production becomes feasible. The task for radical democrats is to harness the contradictory but democratizing tendencies of advanced capitalism towards new political arrangements and recognition of group rights. As Zweigenhaft and Domhoff (1998) have illustrated quite well for the United States, this is not an easy task: in many Western nations, despite three decades of struggles, women, gays, ethnic and racial minorities are still excluded from the corridors of power, status and wealth.

Limits of Modern Citizenship

Although the debate over globalization emphasized the declining sphere of influence of the modern nation-state, recent work on nations as imagined communities and their invented traditions highlights a significant fact: there is more to the nation-state than the state. Nationalism is a powerful imaginary that frames people's perception of their social and political space and identity (B. Anderson, 1991; A.D. Smith, 1996). Similarly, this cautious disposition towards the putative decline of the nation-state underscored the symbolic importance of citizenship as a national identity beyond being merely a legal status (Turner, 1994b). Without simplistically assuming that the nation-state is on the wane, nevertheless, it is equally important to recognize that postmodernization and globalization have imposed severe *upward* and *downward* limits on modern citizenship not only as a form of political and national identity but also as a legal status capable of mobilizing and accommodating the fragmented identities and groups of the late modern condition.

The new cultural politics has effectively questioned the master identity imposed by the modern nation-state. The most important political and constitutional challenge that lies ahead in democratic societies is to recognize diverse group rights in their constitutions (Tully, 1995). At the end of the twentieth century, modern citizenship as described by Marshall can no longer be considered an adequate framework (Turner, 1993a). What does it mean to be political in an age of postmodernization and globalization? What does it mean to be a citizen in an economy and culture of 'being digital' and 'being a consumer'? The question of citizenship arises from significant transformations towards the postmodern condition characterized by several, intertwined shifts since the 1970s: to an advanced capitalism where production of images, sounds, experiences and knowledge has become inseparable from the production of material commodities; to an increasingly global culture where the rise of a space of flows of such images, sounds, experiences and knowledge has integrated and incorporated different places across the globe; to a postmodern politics where the struggles over wealth, political status and access that characterized bourgeois and working-class politics throughout the nineteenth century and the first half of the twentieth century have been displaced by struggles over race, ethnicity, sexuality and ecology, represented by movements rather than traditional parties; to an increasing aestheticization of everyday life where consumption has become a constitutive aspect of identity formation.

In the West, every age since the ancient Greeks has fashioned a new image of the citizen. Above all, citizenship has expressed a right to deliberate with others and participate in determining the fate of the polity to which one belongs. Citizenship emerged as a series of practices (political, juridical and social) that define and constitute individuals as competent members of a polity. Modernity constituted the citizen essentially as a member of a nation-state and effectively juxtaposed nationality and identity as citizenship (Preuß, 1995). The modern nation-state and its sovereignty are being challenged by the rise of new groups and classes, the postmodernization and globalization of politics, economy, culture and society, and the rise of new technologies; these transformations effectively problematize the meaning of citizenship, given its fundamental link to the socio-economic structure of capitalism.

Globalization and Cosmopolitan Citizenship

There is considerable anxiety about the decline of the sovereignty of nation-states in formulating and implementing public policy independent of transnational corporations and organizations. It has been argued that with the rise of flexible or reflexive accumulation under advanced capitalism and the increasing globalization of production and consumption not only of industrial products, but also of financial, consultancy and legal services, the capacity of modern nation-states to regulate economic and social matters has been significantly curtailed (Harvey, 1989; Jameson, 1991). The debate over globalization, therefore, raised the issue of the changing status of the citizen as a member of the nation-state (Amin and Thrift, 1995; Falk, 1994; Held, 1995; Mlinar, 1992; Robertson, 1992; Sassen, 1996b). While globalization is a contested term and there are those who argue that the increased intensity and interconnectedness of flows is exaggerated, it is fairly safe to say that our age is global at least to the extent that it is marked by talk of globalization. At issue from the perspective of citizenship is really not so much the existence of 'globalization' as an objective process as the rise of the institutions of global regimes of governance (and their accountability) that redefine the rights and obligations of citizens as members of nation-states. Globalization cuts both ways. While it may be weakening the nation-state, it is also opening up new spaces for groups to enact new types of politics. Moreover, it is making it possible to raise new claims at the level of the nation-state.

Thus, it is important to recognize that while globalization has been often talked about as a process in which nation-states appear to be acting as pieces on a chessboard, much of the acting is done by agents whose dispositions and positions are different than either the modern bourgeoisie or the modern working class. There are new types of agents under advanced capitalism whose *modus operandi*, occupational status, lifestyle and social and political outlook are very different from what modern sociological and political theories have come to understand as classes. Variously labelled as the 'new class', 'information elite' or the 'knowledge class', the formation of these new identities is as important as the identities that flow from the new social movements (Eder, 1993). In fact, how each group is constituted via the other should be the proper object of sociological and political analysis. The reconfiguration of class and the rise of new groups based on occupation, lifestyle and outlook, civil, political, social and cultural rights are being negotiated anew (Glassman, 1995, 1997; Lash and Urry, 1987, 1994). Whether or not a cosmopolitan virtue will prevail over territorial claims to sovereignty will determine the types of cosmopolitan political regimes and arrangements that will arise in the next few decades.

Postmodernization and Cultural Citizenship

Parallel to the anxiety about globalization but distinct from it has been another anxiety about the decline of faith in democratic institutions and the rise of electoral cynicism, the aestheticization of everyday life and the rise of consumerism, fragmentation and pluralization of lifestyles, and the proliferation of tastes and identities. This debate has been captured by the term 'postmodernism', implying both a fundamental change in our era as well as the rise of a new way of thinking about that change (J. Anderson, 1996; Bauman, 1993, 1995; Best and Kellner, 1991; Bridges, 1994; Featherstone, 1991, 1992; Giddens, 1990, 1991; Lash and Friedman, 1992; McGowan, 1991). The interesting thing about the debate over postmodernity is that whether one is a critic or an advocate of 'postmodernism', the conditions it has described have become conditions of our existence: pluralization of identities, the decline of master narratives, fragmentation of worldviews and localization of critiques. At the same time, postmodernization has created its own counter-movements, engendering various religious, social, political and cultural groups. With the pluralization of identities and the rise of new forms of allegiances and loyalties, citizenship entails not only membership in the nation-state but also the right to participate in the cultural field both as a producer and as a consumer.

Consumer Citizenship and the End of History

There is no doubt that the collapse of 'actually existing socialism' in Eastern Europe and the Soviet Union, while prematurely celebrated by some as the end of history, had at least three significant and unexpected repercussions for democracy in the West (Ekins, 1992; Elkin, 1990; Habermas, 1992). First, the declaration that the new regimes that replaced socialist regimes were 'democracies' raised questions about democratic citizenship and government in the West in the sense of reminding the Western democrats how far 'actually existing liberalism' had moved away from liberal philosophy. Second, the democratic revolutions also brought out a crisis of identity in the West since it had been largely defined against its 'other'. With the disappearance of socialism and communism, Islamic fundamentalism began to fill this vacuum (Barber, 1995). It also spurred a search for new others (Huntington, 1996). Third, perhaps more importantly, its rapid movement, with shock-therapy neoliberalism, into Eastern Europe, coupled with the defeat of socialism as an alternative, has made capitalism much more aggressive on a world scale, particularly in Western countries. This has been accompanied with the rise of a new programme of government, neoliberalism, that dramatically attacked the welfare state in Australia, Britain, Canada, New Zealand and the United States and created a new consumer ethic, which has become the guiding principle of many governments. But, paradoxically, the new social movements, especially ecological movements, had already worked out a conception of environmentally conscious consumption to which socially and politically conscious consumption has been added. What may have begun as a drive towards consumer sovereignty in advanced capitalism can also move in the direction of consumer citizenship in which individuals constitute consumption as an active political, social and ecological practice.

New Ethics of Care and Ecological Citizenship

While the new ethics of care towards 'nature' is an important aspect of ecological citizenship, the struggle to strike a balance between social and ecological citizenship—between the ostensible rights of groups and 'rights of nature'—is perhaps the most significant battleground. We have raised serious doubts about the definition of rights for nature, but that does not mean that we advocate abandoning an ethic of care towards nature. The dilemma is to reconcile addressing the already existing class, ethnic, racial, gender and geographic inequalities with those demands of ecological justice, and articulate rights to nature rather than rights for or of nature.

New Social Movements and Sexual Citizenship

In the past two decades, feminist, gay and lesbian movements have demanded new rights, redefining the sphere and application of citizenship rights and creating new modes of political enactment and activism (Eder, 1993; Lyman, 1995). These movements have not only demanded new rights and extended the definition of citizenship rights but also redefined the very concept of being political. The politics of recognition in which new alliances and group solidarities have been formed on the basis of gender, ethnicity, sexuality, race and ecology is closely associated with the postmodernization of culture and it has splintered modern citizenship as a master identity. These movements have crystallized into powerful social and transnational networks which now constitute a significant aspect of politics in the West. Nevertheless, sexual citizenship faces uphill battles in the next century. Not only have the neoliberal governments mentioned above made these groups their first target for a new disciplinary regime, but constitutional and legal regimes have also been very slow in granting even basic rights such as common law partnerships for same-sex couples. As well, the struggles for rights have taken rather different trajectories for women and gays: while the former have made some gains, the latter face stiff resistance from the new right.

Computers and Technological Citizenship

The impact of digital information technologies on boundaries of what can be known, transmitted and permitted, thereby restricting the modern monopoly of nation-states in this sphere, certainly raises questions about what the nation-state can and cannot regulate regarding its citizens (Castells, 1989; Morley and Robins, 1995; Robins, 1988). In the 1990s, regulation of the Internet has become one of the main fields of social struggle among nations. Computer-mediated communications introduce new issues of privacy, accessibility, surveillance and other political, civil and social rights. While attention has been focused on the Internet and the possibilities and dangers of cyberdemocracy, the rapid proliferation of identification technologies also raises serious concerns about civil and political rights (McBeath and Webb, 1997; Tsagarousianou. Tambini and Ryan, 1998). These technologies of identification (and biology) are perhaps more significant than either surveillance technologies or even computer-mediated communications because they begin to blur the boundaries between the regulation and modulation of behaviour and push the cyborg metaphor onto a new plain. Technological citizenship is therefore not simply about how to harness new technologies for new forms of political enactment or about how to limit the uses of technology that encroach upon civil and political rights, but also about limiting the cybernetic use of modulating behaviour and defining identity.

Postcolonial Identities and Diasporic Citizenship

Movements of immigrants and refugees from economically depressed or politically repressed regimes to democratic societies, and the resultant tensions in definitions of 'inside' and 'outside', have raised critical questions about the extension of citizenship rights to immigrants and other aliens (Soysal, 1994). The struggles over the rights of 'minorities' in the United States, Canada, Australia and Europe are signs of such tensions. This has given rise to a whole new politics of multiculturalism and the rights of minorities (Anthias, 1993; Kymlicka, 1995; I. M. Young, 1990). While the rise of postcolonial identities and demand for new rights and the refusal of minority status have marked this new politics, the question is not simply to accommodate these new groups without a fundamental alteration of the old colonial and imperial political but how to radically alter such arrangements to recognize not minorities but differences (Tully, 1995). This is a major challenge because mainstream discourse does not even pose the question of recognition; or, to put it differently, even the acknowledgement of the question of recognition faces significant challenges in Western liberal democracies.

Global Cities and Urban Citizenship

It has become quite clear that globalization, telecommunications technologies, global immigration and social movements by and large impact specifically on cities and their ability to govern under these rapidly changing conditions (Featherstone, 1993; George, 1994; Harvey, 1993; A.D. King, 1990; Knight and Gappart, 1989; Sassen, 1991, 1994). But the issue is not merely how these broader political, social and economic transformations affect cities but also how cities function as strategic concentration nodes that facilitate or hinder the influence of various new groups and classes in the new global economy (Isin, 1996a). In other words, cities are not merely passive recipients of changes taking place above and beyond their spheres of control, but active participants in accelerating these trends outlined above (Isin, 1996b). The global city literature has arisen in response to this question in an attempt to rethink the city theoretically and to address the impacts of the social changes mentioned above (Friedmann and Wolff, 1982; Knox, 1993a, 1993b; Sassen, 1991; P.J. Taylor, 1995). A tendency in the global city literature has been to regard globalization as ˙a ubiquitous master force, wreaking havoc with local places. The actual process is much more complex than that and localities, particularly local professional-managerial groups, have been instrumental in establishing global networks and thus in articulating 'local' to the 'global'. Global cities are therefore neither a background against which 'globalization' occurs nor a foreground behind which various 'forces' struggle; rather, global cities have become a battleground in which various groups either raise rights-claims or are denied ability to raise such claims.

Coda

The distinctive calling of our time may well be the necessity to negotiate ouī way among the sometimes overlapping, sometimes conflicting identities, and to live with the tension to which multiple loyalties give rise. But the tension that this calling generates has engendered at least two dangerous responses in the West. First, a form of fundamentalism has taken over the social body which urges us to make sacrifices in the name of the absolute certainty of science, time-honoured traditions, non-negotiable beliefs and fixed identities. These new 'orthodoxies of unity' range from anti-immigrant backlashes to new forms of racism, but also afflict the very new movements that have opened up inclusive cultural politics. Radical citizenship is about ongoing vigilance against such tendencies. Second, another form of fundamentalism has arisen to claim, with an illusory lightness of being, that any identity is as good as any other and accessible to any and all. Thus, there is no durability nor relative permanence in our ability to make promises. By contrast, radical citizenship is about maintaining the right to have rights, the ability to make promises and commitment.

Here we have endorsed a third response: a critical responsiveness that embodies an ethos of pluralization. Such a critical responsiveness leads us to assert that if citizenship today is both a status and practice that includes practising safe sex, recycling and reducing waste, demanding social justice, responsible and ethical consumption, care for the self and others, engagement with ever-expanding spirals of politics, and respect, recognition and accommodation, without blinding ourselves with the stabilities and certainties of essential truths about ourselves or deluding ourselves into thinking about the possibilities of the unbearable weightlessness of limitless choices, radical citizenship must then mean discipline and principle. Radical citizenship as an ethos of pluralization must simultaneously mean an openness to multiplicity of identities *and* the recognition of the hard task of cultivating an ethic of making groups. What the new social movements have taught us is a generalization of Weber's conception of politics as a strong and slow boring of hard boards. The work of the citizen and the project of radical citizenship cannot be fulfilled without discipline and principles, without the hard work of activism and engagement, without the tedious but disciplined work of cultivating an ethos of difference/identity.

REFERENCES

Adorno, Theodor W. (1991) *The Culture Industry: Selected Essays on Mass Culture.* London and New York: Routledge.

Albrow, Martin (1996) *The Global Age.* Stanford, CA: Stanford University Press.

Amin, Ash, and Thrift, Nigel (1995) 'Territoriality in the Global Political Economy', *Nordisk Samhällsgeografisk Tidskrift, 20,* 3–16.

Anderson, Benedict (1991[1983]) *Imagined Communities* (2nd ed). London: Verso.

Anderson, James (1996) 'The Shifting Stage of Politics: New Medieval and Postmodern Territorialities', *Environment and Planning D, 14,* 133–153.

Anderson, Kay (1991) *Vancouver's Chinatown: Racial Discourse in Canada, 1875–1980.* Montreal and Kingston: McGill–Queen's University Press.

Anthias, Floya and Yuval-Davis, Nira in association with Cain, Harriet (1993) *Racialized Boundaries: Race, Nation, Gender, Colour and Class and the Anti-Racist Struggle.* London and New York: Routledge.

Anzaldúa, Gloria (1987) *Borderlands: The New Mestiza/La frontera.* San Francisco: Aunt Lute Books.

Applebaum, Anne (1994) *Between East and West: Across the Borderlands of Europe.* New York: Pantheon Books.

Ardener, Shirley (1981) 'Ground Rules and Social Maps for Women: An Introduction', in Shirley Ardener (ed.) *Women and Space.* London: Croom Helm in Association with the Oxford University Women's Studies Committee.

Bahar, Saba (1996) 'Human Rights are Women's Right: Amnesty International and the Family', *Hypatia, 11* (Winter), 105–134.

Balibar, Étienne (1995) 'Culture and Identity', in John Rajchman (ed.) *The Identity in Question.* New York: Routledge.

Bammer, Angelika (ed.) (1994) *Displacements: Cultural Identities in Question.* Bloomington: Indiana University Press.

Barber, Benjamin (1995) *Jihad vs. McWorld.* New York: Times Books.

Barbieri, William A. (1998) *Ethics of Citizenship: Immigration and Group Rights in Germany.* Durham, NC: Duke University Press.

Barry, Andrew, Osborne, Thomas, and Rose, Nikolas (eds) (1996) *Foucault and Political Reason.* Chicago: University of Chicago Press.

Bartelson, Jens (1995) *A Genealogy of Sovereignty.* Cambridge: Cambridge University Press.

Barth, Gunther (1982) *City People: The Rise of City Culture in Nineteenth-Century America.* Oxford: Oxford University Press.

Baudrillard, Jean (1987) *The Evil Demon of Images.* Sydney: Power Institute Publications.

Bauman, Zygmunt (1993) *Postmodern Ethics.* Oxford: Butterworth.

Bauman, Zygmunt (1995) *Life in Fragments: Essays in Postmodern Morality.* Oxford: Butterworth.

Bauman, Zygmunt (1996) 'From Pilgrim to Tourist–or a Short History of Identity', in Stuart Hall and Paul du Gay (eds) *Questions of Cultural Identity.* London: Sage.

Beall, Jo (ed.) (1997) *A City for All: Valuing Difference and Working with Diversity.* London: Zed Books.

Beiner, Ronald (1995) 'Why Citizenship Constitutes a Theoretical Problem in the Last Decade of the Twentieth Century', in Ronald Beiner (ed.) *Theorizing Citizenship.* Albany: State University of New York Press.

Bell, Daniel (1973) *The Coming of the Post-Industrial Society.* New York: Basic Books.

Bell, Daniel (1979) 'The New Class: A Muddled Concept', in B. Bruce Briggs (ed.) *The New Class?* New Brunswick, NJ: Transaction Books.

Ben-David, J. (1964) 'Professions in the Class System of Present-Day Societies', *Current Sociology, 12,* 247–330.

Benhabib, Seyla (1992) *Situating the Self: Gender, Community, and Postmodernism in Contemporary Ethics.* New York: Routledge.

Benhabib, Seyla (ed.) (1996) *Democracy and Difference: Contesting the Boundaries of the Political.* Princeton, NJ: Princeton University Press.

Bennett, Jane, and Chaloupka, William (1993) 'TV Dinners and the Organic Brunch', in Jane Bennett and William Chaloupka (eds) *In the Nature of Things: Language, Politics, and the Environment.* Minneapolis: University of Minnesota Press.

Berlant, Lauren Gail (1997) *The Queen of America Goes to Washington City: Essays on Sex and Citizenship.* Durham, NC: Duke University Press.

Berlin, Isaiah (1969 [1958]) 'Two Concepts of Liberty', *Four Essays on Liberty.* Oxford: Oxford University Press.

Best, Stephen, and Kellner, Douglas (1991) *Postmodern Theory: Critical Interrogations.* New York: Guilford Press.

Bhabha, Homi K. (1996) 'Culture's In-Between', in Stuart Hall and Paul du Gay (eds) *Questions of Cultural Identity.* London: Sage.

Birnbaum, Pierre (1997) 'Citoyenneté et identité: de T.H. Marshall à Talcott Parsons', *Citizenship Studies, 1* (1), 133–151.

Bissoondath, N. (1994) *Selling Illusions: The Cult of Multiculturalism in Canada.* Toronto: Penguin.

Black, Anthony (1984) *Guilds and Civil Society in European Political Thought from the Twelfth Century to the Present.* Ithaca, NY: Cornell University Press.

Blau, Francine D., Ferber, Marianne A., and Winkler, Anne E. (1998) *The Economics of Men, Women and Work* (3rd ed). Upper Saddle River, NJ: Prentice Hall.

Blunt, Alison, and Rose, Gillian (1994) *Writing Women and Space: Colonial and Postcolonial Geographies.* New York: Guilford Press.

Bok, Derek Curtis (1993) *The Cost of Talent: How Executives and Professionals are Paid and How It Affects America.* New York: Free Press.

Bondi, Liz (1990) 'Feminism, Postmodernism, and Geography: Space for Women?', *Antipode, 22* (2), 156–167.

Bookchin, Murray (1992) *Urbanization Without Cities: The Rise and Decline of Citizenship.* Montreal: Black Rose Books.

Boone, Joseph A. (1996) 'Queer Sites in Modernism: Harlem/The Left Bank/Greenwich Village', in Patricia Yaeger (ed.) *The Geography of Identity.* Ann Arbor: University of Michigan Press.

Bottomore, Tom (1992) 'Citizenship and Social Class', in Robert Moore (ed.) *Citizenship and Social Class.* London: Pluto.

Bourdieu, Pierre (1984 [1979]) *Distinction: A Social Critique of the Judgement of Taste.* Cambridge, MA: Harvard University Press.

Bourdieu, Pierre (1986) 'The Forms of Capital', in John G. Richardson (ed.) *Handbook of Theory and Research for the Sociology of Education.* New York: Greenwood Press.

Bourdieu, Pierre (1987) 'What Makes a Social Class? On the Theoretical and Practical Existence of Groups', *Berkeley Journal of Sociology*, *32*, 1–18.

Bourdieu, Pierre (1988 [1984]) *Homo Academicus*. Stanford: Stanford University Press.

Bourdieu, Pierre (1990 [1980]) *The Logic of Practice*. Stanford: Stanford University Press.

Bourdieu, Pierre (1991a) *Language and Symbolic Power*. Cambridge, MA: Harvard University Press.

Bourdieu, Pierre (1991b) 'Political Representation: Elements for a Theory of the Political Field', *Language and Symbolic Power*. Cambridge, MA: Harvard University Press.

Bourdieu, Pierre. (1996 [1989]) *The State Nobility: Elite Schools in the Field of Power*. Oxford: Polity Press.

Bourdieu, Pierre (1998 [1996]) *On Television*. New York: New Press.

Bourdieu, Pierre, and Wacquant, Loïc J.D. (1992) *An Invitation to Reflexive Sociology*. Chicago: University of Chicago Press.

Breslow, Harris (1997) 'Civil Society, Political Economy, and the Internet', in Steven G. Jones (ed.) *Virtual Culture: Identity and Communication in Cybersociety*. London: Sage.

Bridges, Thomas (1994) *The Culture of Citizenship: Inventing Postmodern Civic Culture*. Albany: State University of New York Press.

Brint, Steven (1994) *In an Age of Experts: The Changing Role of Professionals in Politics and Public Life*. Princeton, NJ: Princeton University Press.

Briskin, Linda, and McDermott, Patricia (eds) (1993) *Women Challenging Unions: Feminism, Democracy and Militancy*. Toronto: University of Toronto Press.

Brooks, David (1996) 'Class Politics versus Identity Politics', *The Public Interest*, *125*, 116–124.

Brown, Michael (1995) 'Ironies of Distance: An Ongoing Critique of the Geographies of AIDS', *Environment and Planning D: Society and Space*, *13*, 159–183.

Brown, Michael (1997) *RePlacing Citizenship*. New York and London: Guilford Press.

Brubaker, Rogers (1992) *Citizenship and Nationhood in France and Germany*. Cambridge, MA: Harvard University Press.

Brubaker, Rogers (1996) *Nationalism Reframed: Nationhood and the National Question in the New Europe*. Cambridge: Cambridge University Press.

Bruce-Briggs, B. (ed.) (1979) *The New Class?* New Brunswick, NJ: Transaction Books.

Bulmer, Martin, and Rees, Anthony M. (eds) (1996) *Citizenship Today: The Contemporary Relevance of T.H. Marshall*. London: UCL Press.

Burchell, David (1995) 'The Attributes of Citizens: Virtue, Manners and the Activity of Citizenship', *Economy and Society*, *24* (4), 540–558.

Burchell, Graham (1996) 'Liberal Government and Techniques of Self', in Andrew Barry, Thomas Osborne and Nikolas Rose (eds) *Foucault and Political Reason*. Chicago: University of Chicago Press.

Burchell, Graham, Gordon, Colin, and Miller, Peter (eds) (1991) *The Foucault Effect: Studies in Governmentality*. Chicago: University of Chicago Press.

Burnham, James (1941) *The Managerial Revolution*. New York: Free Press.

Burnheim, J. (1996) 'Power-trading and the Environment', *Environmental Politics*, *4* (4), 49–65.

Burris, Val (1995) 'The Discovery of the New Middle Classes', in Arthur J. Vidich (ed.) *The New Middle Classes: Life-Styles, Status Claims and Political Orientations*. New York: New York University Press.

Butler, Judith (1990) *Gender Trouble: Feminism and the Subversion of Identity*. New York: Routledge.

Button, James W., Rienzo, Barbara Ann, and Wald, Kenneth D. (1997) *Private Lives, Public Conflicts: Battles over Gay Rights in American Communities*. Washington, DC: CQ Press.

Çağlar, Ayşe S. (1997) 'Hyphenated Identities and the Limits of "Culture"', in Tariq Modood and Pnina Werbner (eds) *The Politics of Multiculturalism in the New Europe: Racism, Identity and Community*. London: Zed Books.

Calhoun, Craig (1994a) 'Social Theory and the Politics of Identity', in Craig Calhoun (ed.) *Social Theory and the Politics of Identity*. Oxford: Blackwell.

Calhoun, Craig (ed.) (1994b) *Social Theory and the Politics of Identity*. Oxford: Blackwell.

Callinicos, Alex (1989) *Against Post-Modernism: A Marxist Critique*. Cambridge: Polity.

Carpenter, Joe (1995) 'Regulation Theory, Post-Fordism and Urban Politics', in David Judge, Gerry Stoker and Harold Wolman (eds) *Theories of Urban Politics*. London: Sage.

Castells, Manuel (1989) *The Informational City: Information Technology, Economic Restructuring and the Urban Regional Process*. Oxford: Blackwell.

Castells, Manuel (1996) *The Rise of Network Society*. Cambridge, MA: Blackwell.

Castles, Stephen and Miller, Mark J. (1993) *The Age of Migration: International Population Movements in the Modern World*. New York: Guilford Press.

Chateauvert, Melinda (1998) *Marching Together: Women of the Brotherhood of Sleeping Car Porters*. Urbana: University of Illinois Press.

Churchill, Ward (1996) 'Like Sand in the Wind: The Making of an American Indian Diaspora in the United States', in Dennis Crow (ed.) *Geography and Identity: Living and Exploring Geopolitics of Identity*. Washington, DC: Maisonneuve Press.

Clarke, Paul Barry (1996) *Deep Citizenship*. London: Pluto.

Clement, Wallace, and Myles, John (1994) *Relations of Ruling: Class and Gender in Postindustrial Societies*. Montreal and Kingston: McGill–Queen's University Press.

Clifford, James (1994) 'Diasporas', *Cultural Anthropology*, 9 (3), 302–338.

Cohen, Jean L., and Arato, Andrew (1993) *Civil Society and Political Theory*. Cambridge, MA: MIT Press.

Colley, Linda (1992) *Britons: Forging the Nation, 1707–1837*. New Haven, CT: Yale University Press.

Commission on Global Governance (1995) *Our Global Neighbourhood*. Oxford: Oxford University Press.

Connolly, Clara (1993) 'Culture or Citizenship? Notes from the "Gender and Colonialism" Conference, Galway Ireland. May 1992', *Feminist Review*, 44 (Summer), 104–111.

Connolly, William E. (1988) *Political Theory and Modernity*. Oxford: Butterworth.

Connolly, William E. (1991) *Identity\Difference: Democratic Negotiations of Political Paradox*. Ithaca, NY: Cornell University Press.

Connolly, William E. (1995) *The Ethos of Pluralization*. Minneapolis: University of Minnesota Press.

Cook, Alice H., Lorwin, Val R., and Daniels, Arlene Kaplan (1992) *The Most Difficult Revolution: Women and Trade Unions*. Ithaca, NY: Cornell University Press.

Corvino, John (ed.) (1997) *Same Sex: Debating the Ethics, Science, and Culture of Homosexuality*. Lanham, MD: Rowman & Littlefield.

Cox, Robert (1997) 'Economic Globalization and the Limits of Liberal Democracy', in Anthony McGrew (ed.) *The Transformation of Democracy?* London: Open University Press.

Curran, James (1991) 'Rethinking the Media as a Public Sphere', in Peter Dahlgren and Colin Sparks (eds) *Communication and Citizenship: Journalism and the Public Sphere.* London: Routledge.

Dahlgren, Peter (1995) *Television and the Public Sphere: Citizenship, Democracy and the Media.* London: Sage.

Dahlgren, Peter, and Sparks, Colin (eds) (1991) *Communication and Citizenship: Journalism and the Public Sphere.* London: Routledge.

Davidoff, Leonore (1995) *Worlds Between: Historical Perspectives on Gender and Class.* Cambridge: Polity.

Davis, Ann (1997) 'The Body as Password', *Wired, 5* (7).

Davis, Susan G. (1986) *Parades and Power: Street Theatre in Nineteenth-Century Philadelphia.* Berkeley: University of California Press.

Delaney, C.F. (1994) *The Liberalism-Communitarianism Debate: Liberty and Community Values.* Lanham, MD: Rowman & Littlefield.

Deleuze, Gilles (1995 [1990]) *Negotiations.* New York: Columbia University Press.

de-Shalit, Avner (1995) *Why Posterity Matters: Environmental Policies and Future Generations.* London: Routledge.

Diop, A. Moustapha (1997) 'Negotiating Religious Difference: The Opinions and Attitudes of Islamic Associations in France', in Tariq Modood and Pnina Werbner (eds) *The Politics of Multiculturalism in the New Europe: Racism, Identity and Community.* London: Zed Books.

Dizard, Jan E. (1993) 'Going Wild: The Contested Terrain of Nature', in Jane Bennett and William Chaloupka (eds) *In the Nature of Things: Language, Politics, and the Environment.* Minneapolis: University of Minnesota Press.

Djilas, Milovan (1957) *The New Class.* New York: Praeger.

Downs, Laura Lee (1995) *Manufacturing Inequality: Gender Division in the French and British Metalworkers Industries, 1914–1939.* Ithaca, NY: Cornell University Press.

Drucker, Peter F. (1993) *Post-Capitalist Society.* New York: HarperCollins.

du Gay, Paul (1996) *Consumption and Identity at Work.* London: Sage.

Dunn, Robert G. (1998) *Identity Crises: A Social Critique of Postmodernity.* Minnesota: University of Minnesota Press.

Durkheim, Émile (1984 [1893]) *The Division of Labor in Society.* New York: Free Press.

Durkheim, Émile (1992 [1890–1900]) *Professional Ethics and Civic Morals.* London: Routledge.

Economist (1998) 'The Sinking of the MAI', 14 March.

Eder, Klaus (1993) *The New Politics of Class: Social Movements and Cultural Dynamics in Advanced Societies.* London: Sage.

Eder, Klaus (1996) *The Social Construction of Nature.* London: Sage.

Ekins, Paul (1992) *A New World Order: Grassroots Movements for Social Change.* London: Routledge.

Elkin, Stephen L. (1990) 'Citizenship and Constitutionalism in Post-Communist Regimes', *PS, 23* (June), 163–166.

Elliott, Philip (1972) *The Sociology of the Professions.* London: Macmillan.

Ericson, Richard Victor, and Haggerty, Kevin D. (1997) *Policing the Risk Society.* Oxford: Clarendon Press.

Erni, John Nguyet (1996) 'On the Limits of "Wired Identity" in the Age of Global Media', *Identities, 2,* 419–428.

Esping-Andersen, Gosta (1993) 'Post-Industrial Class Structures: An Analytical Framework', in Gosta Esping-Andersen (ed.) *Changing Classes*. London: Sage.

Evans, David T. (1993) *Sexual Citizenship: The Material Construction of Sexualities*. London and New York: Routledge.

Evans, Sara M. (1979) *Personal Politics: The Roots of Women's Liberation in the Civil Rights Movement and the New Left*. New York: Random House.

Eyal, Gil, Szelényi, Iván, and Townsley, Eleanor (1997) 'The Theory of Post-Communist Managerialism', *New Left Review*, *222*, 60–92.

Faist, Thomas (1994) 'How to Define a Foreigner? The Symbolic Politics of Immigration in German Partisan Discourse, 1978–1992', *West European Politics*, 17 (April), 50–71.

Falk, Richard (1994) 'The Making of Global Citizenship', in Bart van Steenbergen (ed.) *The Condition of Citizenship*. London: Sage.

Faulks, Keith (1998) *Citizenship in Modern Britain*. Edinburgh: Edinburgh University Press.

Featherstone, Mike (ed.) (1988) *Postmodernism*. London: Sage.

Featherstone, Mike (ed.) (1990) *Global Culture: Nationalism, Globalization and Modernity*. London: Sage.

Featherstone, Mike (1991) *Consumer Culture and Postmodernism*. London: Sage.

Featherstone, Mike (1992) 'Postmodernism and Aestheticization of Everyday Life', in Scott Lash and Jonathan Friedman (eds) *Modernity and Identity*. London: Blackwell.

Featherstone, Mike (1993) 'Global and Local Cultures', in Jon Bird, Barry Curtis, Tim Putnam, George Robertson, and Lisa Tickner (eds) *Mapping the Futures: Local Cultures, Global Change*. London: Routledge.

Featherstone, Mike (1995) *Undoing Culture: Globalization, Postmodernism and Identity*. London: Sage.

Featherstone, Mike, and Burrows, Roger (eds) (1995) *Cyberbodies, Cyberspace and Cyberpunk*. London: Sage.

Featherstone, Mike, Lash, Scott, and Robertson, Roland (eds) (1995) *Global Modernities*. London: Sage.

Figes, Kate (1994) *Because of Her Sex: The Myth of Equality for Women in Britain*. London: Macmillan.

Fishman, Robert (1995) 'Megalopolis Unbound', in Philip Kasinitz (ed.) *Metropolis: Center and Symbol of Our Times*. New York: New York University Press.

Flores, William Vincent, and Benmayor, Rina (1997) *Latino Cultural Citizenship: Claiming Identity, Space, and Rights*. Boston: Beacon Press.

Foley, Conor, and Wilkinson, Kate (1994) *Sexuality and the State: Human Rights Violations Against Lesbians, Gays, Bisexuals and Transgendered People*. London: Liberty National Council for Civil Liberties.

Forest, Benjamin (1995) 'West Hollywood as Symbol: The Significance of Place in the Construction of a Gay Identity', *Environment and Planning D: Society and Space*, *13*, 133–157.

Foucault, Michel (1978 [1976]) *The History of Sexuality: An Introduction*. New York: Vintage.

Foucault, Michel (1988) 'Technologies of the Self', in Luther H. Martin, Huck Gutman and Patrick H. Hutton (eds) *Technologies of the Self: A Seminar with Michel Foucault*. Amherst: University of Massachusetts Press.

Foucault, Michel (1997) 'The Birth of Biopolitics', in Paul Rabinow (ed.) *Ethics: Subjectivity and Truth* (Vol. 1). New York: New Press.

Foucault, Michel (1998a) 'Different Spaces', Paul Rabinow (ed.) *Aesthetics, Method, and Epistemology* (Vol. 2). New York: New Press.

Foucault, Michel (1998b) 'What is an Author?', Paul Rabinow (ed.) *Aesthetics, Method, and Epistemology* (Vol. 2). New York: New Press.

Foweraker, Joe, and Landman, Todd (1997) *Citizenship Rights and Social Movements: A Comparative and Statistical Analysis*. Oxford: Oxford University Press.

Frader, Laura L., and Rose, Sonya O. (eds) (1996) *Gender and Class in Modern Europe*. Ithaca, NY: Cornell University Press.

Frances, Rae (1993) *The Politics of Work: Gender and Labour in Victoria 1880–1939*. Cambridge: Cambridge University Press.

Frank, Thomas (1997) *The Conquest of Cool: Business Culture, Counterculture, and the Rise of Hip Consumerism*. Chicago: University of Chicago Press.

Frankenberg, Ruth (1993) *White Women, Race Matters: The Social Construction of Whiteness*. Minneapolis: University of Minnesota Press.

Franzoi, Barbara (1985) *At the Very Least She Pays the Rent: Women and German Industrialization, 1871–1914*. Westport, CT: Greenwood Press.

Fraser, Nancy (1997a) *Justice Interruptus: Critical Reflections on the "Postsocialist" Condition*. New York: Routledge.

Fraser, Nancy (1997b) 'A Rejoinder to Iris Young', *New Left Review*, 223.

Frazer, Elizabeth, and Lacey, Nicola (1993) *The Politics of Community: A Feminist Critique of the Liberal-Communitarian Debate*. Toronto: University of Toronto Press.

Freidson, Eliot (1994) *Professionalism Reborn: Theory, Prophecy, and Policy*. London: Polity.

Friedan, Betty (1970) *The Feminine Mystique*. New York: Dell Publishing.

Friedan, Betty (1991) *The Second Stage*. New York: Dell Publishing.

Friedman, Jonathan (1989) 'Culture, Identity and World Process', *Review*, *12* (1).

Friedmann, John (1995) 'Where We Stand: A Decade of World City Research', in Paul L. Knox and Peter J. Taylor (eds) *World Cities in a World System*. Cambridge: Cambridge University Press.

Friedmann, John, and Wolff, Goetz (1982) 'World City Formation: An Agenda for Research and Action', *International Journal of Urban and Regional Research*, 6, 309–344.

Frow, John (1993) 'Knowledge and Class', *Cultural Studies*, 7 (2), 240–281.

Frow, John (1995) *Cultural Studies and Cultural Value*. Oxford: Oxford University Press.

Gallagher, John, and Bull, Chris (1996) *Perfect Enemies: The Religious Right, the Gay Movement, and the Politics of the 1990s*. New York: Crown Publishers.

García Canclini, Néstor (1995) *Hybrid Cultures: Strategies for Entering and Leaving Modernity*. Minneapolis: University of Minnesota Press.

Gellner, Ernest (1983) *Nations and Nationalism*. Ithaca, NY: Cornell University Press.

George, Jim (1994) *Discourses of Global Politics: A Critical (Re)Introduction to International Relations*. Boulder, CO: Lynne Rienner Publishers.

Giddens, Anthony (1982) 'Class Division, Class Conflict and Citizenship Rights', *Profiles and Critiques and Social Theory*. London: Macmillan.

Giddens, Anthony (1990) *The Consequences of Modernity*. Stanford: Stanford University Press.

Giddens, Anthony (1991) *Modernity and Self-Identity: Self and Society in the Late Modern Age*. Stanford: Stanford University Press.

Gierke, Otto (1900) *Political Theories of the Middle Age.* Cambridge: Cambridge University Press.

Gierke, Otto (1934) *Natural Law and the Theory of Society, 1500–1800.* Cambridge: Cambridge University Press.

Gierke, Otto (1939) *The Development of Political Theory.* London: Allen and Unwin.

Gierke, Otto (1977) *Associations and Law.* Toronto: University of Toronto Press.

Gierke, Otto (1990) *Community in Historical Perspective.* Cambridge: Cambridge University Press.

Gilbert, Rob (1996) 'Identity, Culture and Environment: Education for Citizenship for the 21st Century', in Jack Demaine and Harold Entwistle (eds) *Beyond Communitarianism: Citizenship, Politics, and Education.* New York: St. Martin's Press.

Gilroy, Paul (1991) *'There Ain't no Black in the Union Jack': The Cultural Politics of Race and Nation.* Chicago: University of Chicago Press.

Gilroy, Paul (1993) *The Black Atlantic: Modernity and Double Consciousness.* Cambridge, MA: Harvard University Press.

Glassman, Ronald M. (1995) *The Middle Class and Democracy in Socio-Historical Perspective.* New York: Brill Academic Publishers.

Glassman, Ronald M. (1997) *The New Middle Class and Democracy in Global Perspective.* New York: St Martin's Press.

Glazer, Nathan (1997) *We are All Multiculturalists Now.* Cambridge, MA: Harvard University Press.

Gogwilt, Christopher Lloyd (1995) *The Invention of the West: Joseph Conrad and the Double-Mapping of Europe and Empire.* Stanford: Stanford University Press.

Goodnow, Jacqueline J. (1994) *Men, Women, and Household Work.* Melbourne and New York: Oxford University Press.

Gordon, Colin (1987) 'The Soul of the Citizen: Max Weber and Michel Foucault on Rationality and Government', in Sam Whimster and Scott Lash (eds) *Max Weber, Rationality and Modernity.* London: Allen and Unwin.

Gottdiener, Mark (1994) *The Social Production of Urban Space* (2nd ed). Austin: University of Texas Press.

Gottdiener, Mark, and Kephart, George (1991) 'The Multinucleated Metropolitan Region', in Rob Kling, Spencer Olin and Mark Poster (eds) *Postsuburban California: The Transformation of Orange County since World War II.* Berkeley and Los Angeles: University of California Press.

Gouldner, Alvin W. (1979) *The Future of Intellectuals and the Rise of the New Class.* New York: Oxford University Press.

Gouldner, Alvin W. (1985) *Against Fragmentation: The Origins of Marxism and the Sociology of Intellectuals.* New York: Oxford University Press.

Gower, Barry S. (1995) 'The Environment and Justice for Future Generations', in David E. Cooper and Joy A. Palmer (eds) *Just Environments.* London: Routledge.

Graham, Steven, and Marvin, Simon (1996) *Telecommunications and the City: Electronic Spaces, Urban Places.* London: Routledge.

Gray, John (1995) *Liberalism* (2nd ed). Minneapolis: University of Minnesota Press.

Grube, J. (1997) '"No More Shit": The Struggle for Democratic Gay Space in Toronto', in G.B. Ingram, A.M. Bouthillette and Y. Retter (eds) *Queers in Space: Communities, Public Places, Sites of Resistance.* Seattle: Bay Press.

Gutiérrez-Jones, Carl Scott (1995) *Rethinking the Borderlands: Between Chicano Culture and Legal Discourse.* Berkeley: University of California Press.

Habermas, Jürgen (1989 [1962]) *The Structural Transformation of the Public Sphere: An Inquiry into a Category of Bourgeois Society*. Cambridge, MA: MIT Press.

Habermas, Jürgen (1992) 'Citizenship and National Identity: Some Reflections on the Future of Europe', *Praxis International, 12* (1), 1–19.

Hacking, Ian (1986) 'Making Up People', in Christine Brooke-Rose and Thomas C. Heller (eds) *Reconstructing Individualism*. Stanford: Stanford University Press.

Hall, John R. (ed.) (1997) *Reworking Class*. Ithaca, NY: Cornell University Press.

Hall, Peter (1996) *Cities of Tomorrow: An Intellectual History of Urban Planning and Design in the Twentieth Century* (2nd ed). Oxford: Blackwell.

Hall, Stuart (1996) 'Who Needs "Identity"?', in Stuart Hall and Paul du Gay (eds) *Questions of Cultural Identity*. London: Sage.

Hall, Stuart (1997) 'The Local and the Global: Globalization and Ethnicity', in Anne McClintock, Aamir Mufti and Ella Shohat (eds) *Dangerous Liaisons: Gender, Nation, and Postcolonial Perspectives*. Minneapolis: University of Minnesota Press.

Hall, Stuart, and du Gay, Paul (eds) (1996) *Questions of Cultural Identity*. London: Sage.

Hannerz, Ulf (1990) 'Cosmopolitans and Locals in World Culture', in Mike Featherstone (ed.) *Global Culture: Nationalism, Globalization and Modernity*. London: Sage.

Hannerz, Ulf (1996) *Transnational Connections*. London: Routledge.

Haraway, Donna J. (1991) *Simians, Cyborgs, and Women: The Reinvention of Nature*. New York: Routledge.

Harvey, David (1985) *Consciousness and the Urban Experience*. Baltimore: Johns Hopkins University Press.

Harvey, David (1989) *The Condition of Postmodernity: An Inquiry into the Origins of Cultural Change*. Cambridge: Butterworth.

Harvey, David (1993) 'From Space to Place and Back Again: Reflections on the Condition of Postmodernity', in Jon Bird, Barry Curtis, Tim Putnam, George Robertson and Lisa Tickner (eds) *Mapping the Futures: Local Cultures, Global Change*. London: Routledge.

Harvey, David (1994) 'Flexible Accumulation through Urbanization', in Ash Amin (ed.) *Post-Fordism*. London: Blackwell.

Harvey, David (1996) *Justice, Nature and the Geography of Difference*. London: Blackwell.

Hatab, Lawrence J. (1995) *A Nietzschean Defense of Democracy: An Experiment in Postmodern Politics*. Chicago: Open Court.

Hayden, Delores (1981) *The Grand Domestic Revolution*. Cambridge, MA: MIT Press.

Heater, Derek (1990) *Citizenship: The Civic Ideal in World History, Politics, and Education*. London: Longman Group.

Heater, Derek (1996) *World Citizenship: Cosmopolitan Ideas in the History of Western Political Thought*. London: Macmillan.

Held, David (1995) *Democracy and the Global Order: From the Modern State to Cosmopolitan Governance*. Stanford: Stanford University Press.

Held, David (1997) 'Democracy and Globalization', *Global Governance, 3*, 251–267.

Heuberger, Frank W. (1992) 'The New Class: On the Theory of a No Longer Entirely New Phenomenon', in Hansfried Kellner and Frank W. Heuberger (eds) *Hidden Technocrats: The New Class and New Capitalism*. New Brunswick, NJ: Transaction Books.

Heyck, Denis Lynn Daly (ed.) (1994) *Barrios and Borderlands: Cultures of Latinos and Latinas in the United States*. New York: Routledge.

Hinsley, F.H. (1986) *Sovereignty*. Cambridge: Cambridge University Press.

Hobsbawm, E.J. (1990) *Nations and Nationalism since 1780: Programme, Myth, Reality.* Cambridge and New York: Cambridge University Press.

Hodges, David C. (1998) 'Post-Marxist Political Economy and the Culture of the Left', in Cynthia Willett (ed.) *Theorizing Multiculturalism: A Guide to the Current Debate.* Oxford: Blackwell.

Hoerder, Dirk, and Moch, Leslie Page (eds) (1996) *European Migrants: Global and Local Perspectives.* Boston: Northeastern University Press.

Hoerder, Dirk, Rössler, Horst, and Blank, Inge (eds) (1994) *Roots of the Transplanted.* New York: Columbia University Press.

Holt, Thomas C. (1992) *The Problem of Freedom: Race, Labor, and Politics in Jamaica and Britain, 1832–1938.* Baltimore and London: Johns Hopkins University Press.

Holton, Robert J., and Turner, Bryan S. (1989) 'Has Class Analysis a Future? Max Weber and the Challenge of Liberalism to *Gemeinschaftlich* Accounts of Class', *Max Weber on Economy and Society.* London: Routledge.

Honneth, Axel (1996a) *The Fragmented World of the Social: Essays in Social and Political Philosophy.* Albany, NY: State University of New York Press.

Honneth, Axel (1996b) *The Struggle for Recognition: The Moral Grammar of Social Conflicts.* Cambridge, MA: MIT Press.

hooks, bell (1981) *Ain't I a Woman: Black Women and Feminism.* Boston: South End Press.

hooks, bell (1989) *Talking Back: Thinking Feminist, Thinking Black.* Boston: South End Press.

hooks, bell (1990) *Yearning: Race, Gender, and Cultural Politics.* Toronto: Between-The-Lines.

hooks, bell (1992) *Black Looks: Race and Representation.* Toronto: Between-The-Lines.

Huntington, Samuel P. (1996) *The Clash of Civilizations and the Remaking of World Order.* New York: Simon & Schuster.

Ignatiev, Noel (1995) *How the Irish Became White.* New York: Routledge.

Isin, Engin F. (1992) *Cities without Citizens: Modernity of the City as a Corporation.* Montreal: Black Rose Books.

Isin, Engin F. (1996a) 'Global City-Regions and Citizenship', in David Bell, Roger Keil, and Gerda Wekerle (eds) *Global Processes, Local Places.* Montreal: Black Rose Books.

Isin, Engin F. (1996b) 'Metropolis Unbound: Legislators and Interpreters of Urban Form', in Jon Caulfield and Linda Peake (eds) *City Lives and City Forms: Critical Urban Research and Canadian Urbanism.* Toronto: University of Toronto Press.

Isin, Engin F. (1997) 'Who Is the New Citizen? Toward a Genealogy', *Citizenship Studies, 1* (1), 115–132.

Jackson, Kenneth (1985) *Crabgrass Frontier: The Suburbanization of the United States.* New York: Oxford University Press.

Jacobs, Jane M. (1996) *Edge of Empire: Postcolonialism and the City.* London and New York: Routledge.

Jacobson, David (1996) *Rights across Borders: Immigration and the Decline of Citizenship.* Baltimore: Johns Hopkins University Press.

Jacoby, Robin Miller (1994) *The British and American Women's Trade Union Leagues, 1890–1925: A Case Study of Feminism and Class.* Brooklyn, NY: Carlson Publications.

Jameson, Frederic (1991) *Postmodernism: Or the Cultural Logic of Late Capitalism.* Durham, NC: Duke University Press.

Janoski, Thomas (1998) *Citizenship and Civil Society: A Framework of Rights and Obligations in Liberal, Traditional, and Social Democratic Regimes.* Cambridge: Cambridge University Press.

Jenkins, Richard (1992) *Pierre Bourdieu.* London: Routledge.

Jenkins, Richard (1996) *Social Identity.* London: Routledge.

Jenkins, Richard (1997) *Rethinking Ethnicity: Arguments and Explorations.* London: Sage.

Jennings, Cheri Lucas, and Jennings, Bruce H. (1993) 'Green Fields/Brown Skin: Posting as a Sign of Recognition', in Jane Bennett and William Chaloupka (eds) *In the Nature of Things: Language, Politics, and the Environment.* Minneapolis: University of Minnesota Press.

John, Angela V. (1986) *Unequal Opportunities: Women's Employment in England 1800–1918.* Oxford: Blackwell.

Johnson, David R., and Post, David G. (1997) 'The Rise of Law on the Global Network', in Brian Kahin and Charles Nesson (eds) *Borders in Cyberspace: Information Policy and the Global Information Structure.* Cambridge, MA: MIT Press.

Joppke, Christian (1998) 'Multiculturalism and Immigration: A Comparison of the United States, Germany, and Great Britain', in David Jacobson (ed.) *Immigration Reader: America in a Multidisciplinary Perspective.* Oxford: Blackwell.

Jordan, Tim (1994) *Reinventing Revolution: Value and Difference in New Social Movements and the Left.* Aldershot: Avebury.

Kaplan, Morris B. (1996) *Sexual Justice: Democratic Citizenship and the Politics of Desire.* New York: Routledge.

Katz, Eric (1997) *Nature as Subject: Human Obligation and Natural Community.* Lanham, MD: Rowman & Littlefield.

Katz, M.B. (1972) 'Occupational Classification in History', *Journal of Interdisciplinary History,* 3, 63–88.

Keith, Michael, and Pile, Steve (eds) (1993) *Place and the Politics of Identity.* London: Routledge.

Kellner, Douglas (1995) *Media Culture: Cultural Studies, Identity and Politics Between the Modern and the Postmodern.* London: Routledge.

Kellner, Hansfried, and Berger, Peter L. (1992) 'Life-style Engineering', in Hansfried Kellner and Frank W. Heuberger (eds) *Hidden Technocrats: The New Class and New Capitalism.* New Brunswick, NJ: Transaction Books.

Kellner, Hansfried, and Heuberger, Frank W. (eds) (1992) *Hidden Technocrats: The New Class and New Capitalism.* New Brunswick, NJ: Transaction Books.

Kelly, Rita Mae (1991) *The Gendered Economy: Work, Careers, and Success.* London: Sage.

King, Anthony D. (1990) *Global Cities: Postimperialism and the Internationalization of London.* London: Routledge.

King, Anthony D. (1991) 'Introduction: Spaces of Culture, Spaces of Knowledge', in Anthony D. King (ed.) *Culture, Globalization and the World-System.* London: Macmillan.

King, Russell (1992) 'Italy: From Sick Man to Rich Man of Europe', *Geography,* 77 (April), 153–169.

Knight, Richard V., and Gappart, Gary (eds) (1989) *Cities in a Global Society.* London: Sage.

Knox, Paul L. (1993a) 'Capital, Material Culture and Socio-Spatial Differentiation', in Paul L. Knox (ed.) *The Restless Urban Landscape.* Englewood Cliffs, NJ: Prentice-Hall.

Knox, Paul L. (ed.) (1993b) *The Restless Urban Landscape*. Englewood Cliffs, N.J.: Prentice-Hall.

Kobayashi, Audrey (1993) 'Multiculturalism: Representing a Canadian Institution', in James Duncan and David Ley (eds) *Place/Culture/Representation*. New York: Routledge.

Krasner, Saul (1995) 'Compromising Westphalia', *International Security*, *20* (3), 115–151.

Kriesi, Hanspeter (1995) *New Social Movements in Western Europe: A Comparative Analysis*. Minneapolis: University of Minnesota Press.

Kwolek-Folland, Angel (1994) *Engendering Business: Men and Women in the Corporate Office, 1870–1930*. Baltimore: Johns Hopkins University Press.

Kymlicka, Will (1995) *Multicultural Citizenship*. Oxford: Oxford University Press.

Kymlicka, Will, and Wayne, Norman (1994) 'Return of the Citizen: A Survey of Recent Work on Citizenship Theory', *Ethics*, *104* (January), 352–381.

Laclau, Ernesto (1995) 'Universalism, Particularism and the Question of Identity', in John Rajchman (ed.) *The Identity in Question*. New York: Routledge.

Laguerre, Michel S. (1997) *Diasporic Citizenship: Haitian Americans in Transnational America*. New York: St Martin's Press.

Lash, Scott, and Friedman, Jonathan (eds) (1992) *Modernity and Identity*. London: Blackwell.

Lash, Scott, and Urry, John (1987) *The End of Organized Capitalism*. London: Polity.

Lash, Scott, and Urry, John (1994) *Economies of Signs and Space*. London: Sage.

Leca, Jean (1992) 'Questions of Citizenship', in Chantal Mouffe (ed.) *Dimensions of Radical Democracy: Pluralism, Citizenship, Community*. London: Verso.

Lecker, Robert (1991) *Borderlands: Essays in Canadian–American Relations*. Toronto: ECW Press.

Lefebvre, Henri (1996) *Writings on Cities*. Oxford: Blackwell.

Levy, Jacob T. (1997) 'Classifying Cultural Rights', in Ian Shapiro and Will Kymlicka (eds) *Ethnicity and Group Rights* (Vol. XXXIX). New York: New York University Press.

Lewis, Diane (1977) 'A Response to Inequality: Black Women, Racism and Sexism', *Signs*, *3* (2), 339–361.

Linklater, Andrew (1996) 'Citizenship and Sovereignty in the Post-Westphalian State', *European Journal of International Relations*, *2* (1), 77–103.

Lister, Ruth (1997a) *Citizenship: Feminist Perspectives*. New York: New York University Press.

Lister, Ruth (1997b) 'Dialectics of Citizenship', *Hypatia*, *12* (4), 6–26.

Littleton, James (ed.) (1996) *Clash of Identities: Essays on Media, Manipulation, and Politics of the Self*. Englewood Cliffs, NJ: Prentice-Hall.

Loader, Brian (1997) *The Governance of Cyberspace: Politics, Technology and Global Restructuring*. London: Routledge.

Longhurst, Brian, and Savage, Mike (1996) 'Social Class, Consumption and the Influence of Bourdieu: Some Critical Issues', in Stephen Edgell, Kevin Hetherington and Alan Warde (eds) *Consumption Matters*. London: Blackwell.

Lowe, Graham S. (1980) 'Women, Work and the Office: The Feminization of Clerical Occupations in Canada, 1901–1931', *Canadian Journal of Sociology*, *5* (4), 361–379.

Lyman, Stanford M. (ed.) (1995) *Social Movements: Critiques, Concepts, Case-Studies*. New York: New York University Press.

Lyotard, Jean-François (1984 [1979]) *The Postmodern Condition: A Report on Knowledge*. Minneapolis: University of Minnesota Press.

McBeath, Graham B., and Webb, Stephen A. (1997) 'Cities, Subjectivity and Cyberspace', in Sallie Westwood and John Williams (eds) *Imagining Cities: Scripts, Signs, Memory*. London: Routledge.

Macdonald, Keith M. (1995) *The Sociology of the Professions*. London: Sage.

McGowan, John (1991) *Postmodernism and Its Critics*. Ithaca, NY: Cornell University Press.

McGrew, Anthony (1997) 'Democracy beyond Borders? Globalization and the Reconstruction of Democratic Theory and Practice', in Anthony McGrew (ed.) *The Transformation of Democracy?* London: Open University Press.

Mackenzie, Suzanne (1986) 'Building Women, Building Cities', in Caroline Andrew and Beth Moore Milroy (ed.) *Life Spaces: Gender, Household, Employment*. Vancouver: University of British Columbia Press.

Macnaghten, Phil, and Urry, John (1998) *Contested Natures*. London: Sage.

Magnusson, Warren (1996) *The Search for Political Space: Globalization, Social Movements, and the Urban Political Experience*. Toronto: University of Toronto Press.

Maitland, Frederic W. (1898) *Township and Borough*. Cambridge: Cambridge University Press.

Malcomson, Scott L. (1994) *Borderlands: Nation and Empire*. Boston: Faber and Faber.

Mann, Michael (1987) 'Ruling Strategies and Citizenship', *Sociology, 21* (3), 339–354.

Manning, Nick (1993) 'T.H. Marshall, Jürgen Habermas, Citizenship and Transition in Eastern Europe', *World Development, 21* (August), 1313–1328.

Marcuse, Herbert (1964) *One-Dimensional Man: Studies in the Ideology of Advanced Industrial Society*. Boston: Beacon Press.

Marshall, T.H. (1981) 'Reflections of Power', *The Right to Welfare and Other Essays*. London: Heinemann.

Marshall, T.H. (1992 [1950]) *Citizenship and Social Class*. London: Pluto.

Marston, S.A. (1990) 'Who are "the People"? Gender, Citizenship, and the Making of the American Nation', *Environment and Planing D: Society and Space, 8*, 449–458.

Martínez, Oscar J. (1996) *U.S.–Mexico Borderlands: Historical and Contemporary Perspectives*. Wilmington, DE: Scholarly Resources.

Marx, Karl (1967a [1867]) *Capital: A Critical Analysis of Capitalist Production*. New York: International Publishers.

Marx, Karl (1967b) *Theories of Surplus Value*. Moscow: Progress Publishers.

Marx, Karl (1977) *Selected Writings*. Oxford: Oxford University Press.

Marx, Karl, and Engels, Friedrich (1967 [1848]) *The Communist Manifesto*. London: Penguin.

Massey, Doreen (1991) 'A Global Sense of Place', *Marxism Today*, June.

Massey, Doreen (1994) 'Double Articulation: A Place in the World', in Angelika Bammer (ed.) *Displacements: Cultural Identities in Question*. Bloomington: Indiana University Press.

Massey, Doreen (1995) 'Rethinking Radical Democracy Spatially', *Environment and Planning D: Society and Space, 13*, 283–288.

Matustik, Martin J. Beck (1998) 'Ludic, Corporate, and Imperial Multiculturalism: Imposters of Democracy and Cartographers of the New World Order', in Cynthia Willett (ed.) *Theorizing Multiculturalism: A Guide to the Current Debate*. Oxford: Blackwell.

Mayhew, Leon H. (1997) *The New Public: Professional Communication and the Means of Social Influence.* New York: Cambridge University Press.

Milkman, Ruth (1987) *Gender at Work: The Dynamics of Job Segregation by Sex during World War II.* Urbana: University of Illinois Press.

Miller, Toby (1998) *Technologies of Truth: Cultural Citizenship and the Popular Media.* Minneapolis: University of Minnesota Press.

Mills, C. Wright (1951) *White Collar.* Oxford: Oxford University Press.

Mills, C. Wright (1959) *The Sociological Imagination.* London: Oxford University Press.

Mills, C. Wright (1995 [1951]) 'The New Middle Class', in Arthur J. Vidich (ed.) *The New Middle Classes.* New York: New York University Press.

Mills, C. Wright, and Gerth, H.H. (1942) 'A Marx for the Managers', *Ethics: An International Journal of Legal, Political and Social Thought,* 52 (2).

Mlinar, Zdravko (1992) *Globalization and Territorial Identities.* Aldershot: Avebury.

Modood, Tariq, and Werbner, Pnina (eds) (1997) *The Politics of Multiculturalism in the New Europe: Racism, Identity and Community.* London and New York: Zed Books.

Morgan, Robin (ed.) (1984, 1996) *Sisterhood is Global.* New York: The Feminist Press at The City University of New York.

Morley, David, and Robins, Kevin (1995) *Spaces of Identity: Global Media, Electronic Landscapes and Cultural Boundaries.* London: Routledge.

Morris, Lydia (1994) *Dangerous Classes: The Underclass and Social Citizenship.* London: Routledge.

Morse, Margaret (1998) *Virtualities: Television, Media Art, and Cyberculture.* Bloomington: Indiana University Press.

Mouffe, Chantal (1992a) 'Democratic Citizenship and the Political Community', in Chantal Mouffe (ed.) *Dimensions of Radical Democracy: Pluralism, Citizenship, Community.* London: Verso.

Mouffe, Chantal (1992b) 'Democratic Politics Today', in Chantal Mouffe (ed.) *Dimensions of Radical Democracy: Pluralism, Citizenship, Community.* London: Verso.

Mouffe, Chantal (ed.) (1992c) *Dimensions of Radical Democracy: Pluralism, Citizenship, Community.* London: Verso.

Mouffe, Chantal (1993) *The Return of the Political.* London: Verso.

Mouffe, Chantal (1995) 'Democratic Politics and the Question of Identity', in John Rajchman (ed.) *The Identity in Question.* New York: Routledge.

Mouffe, Chantal (1996) 'Radical Democracy or Liberal Democracy?', in David Trend (ed.) *Radical Democracy: Identity, Citizenship, and the State.* London: Routledge.

Mulhall, Stephen, and Swift, Adam (1996) *Liberals and Communitarians* (2nd ed). Oxford: Blackwell.

Mumford, Lewis (1938) *The Culture of Cities.* New York: Harcourt, Brace and World.

Mumford, Lewis (1961) *The City in History: Its Origins, Its Transformations, and Its Prospects.* London: Harcourt Brace Jovanovich.

Nair, Sami (1996) 'France: A Crisis of Integration', *Dissent,* 43 (Summer), 75–78.

Nava, Michael, and Dawidoff, Robert (1994) *Created Equal: Why Gay Rights Matter to America.* New York: St Martin's Press.

Nederveen Pieterse, Jan (1995) 'Globalization as Hybridization', in Mike Featherstone, Scott Lash and Roland Robertson (eds) *Global Modernities.* London: Sage.

Neuman, W. Russell (1991) *The Future of the Mass Audience.* Cambridge: Cambridge University Press.

New, William H. (1998) *Borderlands: How We Talk About Canada*. Vancouver: University of British Columbia Press.

Nicholson, Linda (ed.) (1990) *Feminism/Postmodernism*. New York: Routledge.

Oakeshott, Michael (1975) *On Human Conduct*. Oxford: Oxford University Press.

Offen, Karen (1984) 'Depopulation, Nationalism, and Feminism in Fin-de-Siècle France', *The American Historical Review, 89* (June), 648–676.

Oldfield, Adrian (1990) *Citizenship and Community: Civic Republicanism and the Modern World*. London: Routledge.

O'Neill, John (1995) *The Poverty of Postmodernism*. London: Routledge.

Ong, Aihwa (1996) 'Cultural Citizenship as Subject-Making: Immigrants Negotiate Racial and Cultural Boundaries in the United States', *Current Anthropology, 37* (5), 737–763.

Oommen, T.K. (1997) *Citizenship, Nationality and Ethnicity*. London: Blackwell.

Pakulski, Jan (1997) 'Cultural Citizenship', *Citizenship Studies, 1* (1), 73–86.

Pakulski, Jan, and Waters, Malcolm (1996) *The Death of Class*. London: Sage.

Parr, Joy (1990) *The Gender of Breadwinners: Women, Men, and Change in Two Industrial Towns*. Toronto: University of Toronto Press.

Parsons, Talcott (1939) 'The Professions and Social Structure', *Social Forces, 17*, 457–467.

Peddicord, Richard (1996) *Gay and Lesbian Rights: A Question of Sexual Ethics or Social Justice?* Kansas City: Sheed & Ward.

Perkin, Harold (1989) *The Rise of Professional Society: England since 1880*. London: Routledge.

Perkin, Harold (1996) *The Third Revolution: Professional Elites in the Modern World*. London: Routledge.

Peterson, Cynthia (1996) 'Canada', in Rachel Rosenbloom (ed.) *Unspoken Rules: Sexual Orientation and Women's Human Rights*. London: Cassell.

Phillips, Anne (1997) 'From Inequality to Difference: A Severe Case of Displacement', *New Left Review*, 224, 143–153.

Phillips, Derek L. (1993) *Looking Backward: A Critical Appraisal of Communitarian Thought*. Princeton, NJ: Princeton University Press.

Pierson, Ruth Roach (1986) *"They're Still Women After All": The Second World War and Canadian Womanhood*. Toronto: McClelland and Stewart.

Pirenne, Henri (1925) *Medieval Cities: Their Origins and the Revival of Trade*. Princeton, NJ: Princeton University Press.

Poster, Mark (1997) 'Cyberdemocracy: The Internet and the Public Sphere', in David Holmes (ed.) *Virtual Politics: Identity and Community in Cyberspace*. London: Sage.

Preuß, Ulrich K. (1995) 'Citizenship and Identity: Aspects of a Political Theory of Citizenship', in Richard Bellamy, V. Buffachi and Dario Castiglione (eds) *Democracy and Constitutional Culture in the Union of Europe*. London: Lothian Foundation Press.

Rajchman, John (ed.) (1995) *The Identity in Question*. New York: Routledge.

Rawls, John (1996) *Political Liberalism*. New York: Columbia University Press.

Rees, Anthony M. (1996) 'T.H. Marshall and the Progress of Citizenship', in Martin Bulmer and Anthony M. Rees (eds) *Citizenship Today: The Contemporary Relevance of T.H. Marshall*. London: UCL Press.

Reich, Robert B. (1992) *The Work of Nations: Preparing Ourselves for Twenty-First-Century Capitalism*. New York: Vintage Books.

Rheingold, Howard (1993) *The Virtual Community*. Reading, MA: Addison-Wesley.

Rheingold, Howard (1996) Citizens' Databases Reveal Who Owns Who in D.C. http://www.well.com/user/hlr/tomorrow/mojowire.html.

Riberio, Gustavo Lins (1998) 'Cybercultural Politics: Political Acitivism at a Distance in a Transnational World', in Sonia E. Alvarez, Evelina Dagnino, and Arturo Escobar (eds) *Cultures of Politics/Politics of Cultures: Re-visioning Latin American Social Movements*. Boulder, CO: Westview Press.

Richardson, Boyce (1993) *People of Terra Nullius: Betrayal and Rebirth in Aboriginal Canada*. Vancouver: Douglas & McIntyre.

Riley, Denise (1990 [1988]) *Am I That Name? Feminism and the Category of Women in History*. Minneapolis: University of Minnesota Press.

Robertson, Roland (1992) *Globalization: Social Theory and Global Culture*. London: Sage.

Robins, Mark (1988) 'Electronic Spaces: New Technologies and the Future of Cities', *Futures*, 20 (2), 155–176.

Rocco, Raymond A. (1996) 'Latino Los Angeles: Reframing Boundaries/Borders', in Allen John Scott and Edward W. Soja (eds) *The City: Los Angeles and Urban Theory at the End of the Twentieth Century*. Berkeley, CA: University of California Press.

Roche, Maurice (1992) *Rethinking Citizenship: Welfare, Ideology and Change in Modern Society*. Cambridge: Polity.

Roediger, David (1991) *The Wages of Whiteness: Race and the Making of the American Working Class*. London: Verso.

Root, Maria P.P. (ed.) (1996) *The Multiracial Experience: Social Borders as the New Frontier*. London: Sage.

Rose, Gillian (1993) *Feminism and Geography: The Limits of Geographical Knowledge*. Minneapolis: University of Minnesota Press.

Rose, Nikolas (1990) *Governing the Soul: The Shaping of the Private Self*. London: Routledge.

Rose, Nikolas (1996a) 'The Death of the Social? Re-figuring the Territory of Government', *Economy and Society*, 25 (3), 327–356.

Rose, Nikolas (1996b) 'Governing "Advanced" Liberal Democracies', in Andrew Barry, Thomas Osborne and Nikolas Rose (eds) *Foucault and Political Reason*. Chicago: University of Chicago Press.

Rose, Nikolas (1996c) 'Government, Authority and Expertise in Advanced Liberalism', *Economy and Society*, 22 (3), 283–299.

Rosenau, James N., and Czempiel, Ernst-Otto (1992) *Governance Without Government: Order and Change in World Politics*. Cambridge: Cambridge University Press.

Ross, George (1978) 'Marxism and the New Middle Class', *Theory and Society*, 5, 163–180.

Rothblatt, Donald N., Garr, Daniel J., and Sprague, Jo (1979) *The Suburban Environment and Women*. New York: Praeger.

Ryan, Mary P. (1990) *Women in Public: Between Banners and Ballots, 1825–1880*. Baltimore: Johns Hopkins University Press.

Ryan, Mary P. (1997) *Civic Wars: Democracy and Public Life in the American City During the Nineteenth Century*. Berkeley: University of California Press.

Said, Edward W. (1978) *Orientalism*. New York: Random House.

Said, Edward W. (1993) *Culture and Imperialism*. New York: Vintage Books.

Sancton, Thomas (1997) 'Further Right', *Time*, 149 (March 10).

Sandel, Michael J. (1996) *Democracy's Discontent: America in Search of a Public*. Cambridge, MA: Harvard University Press.

Sandel, Michael J. (1998 [1982]) *Liberalism and the Limits of Justice* (2nd ed). Cambridge: Cambridge University Press.

Sandercock, Leonie (1998) *Towards Cosmopolis: Planning for Multicultural Cities.* New York: John Wiley.

Sassen, Saskia (1991) *The Global City: New York, London, Tokyo.* Princeton, NJ: Princeton University Press.

Sassen, Saskia (1994) 'Urban Impacts of Economic Globalization', in Engin F. Isin (ed.) *Toronto Region in the World Economy.* Toronto: York University.

Sassen, Saskia (1996a) *Losing Control? Sovereignty in an Age of Globalization.* New York: Columbia University Press.

Sassen, Saskia (1996b) 'Whose City Is It? Globalization and the Formation of New Claims', *Public Culture, 8*, 205–223.

Saunders, Peter (1993) 'Citizenship in a Liberal Society', in Bryan S. Turner (ed.) *Citizenship and Social Theory.* London: Sage.

Schlesinger, Arthur M. (1992) *The Disuniting of America.* New York: Norton.

Scott, Joan Wallach (1988) *Gender and the Politics of History.* New York: Columbia University Press.

Sennett, Richard (1974) *The Fall of Public Man.* New York: W.W. Norton.

Shafir, Gershon (ed.) (1998) *The Citizenship Debates: A Reader.* Minneapolis: University of Minnesota Press.

Shapiro, Ian, and Kymlicka, Will (eds) (1997) *Ethnicity and Group Rights.* New York: New York University Press.

Shelton, Beth Anne (1992) *Women, Men and Time: Gender Differences in Paid Work, Housework and Leisure.* New York: Greenwood Press.

Shields, Rob (1996) 'Virtual Spaces, Real Histories and Living Bodies', in Rob Shields (ed.) *Cultures of Internet.* London: Sage.

Shilts, Randy (1987) *And the Band Played On: Politics, People, and the AIDS Epidemic.* New York: St Martin's Press.

Silbergleid, Robin (1997) 'Women, Utopia, and Narrative: Toward a Feminist Postmodern Citizenship', *Hypatia, 12* (4), 156–177.

Siltanen, Janet (1994) *Locating Gender: Occupational Segregation, Wages, and Domestic Responsibilities.* London: UCL Press.

Simons, Margaret (1979) 'Racism and Feminism: A Schism in the Sisterhood', *Feminist Studies, 5* (2), 384–402.

Slater, Don R. (1997) *Consumer Culture and Modernity.* London: Polity.

Smith, Anthony D. (1986) *The Ethnic Origin of Nations.* Oxford: Butterworth.

Smith, Anthony D. (1996) *Nations and Nationalism in a Global Era.* Cambridge: Polity.

Smith, Michael Peter (1997) 'Looking for Globality in Los Angeles', in Ann Cvetkovitch and Douglas Kellner (eds) *Articulating the Global and the Local.* Boulder, CO: Westview Press.

Smith, Neil (1992) 'New City, New Frontier: The Lower East Side as Wild, Wild West', in Michael Sorkin (ed.) *Variations on a Theme Park: The New American City and the End of Public Space.* New York: Hill and Wang.

Soja, Edward W. (1992) 'Inside Exopolis: Scenes from Orange County', in Michael Sorkin (ed.) *Variations on a Theme Park: The New American City and the End of Public Space.* New York: Hill and Wang.

Soja, Edward W. (1996) *Thirdspace.* Cambridge, MA: Blackwell.

Soja, Edward W. (1997) 'Six Discourses on the Postmetropolis', in Sallie Westwood and John Williams (eds) *Imagining Cities: Scripts, Signs, Memory.* London: Routledge.

Sorkin, Michael (ed.) (1992) *Variations on a Theme Park: The New American City and the End of Public Space*. New York: Hill and Wang.

Soysal, Yasemin (1994) *Limits of Citizenship: Migrants and Postnational Membership in Europe*. Chicago: University of Chicago Press.

Spahr, Jane Adams (ed.) (1995) *Called Out: The Voices and Gifts of Lesbian, Gay, Bisexual, and Transgendered Presbyterians*. Gaithersburg, MD: Chi Rho Press.

Spain, Daphne (1992) *Gendered Spaces*. Chapel Hill: University of North Carolina Press.

Sparks, Holloway (1997) 'Dissident Citizenship: Democratic Theory, Political Courage, and Activist Women', *Hypatia, 12* (4), 74–110.

Spinner, Jeff (1994) *The Boundaries of Citizenship: Race, Ethnicity, and Nationality in the Liberal State*. Baltimore: Johns Hopkins University Press.

Stansell, Christine (1986) *City of Women: Sex and Class in New York, 1789–1860*. Urbana: University of Illinois Press.

Starr, Paul (1987) 'The Sociology of Official Statistics', in William Alonso and Paul Starr (eds) *The Politics of Numbers*. New York: Russell Sage Foundation.

Stasiulis, Daiva K., and Yuval-Davis, Nira (eds) (1995) *Unsettling Settler Societies: Articulations of Gender, Race, Ethnicity and Class*. London: Sage.

Steedman, Mercedes (1997) *Angels of the Workplace: Women and the Construction of Gender Relations in the Canadian Clothing Industry, 1890–1940*. Toronto: University of Toronto Press.

Steenbergen, Bart van (ed.) (1994) *The Condition of Citizenship*. London: Sage.

Stehr, Nico (1994) *Knowledge Societies*. London: Sage.

Stevenson, Nick (1997) 'Globalization, National Cultures and Cultural Citizenship', *The Sociological Quarterly, 38* (1), 41–67.

Strange, Carolyn (1995) *Toronto's Girl Problem: The Perils and Pleasures of the City, 1880–1930*. Toronto: University of Toronto Press.

Strong-Boag, Veronica (1991) 'Home Dreams: Women and the Suburban Experiment in Canada, 1945–60', *Canadian Historical Review, LXXII* (4), 471–504.

Swartz, David (1997) *Culture and Power: The Sociology of Pierre Bourdieu*. Chicago: University of Chicago Press.

Szelényi, Iván, and Martin, Bill (1990) 'The Three Waves of New Class Theories and a Postscript', in Charles C. Lemert (ed.) *Intellectuals and Politics*. London: Sage.

Takaki, Ronald T. (1993) *A Different Mirror: A History of Multicultural America*. Boston: Little, Brown and Company.

Tambini, Damian (1998) 'Civic Networking and Universal Rights to Connectivity: Bologna', in Roza Tsagarousianou, Damian Tambini and Cathy Bryan (eds) *Cyberdemocracy: Technology, Cities, and Civic Networks*. London: Routledge.

Tasmanian Gay and Lesbian Rights Group (1998) Current Campaigns. http://www.tased.edu.au/tasonline/tasqueer/tasqueer.html.

Taylor, Charles (1989) *Sources of the Self: The Making of the Modern Identity*. Cambridge, MA: Harvard University Press.

Taylor, Charles (1994) 'The Politics of Recognition', in Amy Gutman (ed.) *Multiculturalism: Examining the Politics of Recognition*. Princeton, NJ: Princeton University Press.

Taylor, Peter J. (1995) 'World Cities and Territorial States: The Rise and Fall of Their Mutuality', in Paul L. Knox and Peter J. Taylor (eds) *World Cities in a World System*. Cambridge: Cambridge University Press.

Thelen, David P. (1996) *Becoming Citizens in the Age of Television: How Americans Challenged the Media and Seized Political Initiative During the Iran–Contra Debate*. Chicago: University of Chicago Press.

Thomashow, Mitchell (1995) *Ecological Identity: Becoming a Reflective Environmentalist*. Cambridge, MA: MIT Press.

Tilly, Charles (ed.) (1990) *Coercion, Capital and European States: 990–1990*. Cambridge, MA: Blackwell.

Tilly, Charles (ed.) (1996) *Citizenship, Identity and Social History*. Cambridge: Cambridge University Press.

Tönnies, Ferdinand (1963 [1887]) *Community and Association*. New York: Harper and Row.

Trend, David (ed.) (1996) *Radical Democracy: Identity, Citizenship, and the State*. London: Routledge.

Tsagarousianou, Roza, Tambini, Damian, and Bryan, Cathy (1998) *Cyberdemocracy: Technology, Cities, and Civic Networks*. London: Routledge.

Tully, James (1995) *Strange Multiplicity: Constitutionalism in an Age of Diversity*. Cambridge: Cambridge University Press.

Turkle, Sherry (1995) *Life on the Screen: Identity in the Age of the Internet*. New York: Simon & Schuster.

Turner, Bryan S. (1986) *Citizenship and Capitalism: The Debate Over Reformism*. London: Allen and Unwin.

Turner, Bryan S. (1990) 'Outline of a Theory of Citizenship', *Sociology*, 24 (2), 189–217.

Turner, Bryan S. (ed.) (1993a) *Citizenship and Social Theory*. London: Sage.

Turner, Bryan S. (1993b) 'Contemporary Problems in the Theory of Citizenship', in Bryan S. Turner (ed.) *Citizenship and Social Theory*. London: Sage.

Turner, Bryan S. (1994a) *Orientalism, Postmodernism and Globalism*. London: Routledge.

Turner, Bryan S. (1994b) 'Postmodern Culture/Modern Citizens', in Bart van Steenbergen (ed.) *The Condition of Citizenship*. London: Sage.

Turner, Bryan S. (1997) 'Citizenship Studies: A General Theory', *Citizenship Studies, 1* (1), 5–18.

Turner, Stephen P., and Factor, Regis A. (1994) *Max Weber: The Lawyer as Social Thinker*. London: Routledge.

Ullmann, Walter (1968) 'Juristic Obstacles to the Emergence of the Concept of State in the Middle Ages', *Annali di Storia diritto*, *12–13*, 43–64.

Vaid, Urvashi (1995) *Virtual Equality: The Mainstreaming of Gay and Lesbian Liberation*. New York: Anchor Books.

Vidich, Arthur J. (ed.) (1995) *The New Middle Classes*. New York: New York University Press.

Voet, Rian (1998) *Feminism and Citizenship*. London: Sage.

Waaldijk, Kees and Clapham, Andrew (eds) (1993) *Homosexuality, a European Community Issue: Essays on Lesbian and Gay Rights in European Law and Policy*. Dordrecht: Martinus Nijhoff Publishers.

Walby, Sylvia (1986) *Patriarchy at Work: Patriarchal and Capitalist Relations in Employment*. Cambridge: Polity.

Walby, Sylvia (1990) *Theorizing Patriarchy*. Oxford: Blackwell.

Wald, Priscilla (1995) *Constituting Americans: Cultural Anxiety and Narrative Form*. Durham, NC: Duke University Press.

Walker, Brian (1997) 'Plural Cultures, Contested Territories: A Critique of Kymlicka', *Canadian Journal of Political Science, XXX* (2).

Walker, R.B.J. (1988) *One World, Many Worlds: Struggles for a Just World Peace.* Boulder, CO: Lynne Rienner Publishers.

Wallerstein, Immanuel (1995) 'The Insurmountable Contradictions of Liberalism: Human Rights and the Rights of Peoples in the Geoculture of the Modern World-System', *The South Atlantic Quarterly, 94* (Fall), 1161–1178.

Waters, Malcolm (1995) *Globalization.* London: Routledge.

Weber, Max (1927) 'Citizenship', *General Economic History.* London: George Allen & Unwin.

Weber, Max (1930 [1905]) *The Protestant Ethic and the Spirit of Capitalism.* London: Unwin.

Weber, Max (1958 [1921]) *The City.* New York: Free Press.

Weber, Max (1978 [1921]) *Economy and Society: An Outline of Interpretive Sociology.* Berkeley: University of California Press.

Weigel, George (1995) 'Are Human Rights Still Universal?', *Commentary, 99* (February), 41–45.

Williams, Raymond (1990) *Television: Technology and Cultural Form* (2nd ed). London: Routledge.

Wolch, J.R. (1989) 'The Shadow State: Transformations in the Voluntary Sector', in J.R. and M. Dear Wolch (ed.) *The Power of Geography: How Territory Affects Social Life.* Boston: Unwin Hyman.

Wood, Patricia K. (1995) 'Nationalism from the Margins: The Development of National and Ethnic Identities among Italian Immigrants in Alberta and British Columbia, 1880–1980', Unpublished Ph.D. dissertation, Duke University, Durham, North Carolina.

Wood, Patricia K. (1999) 'Outside the Lines: Borders and Identities among Italian Immigrants in the Pacific Northwest, 1880–1938', in John and Kenneth Coates Findlay (eds) *'On Brotherly Terms': Canadian–American Relations in the Pacific Northwest.* Seattle: University of Washington Press.

Wright, Erik Olin (1985) *Classes.* London: Verso.

Wright, Erik Olin (1997) *Class Counts: Comparative Studies in Class Analysis.* Cambridge: Cambridge University Press.

Wright, Ronald (1992) *Stolen Continents: The 'New World' through Indian Eyes.* Toronto: Penguin.

Yalçin-Heckman, Lale (1997) 'The Perils of Ethnic Associational Life in Europe: Turkish Migrants in Germany and France', in Tariq Modood and Pnina Werbner (eds) *The Politics of Multiculturalism in the New Europe: Racism, Identity and Community.* London and New York: Zed Books.

Yingling, Thomas E. (1997) *AIDS and the National Body.* Durham, NC: Duke University Press.

Young, Iris Marion (1989) 'Polity and Group Difference: A Critique of the Ideal of Universal Citizenship', *Ethics, 99* (January), 250–274.

Young, Iris Marion (1990) *Justice and the Politics of Difference.* Princeton, NJ: Princeton University Press.

Young, Iris Marion (1997) 'Unruly Categories: A Critique of Nancy Fraser's Dual Systems Theory', *New Left Review,* 222, 147–160.

Young, Oran R. (1994) *International Governance: Protecting the Environment in a Stateless Society.* Ithaca, NY: Cornell University Press.

Young, Oran R. (ed.) (1997) *Global Governance: Drawing Insights from the Environmental Experience*. Cambridge, MA: MIT Press.

Young, Robert J.C. (1995) *Colonial Desire: Hybridity in Theory, Culture and Race*. London: Routledge.

Yuval-Davis, Nira (1997) *Gender & Nation*. London: Sage.

Zolo, Danilo (1997) *Cosmopolis: Prospects for World Government*. London: Polity.

Zweigenhaft, Richard L., and Domhoff, G. William (1998) *Diversity in the Power Elite: Have Women and Minorities Reached the Top?* New Haven: Yale University Press.

Zylberberg-Hocquard, Marie-Hélène (1978) *Féminisme et syndicalisme en France*. Paris: Anthropos.

Zylberberg-Hocquard, Marie-Hélène (1981) *Femmes et féminisme dans le mouvement ouvrier français*. Paris: Éditions ouvrières.

INDEX

Printed in the United Kingdom
by Lightning Source UK Ltd.
9792600001B/4-48